Chronometer Jack

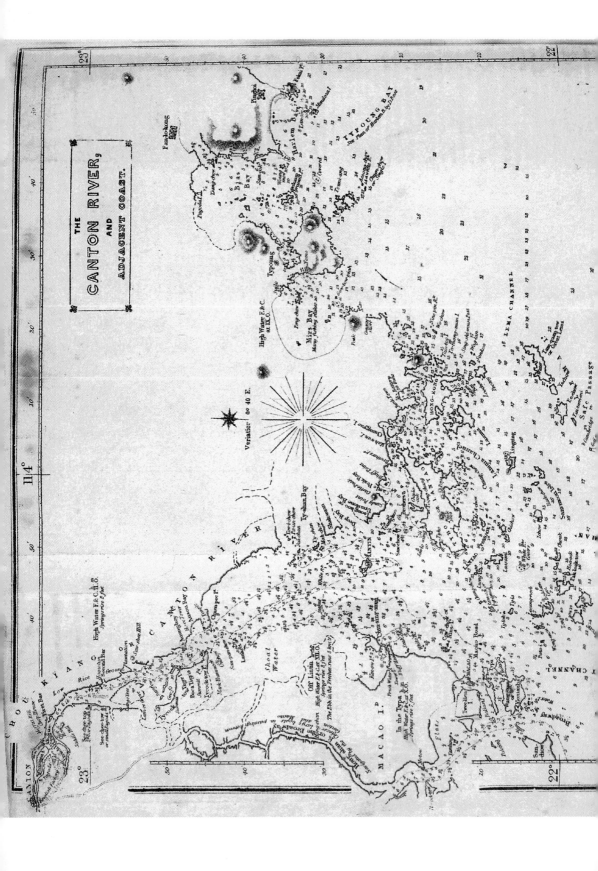

THE
CANTON RIVER,
AND
ADJACENT COAST.

Chronometer Jack

The Autobiography of the Shipmaster

John Miller of Edinburgh

(1802–1883)

Edited by Robin Craig, Ann Nix and Michael Nix

Whittles Publishing

Published by
Whittles Publishing,
Dunbeath,
Caithness KW6 6EY,
Scotland, UK
www.whittlespublishing.com

Design and typesetting by Scotty-Dog Pictures

Printed and bound in Poland, EU
Produced by Polskabook

Frontispeice:
'Chart of the Canton River and adjacent coast', adapted, with permission,
from the original published in *Nautical Magazine*, 1841, facing p. 473.
(The Trustees of the National Library of Scotland.)

*In memory of Robin Craig – a good
friend and a fine maritime historian*

Contents

Introduction

Many years ago a secondhand bookseller, knowing my deep interest in the sea and ships, offered me a battered leather-bound notebook. Its size was 22 x 13 cm and a large number of pages had been left blank. But there were 422 pages of text, which forms the matter of this book. A cursory examination of the text revealed a narrative both extensive in its interest and extremely well written in a good firm hand. Its author was plainly an educated man. Authenticity of the text was soon established. In studying the manuscript I concentrated on the shipping aspects and traced the life Captain Miller had as a midshipman in the East India Company, through to the time when he owned his own vessels and settled in Tasmania. Miller's narrative is both detailed and remarkably accurate throughout.

I confess that I did not pay sufficient attention to other aspects of the journal among which were many references to people whose identity was signified only by an initial letter of their name. It had not really occurred to me that a substantial number of the people described in the text were identifiable.

At this point my friend, Michael Nix, approached me to see the manuscript in connection with his research into the Australian Company's ship *Portland* which Miller commanded for a voyage to India. He examined the manuscript and subsequently his wife, Ann, requested a photocopy of the text to add to the collection of manuscripts in the City of Edinburgh Central Library, where she was local studies librarian.

Fortunately, I had arranged for the manuscript to be transcribed and typed. This onerous task was undertaken by Mrs Julia Walker (née Cornes) who was about to resign her position of Assistant Secretary, Department of History, University College London. She did a highly commendable job and her transcription proved to be accurate despite the fact that very often Captain Miller was dealing with matters maritime, of which Mrs Walker had no expert knowledge.

Michael is a maritime historian and, like Ann, quickly perceived the interest and value of the text and he took the initiative in discussing with publishers the possibility of a book. Michael and Ann undertook a complete editing of the text to improve the flow of the narrative. Miller wrote as he recalled the people and incidents described and the resulting text contained some rather long, rambling sentences. These have been simplified while remaining as faithful as possible to the wording of the original in order to preserve Miller's distinctive style of writing. In the meantime Ann did a spectacular job in identifying people mentioned in Miller's text and providing his narrative with well attested circumstantial context. In this, Michael and Ann, during their visit to Launceston in Tasmania, were able to research and enhance our understanding of Miller's sojourn there.

There have been innumerable narratives of merchant seamen, notably the *Barlow Journal*, edited by Basil Lubbock and published in two volumes in 1934. A much slimmer volume was rescued by E.H.W. Meyerstein as *Adventures by Sea* of Edward Coxere (1945). Through much of the nineteenth and twentieth centuries, seafarers have bequeathed us a substantial body of work, though variable in quality, which testifies to the interest of a wide range of readers. We make no apologies for adding to their number. Few have enjoyed the care, enterprise and initiative bestowed on Captain Miller's text by Michael and Ann, and I have never had the slightest reservation in preserving a narrative unique in comprehensiveness and interest.

Robin Craig

Acknowledgements

The editors would like to thank the following for all their help and assistance: Julia Walker who first transcribed the manuscript; Eileen Stage who undertook some research into Captain Miller's career in the Coast Guard; Kenneth Dunn for his Latin translations; the staffs of the: National Archives, Kew; National Library of Scotland, Edinburgh; the Edinburgh Room, Edinburgh Central Library; the Local History Library, Lincoln Central Library; the Local History Library, Newcastle Central Library; Morpeth Library, Northumberland; RNLI Library, Poole; the State Library of Victoria, Melbourne; the State Library of Tasmania, Hobart; the Mitchell Library, Sydney; the Launceston Library, Tasmania.

Abbreviations

ADB	*Australian Dictionary of Biography*
AJ	*Asiatic Journal*
BL	British Library
DNB	*Dictionary of National Biography*
LCL	*Leith Commercial List*
LL	*Lloyd's List*
LR	*Lloyd's Register*
NA	National Archives, London
OED	*Oxford English Dictionary*

Preface

The following pages were originally intended for the information and amusement of my family and friends only, having a wholesome dread of appearing before the public as an author, as well as an instinctive feeling of inability for such in any shape. But being advised by sundry folks to let 'the world' judge for itself, I have agreed to 'cast my bread upon the waters' and trust to the mercy of my readers, if I should ever be fortunate enough to have any.

I make no pretensions to the 'Grand' or 'Picturesque', and those who expect sensational descriptions of love or romance would do well to go no further as they will not find them here.

My object has been merely to write down some of the leading facts and occurrences of 50 years of my life, exactly as they came to my memory, without the aid of a single note or book of any kind, making a few remarks occasionally on such subjects as required them.

To nautical men there may be some things to create interest, and to the general reader somewhat of amusement from a variety of incident shown in a sailor's life both at sea and on shore; but whatever the results, I pledge myself to the unvarnished truth of all that is herein contained.

London 1st March 1874
JM

CHAPTER 1

How anxiously did I wish to belong to that ship

(1802–1819)

I was born in Edinburgh on the 11th September 1802, my father being a Writer to the Signet (WS), besides holding a public law office there.[1] At the age of eight years I was sent to a private Latin school in St James Square for a few months and, on the 1st October 1810, duly installed at the High School under Mr Carson. I remained with him for four years, as was usual, and after that time with Mr Pillans, the Rector, for two years.[2] Now I have no intention of writing a long story about my school days, like 'Tom Brown', yet I cannot pass over six years of my life without a few remarks concerning that ever memorable period to all rising generations.

Touching the master, Carson, who was afterwards many years Rector of the new High School on the Calton Hill, I believe he was a kind-hearted man in the main and also a just one, but certainly a very severe disciplinarian and a first rate hand at 'palming'. It was of no use for the boys to shove their cuffs over their hands to save them from the tawse: Carson would hit the fingers if there was only one such left bare, and 'whack whack' was the order of the day. It was customary to fall into divisions for the purpose of the boys being heard reciting the lessons of the day by one of the head boys as monitor who, in grammar, had to report every error made by each boy. Carson used to go round the whole class daily with each monitor at his side calling out the number of errors made by those he came to in succession for every one of which a palming was given by Carson, the whole process occupying fully half an hour daily.

Sometimes, when a crime of some sort had been committed, the boy would receive his 'palmies' with his hand laid on a brush on the desk! And in cases of a serious nature the janitor was sent for and the boy stripped and flogged on his nether-end, although this last I may say was a rare occurrence.

My place in the class of 160 boys was, during the whole four years, generally between 40 and 50 where about 20 of the 'choice spirits' used to hobble; in other words those boys who were idle and lazy at their lessons and who ought to have stood higher but preferred play and amusement. The late Lord Dundas of the Court of Session[3] was one of the 'dunces' of my class and a very good fellow he was, as also his brother John, a WS for many years,[4] Sir David Dundas[5] and Sir Francis Grant, RA.[6]

Carson was a capital scholar and teacher and with all his severity in punishing he had the good will of all the class, as he did his work in a jocular and amusing style, and always acted justly and without favour or affection. Not so Pillans, the Rector, who was a man of a totally different stamp. More polished both in appearance and manner and also an excellent teacher and a clever man, he had one of the worst faults which can belong to an instructor of youth, especially with 220 boys under him in his individual class: it was partiality! Such was the extent to which it was carried that (in my day) no one could mistake it and a most lasting impression to his detriment remained in the breasts of nearly all who did not happen to belong to the favoured few of aristocrats. I need hardly say that they or the upper grades were the boys who carried all before them! He toadied to the great

THE SECOND HIGH SCHOOL, 1820. (*After Storer.*)

Royal High School, Edinburgh, showing the building in Infirmary Street which
Miller attended, from James Grant *Old and New Edinburgh*, *c*.1880–1883.

through their sons and uniformly reminded me of the truth of the appellation given to him by Byron in his *English Bards and Scots Reviewers*, viz. 'paltry Pillans'.[7]

During my six years at the High School play and amusement of all kinds were not omitted whenever it was possible to get a hand in, but the half holiday Saturdays were very often used for a trip to Leith. There I learned to go aloft on board ships in the docks and, along with a few intimates, a London smack's boat would often be borrowed and a pull out to the men-o-war in the Roads made us fancy ourselves sailors or midshipmen and no mistake! Sure enough practice soon made perfection (or something akin to it) and we did many a time put our four-oared boat alongside of the old *Ramillies* in as good style as those belonging to her.[8] On one of these occasions it so happened that it was close upon the time when the ship was to fire a salute, and we were told by a midshipman of the deck that three of the five of us might come on board and the other two drop the boat astern and make her fast to the hanging stern ladder. This was accordingly done by myself and another who had to perform the grand feat of climbing up the ladder onto the poop, about 30 feet from the water, in time to see the salute fired after all.

How anxiously did I wish to belong to that ship, or any other in the Navy, for all the three years which she lay guard ship in Leith Roads! But such was not my fate. After being a year and a half at mathematics and having secretly written to the Admiralty to appoint me to a ship without success, I went to Mr Alex Reid's office in Leith at the earnest wish of my parents.[9] There I remained for six months, when I could stay on shore no longer and succeeded in getting my father to use his influence to obtain me an appointment as midshipman in an East India Company ship, which was shortly procured for me on board the *Lord Castlereagh* bound for China direct.

While in the merchant's office I had persuaded my father to allow me to learn navigation and, as I had also studied a book on seamanship and constantly saw many of the problems carried out in ships in the docks, besides having read all and sundry books of voyages and naval battles, I felt little fear of being able to stand my ground with any green messmates at least. With that state of preparation touching the internal man, I proceeded to do somewhat of the same to the external which, with the help of a tailor and a friend who had shortly before been a midshipman in the very ship I was appointed to, I was not long in accomplishing. Early in February 1819 I bid adieu to my paternal home in Edinburgh[10] and, escorted by half a dozen of my old boat's crew on half holidays, I sped to Leith and joined a smack bound for London full of life and hope and kindly feeling to everybody.

My old chums went with me as far as Leith Roads then, when leaving in the pilot's boat, gave me three hearty cheers and we started for London. After a pleasant passage of four days I arrived at the great city and soon found out the lodgings of my two elder brothers, who had begun business as general agents and brokers a year or two previously.[11] I lived with them a fortnight seeing the sights and wonders of London and enjoying myself very much, of course.

11 York Place, Edinburgh, the Miller family home between 1811 and 1829. (M. Nix, 2006.)

But 'there is an end of all things', and in my case there was no exception to the rule. One fine morning in March, I found it necessary to turn out at 3.30 a.m., bid adieu to all this life of pleasure and trudge down to the East India Docks on foot (no coaches so early) to join the ship *Lord Castlereagh*, which was to sail for Gravesend at 5 a.m. from Blackwall.

I was in good time and found Captain Younghusband, the first four officers and one midshipman already on board. We all breakfasted in the cuddy with the captain after being fairly under way with a fine fair wind: tug steamers were not yet in use. In due time we got to Northfleet and moored ship to the buoys, where the Captain left to return to London.

In the evening after the sails were unbent, the decks cleared and all things pretty well squared up, I had leisure to take a survey of my new position and shipmates as well as the one messmate who had as yet joined the ship. I shall here make a few observations on the whole so far as I can recollect my feelings at the time of this the first day spent on board the ship I actually belonged to. For several years I had been quite accustomed to ships of various kinds, both men-of-war and merchant, but I had never obtained my desire and really and truly become a part and parcel of the one on which I trod.

The *Lord Castlereagh* was an old vessel of about 900 tons with a poop and top gallant forecastle, and was pierced for 38 guns but, like all other Company ships, only mounted twenty-six 18-pounders in peacetime. In fact she had all the appearance of a 36-gun frigate of the old school, saving the poop.[12] Our crew including officers was 115, and the general duties and discipline of all Company ships were very much the same as in the Navy, the number of a ship's company varying according to the size of the ship from 110 to 150.[13] The number of officers was the same in all, viz. four 'sworn', two junior and five midshipmen (or sometimes six or seven), with warrant and petty officers as in the Navy, besides a doctor, assistant surgeon, purser and clerk. As a general rule the chief officers were in age above 30 and smart, gentlemanly men, which latter quality may be said of all in the Service, with the usual allowance for 'mauvais sujets' [a bad lot]!

Our Captain, William Younghusband, was a very gentlemanly man of about 45 years of age and of an old Northumbrian family. He had commanded the ship for some years, had the reputation of being an excellent officer and was also an exceedingly kind and attentive commander both to officers and men. To this I had ample opportunity of testifying during the whole of the 14 months I served under him.[14]

The chief officer's name was John Manderson, an East Lothian man, or 'Jock' as he was called by those who knew him in the Service. He was a gentleman born, but had no right to that title either for his manners, or language, or feelings generally. He was, however, a good officer and most attentive to his duties, but a great bully to the midshipmen and youngsters who consequently hated him most cordially. His age was about 31 and he was a good looking man with a small compressed mouth and decidedly sharp temper. I may here add, what I only knew some months afterwards, that he was *not* a favourite of the captain who was, in everything except seamanship, his very antithesis.[15]

The second officer was an elderly easy going sort of person called Williams who had been rusting in idleness at home for some years and, although very kindly disposed, was one who neither added to his friends nor made any real enemies. He was about 36 or 38 years of age.[16]

Patrick Lindesay of the family of Wormiston in Fife was the third officer. A fine looking, well made, six foot tall man of about 25 years, he had sailed with Jock previously in the *William Pitt* and they were great friends, which proved to be all against the 'young gentlemen' in the future. Lindesay was a good officer and strict in his duties yet he never omitted asking a midshipman to dine with him at his mess once a week, on which occasions he was always most agreeable. He had some droll ways and whims, such as frequently smiling to himself when walking the deck during his watch. All was easily accounted for when he joined the *Sir David Scott* about a year and a half afterwards, where he became quite mad and died lashed to a ring bolt in his cabin when that ship was lying at Saugor in the Hooghly River near Calcutta.[17]

The fourth officer's name was Legget of whom I can say little either way. He was a nonentity, but did his duty tolerably well.[18] The fifth's name was Whitmarsh,[19] the sixth's Somerville,[20] both very nice young men who I believe never succeeded in 'setting the Thames on fire'. They were a little given to grog drinking, although never to call for the aniseed version, and were great friends of the assistant surgeon, Mr Muir of Edinburgh, who was a pleasant and agreeable fellow at all times.[21]

The doctor was an elderly man called Lorimer, a good and steady red-nosed Scotchman, who troubled himself with no one and was always at his post at meal times, being pleased with good living, if not caring about conversation.[22] E. Bostock, the purser, will complete the list of officers. He was a pleasant, gentlemanly man and liked by all. For many years afterwards he was a merchant in London.[23]

As to the midshipmen, my messmates, we were five in all: Richard Oakes Hardy,[24] John Say Sparkes,[25] Henry Bonham Shepherd,[26] Charles D[27] and myself. The first two had been in the Service about a year and a half and the others were 'Johnnie Newcomes'. Our mess berth was a cabin on the after part of the gun or main deck abreast the after hatchway. It was of the somewhat small dimensions of ten feet by eight with an 18-pounder in it and, of course, a good sized port and scuttle. But in those days 'young gentlemen' were not quite so fastidious as they are now in the Navy, nor did they fare so well in the way of grub generally. Yet in harbour we always managed to have good wholesome food and occasionally an allowance of rum to wash it down. I say 'occasionally' as our friend Jock Manderson thought that 'midshipmen' (as he always called us) had no need of grog to stimulate them to do their duty. It was even very seldom that we afterwards succeeded in getting a dram when the 'main brace' happened to be 'spliced' and we were cold and drenched with wet after reefing topsails or some such work aloft.

Once, indeed, Jock wished to be very kind to me when lying at Northfleet. Before sailing and during my lookout on deck at the dinner hour, in the midst of continued heavy rain, he called me into the cuddy and asked me if I would take a glass of wine! I took this for an invitation to sit down at table and was about to do so by placing a chair. I was soon undeceived by his roaring out in his rough, hoarse voice: 'Oh you needn't sit down, just take it standing! This is something different to walking the streets of Edinburgh!'; and after drinking his health: 'Oh now you can keep your lookout!' at which I hauled out of the cuddy wishing the fellow at the bottom of the river!

Upon another occasion, shortly after the above had occurred, it so happened that there was a difference between the account which I had taken of some stores which had been received on board, and the shipping notes. To show my correctness I handed over my book to Jock who was very wroth. Sitting at the table in the cuddy he took the book and roared out: 'Damn you and your book!' and hove it in my face! I at once went below to ascertain who was rightly counting over the packages of stores in the gun room. In doing so, however, I fell through the bread room scuttle to the bottom of the hold, not knowing or seeing that it was open, a height of about 18 feet. Fortunately for me a plank had been placed across about half way down this abyss, which broke my fall so much that I was only stunned for a short time and a good deal bruised, without any bones being broken. On coming to myself I went up to the quarterdeck to tell Jock that my account was correct, when he met me with the vociferation of: 'What the Devil took you tumbling away down the hold!' This was poor comfort I thought under the circumstances and I merely answered that my account was correct. But 'every dog has his day' and I lived to bring this bully to be my humble servant some few months afterwards.

CHAPTER 2

I takey ship Macao!

(1819–1820)

After six weeks of labour, fitting the ship for sea and taking in cargo at Northfleet, we unmoored about the end of April 1819 and dropped down to the Lower Hope. There we paid ship and started on the following day for the Downs, the wind being easterly. We arrived there just in time to meet a westerly fresh breeze which kept us for some days at anchor off Deal. By this time we had begun to know something of each other and had got the ship into tolerable order and comfort, exercising royal yards morning and evening.[1]

It was customary for the 'young gentlemen' in the East India Company Service, along with two or four mizzentopmen and some idlers[2] to man the mizzen topsail yard and do nearly all the duties connected with the mizzenmast and poop in working ship and exercises. On one of the mornings for crossing royal yards we were all ready on the poop, with the yard rope in our hands, to sway away when the order should be given by Jock, the chief executive. It came into our heads, however, to have a desire to 'steal a bit' and thereby be in good time with the yard for crossing. Our worthy chief having observed us from the quarterdeck, flew up the poop ladder, speaking trumpet in hand and, with a volley of expletives from his mouth, hove the trumpet (as he thought) right in amongst us! But alas, his rage had successfully, for us, affected his steadiness of aim so much as to carry the said trumpet clean over the taffrail into the sea! Seeing which, he kicked every idler one by one off the poop and, when he found the remainder to be composed only of 'young gentlemen', he turned to each and grinned in his face, finishing off with a volley of oaths before taking himself to his duty. All this and some other little escapades on the passage through the Queen's Channel had been performed in the presence of the captain, which seemed to give him great uneasiness and eventually had the effect of causing positive disagreement between them.

At length the day came which carried us not only clear of the Downs, but also of the Channel. After the usual vicissitudes of weather, the general routine of naval duties at sea and a good deal of polishing up of the 'young gentlemen', in three months we made Christmas Island, near Java Head, being the first and only land we had seen since leaving the Lizard.

In a couple of days more we anchored in the Strait of Sunda and next morning got into Anjer Roads. This is a very pretty little Dutch settlement which has a small fort and a few native soldiers. We saw only one solitary European and certainly did not envy him his position in the midst of a mere jungle with a small population of Malays, and the continual heat of a near perpendicular sun throughout the year. We youngsters, however, were much delighted with the splendid fruits brought off by the natives in their canoes of the most primitive 'Crusoe' shape which, with plenty of cheap fowls, made up for many a day's dinner of salt junk and 'duff' [dough].

After filling up our water, we sailed for the Straits of Banka and in a few days arrived at Muntok, without touching the ground, where we found a Dutch 32-gun frigate at anchor. From her officers we very soon learned that she had been boarded on the previous night by the Malays and lost 30 men before they could clear the ship of these unwelcome intruders! Of course vengeance was sworn, but I do not recollect all the retaliation that was to take place, nor do I know what really did occur afterwards as we sailed for Canton the following day and never heard more of our well-beaten friends. But we did not forget the lesson which had been read to us, of the fatal consequences of a bad look out.

Muntok is famous for its extensive tin mines, which at the time I was there in July 1819, were worked by about 2,000 Chinamen and yielded a handsome revenue to the Dutch.

Up the China Sea we had a fine south-west monsoon and in 12 days sighted the Ladrone Islands near the Macao Passage where we fell in with a pilot boat of the true Chinese pattern.[3] He came alongside and, without our heaving to, he laid hold of a rope thrown to him, jumped into the mizzen chains like a rigger and onto the poop in a minute. He sang out in the broken English jargon generally used by the Chinese and as absurdly returned by the English:

'Hey you Messey Captain how you do! Hey you Messey Chief Mate! I takey ship Macao! All right! Steady, so fashion!' (to the quartermaster).

This, with plenty more of a similar sort of talk, along with the rum look of the man's 'tout ensemble', amused us all very much, his plaited tail hanging down his back being not the least of his remarkable points. These men as pilots are quite astonishing in their knowledge and coolness. In working ship or backing and filling across a bar they will match any English pilot on the Thames or elsewhere, and that without steam in any shape or form.

On our passage hence to Whampoa, of course, we passed the island of Lintin and then through the Bocca Tigris.[4] We moored ship at Whampoa abreast of Dane's Island

'Whampoa from Dane's Island', from G.N. Wright, China in a series of views, 1843.
(The Trustees of the National Library of Scotland.)

some time in August, and up to the early part of November, were busily employed in delivering cargo and taking in tea for the homeward voyage to London, besides thoroughly refitting ship in every way. We found several Company ships at Whampoa and in a short time about eight or ten more arrived so that in all our fleet amounted to 21 ships, besides 'Country ships' and a few Dutch.

Our amusements were but few as it was dangerous to go on shore on Dane's Island excepting close to the ships. Yet we had some visiting between different ships and every two or three days some of us were up at Canton either on duty or on leave, which made three months very soon come to an end.

With such a state of things, there was but little that occurred which proved worthy of remark. Our friend Jock Manderson, all along treating us midshipmen with a tough hand, frequently went so far in his ill temper as to 'cuff' some of us, which was not a likely thing to be quietly put up with for any length of time, and we were all on the watch for a slap at him in some way. It fell to my lot to assist the fourth officer with a few men in removing some bags of rice and starting them into some casks in the steerage. Suddenly, Jock made his appearance and, finding that it was the wrong rice that had been started, he was so enraged that he blew up the fourth officer furiously and then, turning to me, he grinned in my face and said: 'And you were there too!' At the same time he gave me a kick with his foot, which he was about to repeat, when I jumped on one side and defied him to touch me again. I told him at the same time in pretty plain terms that he should neither strike me with his hand nor his foot henceforth with impunity, and I should certainly report his dastardly conduct to the Captain, who I knew would never allow him to behave like a bully to any of us. At this harangue he appeared mortally astonished and sneaked away to his cabin double quick. The result was that he never attempted such things again to any midshipman and I may fairly say that he was ever afterwards my humble servant and real friend! Such was the chief officer of the *Lord Castlereagh* who even in his friendly humours was one of the most disagreeable men I ever sailed with.

Towards the end of November[5] we sailed for old England in company with the *Lowther Castle*[6] and, early in April, arrived in the Downs, after what may be termed a fine weather passage. We touched only at Radja Basa in the Straits of Sunda for water and sighted Cape Agulhas and the Cape of Good Hope previous to anchoring at St Helena.[7] Here we found various frigates of 26 guns and brigs cruising about on watch for any move which might be made towards the escape of Napoleon Bonaparte. He was at that time confined on the island, fighting new battles with the Governor Sir H. Lowe on paper as

'St Helena', from Frederick Whymper, *The Sea*, 1882–1885.

well as verbally.[8] So strict were the orders regarding anyone going to Longwood, that no one from our two ships had a single chance of seeing him: we were well pleased when the day came for sailing.

HMS *Conqueror*, 74 guns, flagship of Admiral Lambert,[9] lay off James Town and the *Tees*, 26 guns,[10] off Lemon Valley, rowing guard all night. The *Menai*, 26 guns,[11] with the *Redwing*,[12] *Leveret*[13] and *Rosario*[14] brigs, cruised to the windward of the island, boarding all ships which came near and allowing none to go into anchor save Company ships and men-of-war. Captain Rennie[15] of the *Tees* was a cousin of our magnanimous chief, Jock, who paid him a visit, of course. This officer, we learned, had been tried by court-martial for tyranny and oppression some time before our arrival. We presumed that the two cousins would naturally compare notes!

We were all very much interested in St Helena and wondered much at its fortifications and natural strength from almost continuous cliffs of upwards of 250 feet high at least and 25 miles round. With its remarkable prisoner it formed one of the greatest curiosities of all time.

But I must return to the Downs, where we hove to for a short time to take in our river pilot and started for Gravesend with one of the Company's pilot cutters ahead.[16] The following day found us at Purfleet where, having got leave to quit the ship, Henry Bonham Shepherd and I took a boat and landed on the left bank of the river after having been searched by the Customs raggamuffins, first at the gangway, next on the water and thirdly on stepping on shore, much to our disgust. They found nothing on our persons worth taking. This abominable system was soon after put an end to by an Act of Parliament, I am glad to say.[17] A gentleman, having dared one of these men to touch his person, knocked him down when he attempted it. This general Customs practice was then found to be contrary to the law of England as well as the liberty of the subject, and the new Act substituted. Yet I am aware that such proceedings frequently take place even now, from the ignorance of the public as to the power of these men. Only three years ago I was surprised to find a Collector of Customs at one of the outports arguing that he and his men had this power, when I referred him to the Customs Act, which I hope has since caused him to alter his ways.

Shepherd and I walked to Dartford across the fields and there got a post chaise and drove to my brothers' counting house in Bishopsgate Street, London, and thus ended my first 14 months at sea.

CHAPTER 3

Chronometer Jack

(1820–1821)

The change from a midshipman's berth of those days to a snug lodging with my brothers, James and Andrew, at Camberwell was very pleasing indeed, although I felt no regret at my choice of the sea as a profession, which under any circumstances assuredly enhances by comparison the pleasures of the shore. The discipline and regularity on board of a ship must ever after prove a most useful lesson to all those youngsters who may have been fortunate enough to pass through the ordeal of even a couple of years' trial.

I soon found my way down to my paternal home in Edinburgh by a Leith smack once more, and received that welcome from my parents and sisters which nothing but the purest affection could give. A trip to the Highlands with an old school-fellow to his uncle's place called Kinnaird passed away a month very agreeably. Three more months at Portobello, where my family generally went in autumn, brought the time for my start very near having been appointed as midshipman to the *Marquis Camden*, to sail in December to Bombay and China.[1]

I enjoyed myself very much at Portobello, and was not a little surprised to receive a visit there one day from my old enemy Jock Manderson who professed all sorts of friendship, and gave me an excellent character to my worthy parents who were well acquainted with a lady cousin of his in Edinburgh. I found that he was appointed to the *Repulse*,[2] Captain Paterson, as chief officer once more, the old *Castlereagh* being done up and sold to the ship-breakers.[3]

About the beginning of October 1820 I left, for the second time, York Place having decided to study navigation for a few weeks with Mr Adams at Edmonton where my old messmate Hardy had been formerly. I had every reason to be thankful for his recommendation. We always worked from our own observations with the false horizon, and Mr

'Leith', from Richard Ayton and William Daniell, *Voyage round Great Britain*, 1814–1825. The illustration shows smacks entering the harbour. (The Trustees of the National Library of Scotland.)

Adams was a pleasant and dear teacher and astronomer. The six weeks spent at Edmonton amongst the tombs (the house looking into the churchyard facing the long flat ones for the false horizon to stand on) I have never forgotten both for the result of the studies and the great kindness of the family. Charles Adams, the only son, studied along with me, and he afterwards turned out a clever lecturer on astronomy in London for many years.[4]

Late in November I joined the *Marquis Camden* at Northfleet, which ship I was well aware from what I had seen and heard when in China was one of the smartest in the Company's service. She was still commanded by Captain T. Larkins or 'Tommy', by sobriquet, who was a man of no ordinary kind in several ways, as will be seen.[5] I shall however at present only give his general appearance. He was an acquaintance of my brother William at Bombay, at that time captain of artillery,[6] and at his recommendation I had been appointed by Captain Larkins. He was in height five feet ten inches, of stout and muscular build, good looking, but a little pitted by the smallpox, or as he called it 'rolled over Deal beach'. Nevertheless, he was a gentlemanly and active looking man and powerful enough to cope with anyone, especially with the scum. As many of our ship's company had good reason to know by experience, his strength of arm was such that he could hold out a musket horizontally by the muzzle!

We saw little of him till the ship was dropped down to the Lower Hope to be paid before sailing, as usual, but we had been all very comfortable up to that time under Mr Butler, the chief officer,[7] Mr Fenn,[8] the second, Mr Fox,[9] the third, Mr Hutchinson,[10] the fourth, my old messmate Hardy, the fifth, and Mr Hogarth[11] the sixth, also assistant surgeon Veitch.[12] In our midshipmen's mess we only mustered four in all, the clerk messing with the officers. The doctor, D. Scott,[13] and the purser, Stoddart Drysdale,[14] of course, messed with the captain and chief and second officers, as also three passengers, Major Deschamps, Captain Riddock of the Country service, and Mr Taylor, assistant surgeon in the army.[15] The *Marquis Camden* was not a passenger ship as Tommy could not be troubled with them, and they would not risk their comfort by sailing with such a man as he was usually represented to be. I have omitted to mention another passenger, however, Captain Falconer of the Bombay Artillery, in command of 200 Company recruits, which we had on board and who, belonging to my brother's corps, treated me throughout the passage with great kindness.[16]

For some time before leaving the river we had upwards of 200 men on board in order that the captain might have at least a surplus of 50 to choose from on pay day. Our complement was 150 in all and I believe we sailed with a first-rate ship's company in their different stations. At the Motherbank off the Isle of Wight[17] we were detained about a fortnight by foul winds during which time we brought them into tolerable training and smartness in their duties and exercises. Tommy showed unmistakably that 'he was captain of his own ship' as well as chief officer, boatswain, gunner, etc. He was everywhere and had his eyes upon everyone (very piercing ones too). Indeed, I have heard him boast more than once that he knew what went on in the ship 'from the taffrail to right chock forward in the eyes of her!' But this was to terrify the men against doing certain acts which would as certainly be followed by flogging!

Corporal punishment was then considered so essentially necessary to the keeping up of proper discipline and securing the comfort of all generally, that all Company ships carried letters of marque. These gave captains that power which by the regulations was only to be exercised after the culprit should have been tried by a court of enquiry composed of the 'four sworn officers of the ship'. This, in most ships, was fairly carried out. The captain did not sit as a member of the court, but received the written minutes from the purser, who acted as judge advocate on such occasions, and had discretion to reduce the number of lashes awarded, but no power to increase them.

We had soon good reason for saying, however, that one captain at least did not stick very rigidly to these salutary instructions. For about five years, from first to last, that I served under his command, there never was one court of enquiry called at which Tommy himself did not sit as president, acting throughout as both judge and jury and merely taking the opinion of the officers as a matter of form! Indeed, the whole affair was at all times a matter of form as he seldom failed to tell a man, who had in his idea deserved flogging, that he would next day give him so many dozens. Ordered to be put in irons till tried, the individual might think himself very fortunate if he got only his promised quota.

We had not been many days at sea after leaving Cowes when some of the men incurred the displeasure of the captain, and the solemn farce of a trial was gone through with sundry dozens of lashes inflicted. It was a rare thing for a week to pass over without such acts. The crimes were generally very trifling, but the men were at first after sailing much inclined 'to show their teeth', as it is called, and it was more necessary to punish severely at such times than later on the voyage. A word of smartness or the slightest retort when an order was given was quite a sufficient case, and the slightest drunkenness or disobedience was sure to draw down from two to five dozen. With all this severity, however, Tommy paid due attention to the comforts of the ship's company in every way and rewarded those who did well. The officers were not spared any more than the men. His language was quite as impolite to them on all occasions as to anyone else, the expletives being three to one at least, but to the officers he took care on most occasions to send himself to perdition when using those terms commonly called gross swearing!

No order was given without an oath, even when roared out to the masthead or to the bottom of the hold. This kind of game was kept up 'til we were nearing the Cape of Good Hope from the coast of Brazil, when a row occurred which called forth all the energies not only of Tommy, but of all officers, midshipmen and warrant officers, which I shall here relate to the best of my recollection.

I think we were under all plain sail and wind, in a moderate breeze at sunset, when the boatswain piped to 'stand by the hammocks'. All were reported up from below, but amongst the last was a captain of the forecastle named Lynch, a strong and powerful man of six feet, who came on the quarterdeck to rescue his hammock without his shirt on. The chief officer asked him how he dared to come up in that state, to which he answered he was hot after being in the hold. Mr Butler then told him to take care not to do so again, to which the man very impertinently said he would if he was hot, but if not he would put on his shirt. Mr Butler told him to take his hammock down, and come up to him when he had put on his shirt. Meantime, the boatswain piped down and the deck was cleared. Shortly after, Lynch came up with his shirt on, when Mr Butler ordered him to go on the poop and called the master-at-arms to put him in irons. This order he refused flatly to obey, and Mr Butler and the master-at-arms got hold of him to force him aft, but he burst away from them and ran forward. Seeing what was going on Tommy came out from his cabin.

He at once sent for Lynch and ordered him onto the poop, but he refused. Tommy, who was just his match in strength and well up in pugilism, got hold of him and had succeeded in getting him half along the quarterdeck when three more forecastlemen came to his rescue and dragged him forward. The captain and myself (who had been on deck all the time) followed the men to the forepart of the waist where he again got hold of Lynch, but the latter was immediately laid hold of by Sutherland, one of the other three, who dragged him away. The captain took a pistol out of his pocket and presented it at the man's breast, telling him to let go Lynch or he would fire. He answered: 'Fire and be damned, we can only die once!' Most fortunately, he did not fire, but told me 'to turn the hands out' and 'beat the roll for the soldiers', which were done immediately. Officers and warrant officers rushed down below securing the four prisoners, every one arming himself, and some handing weapons up to the cuddy from the steerage where they were in the racks. Captain Falconer did his best with the troops, many of whom were inclined to side with the mutineers, and in a short time got the whole of them on deck. The prisoners were placed under an armed guard of non-commissioned officers on the quarterdeck, where were now assembled all the officers who were prepared to cut down the first who might dare step over a rope drawn across the gangways to keep the ship's company and soldiers at bay.

By this time it was dark and by lantern light the gratings were rigged and, after a severe tussle, Lynch was tied up and the shirt torn off his back. He then turned his head round and said: 'Well, you've got me at last!' The boatswain and his mates were ordered to 'do their duty forthwith' and this man received seven dozen lashes with only a drink of water two or three times, and without a sound almost from his mouth. Sutherland was then ordered to be tied up, but he had escaped from his guards or sentries and could not be found. Midshipmen and others were ordered below to find him and, after a delay of about ten minutes, I saw something stuffed in between the main chains and a portlid. Poking my cutlass through I found it to be the man, who was dragged out and tied up to the grating where he received six dozen lashes. He roared like a bull all the time, the captain frequently calling to him to 'take his punishment like a man', and calling him 'cowardly scoundrel'.

The next man was a dark coloured, fierce looking fellow called Truman who got six dozen also, and the fourth was a foretopman, whose name I forget, who got five dozen. Then a forecastleman named Earl got one dozen because he did not come aft quick enough on the hands being turned out. He pleaded hard to be let off as he was in the head, but he got his dozen. Then the four prisoners were ordered to be put in irons and placed in the steerage, but no irons were to be found which showed the depth of the plot. A rod for the awning on the main rigging was then ordered to be cut down immediately, and the armourer to make a head and eye to it, the prisoners being placed under sentries till it was finished.[18]

The boatswain was ordered to pipe down about half past eight at night, and thus ended this émeute, which might have been far more serious had Captain Tommy used any temporising measures or delayed execution one single night. It was soon seen who was to be master, and although the same strict discipline and punishments were continued for two and a half years afterwards before reaching England, yet there was never another disturbance. At the present time such severity and decision might be much questioned

'Bombay', by William Daniell, from *Oriental Annual*, 1836.
(The Trustees of the National Library of Scotland.)

even in the Navy, and few naval officers would probably credit it who had never known the late East India Company Service, which was broken up in 1833.

For six weeks the prisoners were kept in irons till we reached Bombay, and then Lynch and the others were released from confinement and put in the afterguard for about three or four weeks more. Lynch was exchanged for a carpenter of a free trader called the *Bombay Merchant*,[19] ours having died of cholera, and the rest returned to their old stations.

On the morning after arrival in Bombay harbour,[20] when on the mizzen topsail yard unbending the topsail, I saw an artillery officer coming alongside in a dinghy. Supposing that he was my brother William, I at once bundled down to the quarterdeck and met him at the gangway. We soon recognised each other although it had been ten years since we had met when I was only eight years old. He asked the Captain to allow me to go on shore with him, which was immediately granted, and after dressing in haste we started for his quarters about half way to Byculla. There I found Captain Falconer who had gone out the evening before. I remained only till the afternoon as I was promised a week's leave in a few days by Captain Tommy, who I may here remark had from the first treated me with most marked kindness.

On leaving England he had asked me if I could 'work a time' to which I answered 'yes'. 'Then come into the cuddy every day and do so along with me at noon,' he ordered, which I did and compared the chronometer with him regularly, thereby getting the name of 'Chronometer Jack' amongst the officers. If anyone ever went with him in his gig it was always I who had that honour; also my invitations to dinner exceeded those of my messmates considerably. Indeed, so much so that one of them by the name of Hollingsworth refused to dine with him one day when asked, which he had good reason to regret for the rest of the time he was in the ship, nearly two years more. I always took care to do my duty well and to his satisfaction, not a very easy matter, but Jock Manderson's former training had a good deal to do in the matter.

One day when at my brother's house on my week's leave, he said to me that he intended to take me to breakfast with 'two very fine young ladies' at Byculla, sisters of a brother officer who had just come from England, and I must take care to 'be on my Ps and Qs', in other words not to make a hole in my manners. The breakfast took place in due course and, as they were all good musicians, a morning concert afterwards, then tiffin. After that we had dinner at the mess in the evening (no ladies there of course) during all of which I hope I did the right thing. But the cause of my particular instructions did not appear for some months afterwards when I was not surprised to learn that my excellent brother, the brigade major, was married to the elder of the two 'very fine young ladies'.[21]

He was a very kind brother to me while at Bombay, and ever after it also, even to his death in 1836 at the Mahabaleshwar Hills, when he had reached the rank of Judge Advocate General of the army. He told me to keep a good mess on board and he would pay our bills when leaving Bombay, which he did. At our parting he sent us two dozen bottles of wine to wind up with. My two messmates were of course very much gratified as well as myself.

While lying at Bombay we had to shift our mainmast, sprung from carrying too much sail at times, which would certainly have agitated, if not frightened, a not very nervous man. This will appear plausible enough when I state that frequently I have seen the *Marquis Camden* tearing away under double-reefed top sails, whole courses, double-reefed topmast studding sail, and reefed lower studding sail, when it was blowing fully half a gale of wind, going 12 knots.

The getting out a mainmast with sheers rigged on board, and another one in, was no trifling job, the latter weighing 12 tons! But our boatswain (who soon after died of cholera) along with his mates, especially the chief, effected the whole without a hitch. The chief boatswain's mate was called William Clark, a thorough seaman of those times, and a great favourite of Captain Tommy, who could not resist being lenient to the man even when he threw a serpent at his head one day in one of his drunken fits. He only put him in irons for the night.

This man was certainly the smartest seaman I ever saw and was a most valuable one on board of a ship. But consistency is most essential to discipline and Tommy was greatly in error in this respect towards Clark who, when drunk, was sometimes dangerous to the Captain himself. He used occasionally to go to the officers' steward and ask for grog and, at one time when refused, he swore he would put him overboard if not given it. Being again denied it, Clark seized the man by the trousers with both hands and held him out at the port at arms length till he agreed to give him the grog, when he brought him in again. Had Clark's strength failed, the man must have been drowned, as he could not swim and the ship was going fast through the water.

When our cargo of cotton was on board and the ship ready for sea we were not sorry to quit Bombay as we had been in almost continuous rain for six weeks and lost nine men by cholera, having had as many as 50 ill at one time with that horrible disease. A few hours was enough with some to put out the lamp of life; the wonder was that we lost so few out of the 50. I recollect Veitch the assistant surgeon telling me how horrified he was one night when one of these poor fellows, a quartermaster named Mosely, came crawling aft to his cot and roused him by putting his cold, clammy hand on his face, telling him that he was dying![22] The man dropped down alongside him and in three hours was a corpse.

The effect was felt so much by the healthy men that we were obliged to get the fiddler to work on one side of the gundeck while they were dying on the other. The people in the town of Bombay and its environs were dying at the rate of 300 per day![23] So as I have already said we were not a little glad to leave that 'Golgotha' and sail for China in July 1821, minus seven men, including the boatswain and carpenter.[24]

The only occurrence worth mentioning before anchoring at Penang was another flogging affair, that is, one of several, rendered remarkable by its severity. A maintop man called Brown was rigging out the topgallant studding sail boom on the topsail yard, when the chief officer sung out to him to 'bear a hand', and he answered rather loudly: 'I am doing it as fast as I can!'

'Come down here directly, sir,' said the chief officer, and called a boatswain's mate aft with a 'point' to be ready to 'start' the man when he should reach the deck. He was ordered to come aft to where the boatswain's mate was with the point in his hand. Seeing what was to be his fate, he at once jumped onto the Jacob's ladder, which he had hardly quitted, and ran up the rigging to the main topmast cross-trees, and there stopped till he saw a couple of quartermasters coming up for him. He started hand-over-hand down the topmast stay into the foretop and up to the foretopmast crosstrees like a monkey. His pursuers then went up forward and down he went to the jib boom end by the jib stay, from whence he was in a little time brought down and put in irons for the night.

Next morning he was tried as usual and got the five dozen which Tommy had promised him he should get if he did not come down directly from the main topmast head. Now this man really got punished (and it was always well laid on) for refusing to come aft to be 'started' which, by the way, was a very common occurrence on board the *Marquis Camden* and, I believe, on many other Company ships of those days, much as it may be wondered at now.

CHAPTER 4

A small opium ship called the Merope

(1821)

The day after anchoring at Penang[1] we were boarded by Captain Richardson of *HMS Topaze*[2] of 44 guns who, after being received by Captain Tommy, said that he had been ordered by Admiral Sir Henry Blackwood[3] to inquire into a 'round robin'. Sent to the Admiral signed or initialled (I forget which) by 20 men, it stated that the usage and discipline of the *Marquis Camden* was a disgrace to the service and they wished to volunteer for the Navy! This caused the hands to be turned out to muster, when the 20 men were called on to come out from the mess. They were placed in a line from the brake of the poop to forward on the opposite side of the quarterdeck by Captain Tommy himself. Captain Richardson then began to ask them from the after end what each man had to complain of, to which they answered according to the number of lashes they had received. The first was Brown, the maintop man, who had been twice flogged, first with four and afterwards, as related, with five dozen, so he said: 'I have received nine dozen, sir!' Another said: 'I have received six dozen, sir' and so on. But I forgot to state that only 19 men of the 20 came forth to claim 'distinction', and the 20th was never known, so I think they had signed their initials only. Captain Richardson said he could only take 13 men out of the 19, and the Admiral himself could not take more. They were counted from the after end leaving six at the forepart to remain on board.

This was a great cut to the six who knew well what to expect afterwards. Captain Richardson made his report to the Admiral which, I was told, was sent home to India House in due form.[4] Captain Tommy cared little about the matter, as he had never returned home from a command without having been severely reprimanded by the Court of Directors for severity. Although it is rather premature to state here what was the result in this case, which could not be noticed by the Court till nearly two years afterwards, I may

'Front of the East India House, Leadenhall Street', by William Griggs, from *Relics of the Honourable East India Company*, 1909. (The Trustees of the National Library of Scotland.)

as well inform the reader that Captain Tommy was hauled up before the Court at Leadenhall Street, in full toggery as was customary and heard the reprimand given him by the Chairman. On departing he wheeled round to walk out from the centre of the hollow horseshoe table, and proceeded a few paces with his coat tails turned up behind, when the Chairman called him back to his place before him to administer a most severe rebuke for such insulting conduct. Many of the members were for dismissing him from the service forthwith and, if the Chairman had not been to some extent a friend of his, it was said that he certainly should have been dismissed.

This digression from the usual current of events will save any further notice of the Court of Directors for some time to come. However, the full force of the insult can only be known by the fact that their orders were, when officers or civil servants were sent before the court to be sworn in or for any other purpose, that they should not turn their backs at all when going out from the centre of the horseshoe table. They had to back out with their face to the Chairman all the way till reaching the door, in nautical parlance, to 'make a stern board of it', the same as a subject does in the presence of majesty. Nothing can excuse this abominable conduct of Captain Tommy, as he was the last man in the world to have looked over such an insult if offered to himself. Indeed, no man was ever a greater stickler for respect and almost 'kowtowing' than he was.

The 'round robin' affair cleared the ship of 13 of the most troublesome characters in her, and in a day or two afterwards we sailed for Singapore and China. At the former, our stay was only a few days, and about the end of August 1821 we arrived at Macao Roads, where we took on board a river pilot and proceeded to Whampoa.[5] The passage generally occupied two or three days, unless detained at Second Bar by neap tides.

At the latter place the usual work of clearing cargo and refitting ship had been carried on for some weeks when I was ordered by the captain to go on board of a small opium ship called the *Merope* with six armed men.[6] There I was to act as a help to the captain and officers in the event of the Chinese boarding the ship and taking the opium, as had been threatened by their Government, along with thundering edicts about driving the 'Fanquais' [foreigners] out of the port. Captain Tommy was a large holder of opium in the vessel, and had been requested to do this by the agent James Matheson and others.[7] The ship was then to go to sea and cruise amongst the Ladrone Islands till her cargo should be delivered into smuggling boats, and thereby avoid a rupture with the Chinese Government.

The six men placed under my command were picked by the Captain himself, and I

'Macao, China', from Robert Elliot, *Views in the East*, 1833.
(The Trustees of the National Library of Scotland.)

had no reason to find fault with his choice. On joining the *Merope* at Whampoa I found her to be commanded by a most gentlemanly man, by name George Parkyns, a lieutenant RN on half pay.[8] The chief mate's name was Lang and the second's Grant, formerly a midshipman RN.

The following morning we got under way without opposition from the Chinese, having previously received Captain Tommy and Mr Matheson on board for a passage to Macao, which was made in a couple of days, passing through the Bocca Tigris without remark. It was our custom in this ship to remain at anchor for a few days or sometimes a week or two off Macao, Lintin, or some of the Ladrone Islands, leaving notice with the fishermen where we were likely to be found by the smugglers, who frequently came from Canton for opium. Occasionally we got under way for practice only and cruised about during the day, coming back to our former anchorage in the evening. At other times we would go on shore at Macao for a day, where Mr Matheson's house was always at our disposal, to see what was going on, or go shooting where there was any game to be got.

On our first visit to Lintin, after Captain Tommy had left us, we found the *Topaze* frigate there and, as Captain Parkyns had by this time begun to take someone with him almost to every place or ship he might visit, I accompanied him on board the frigate frequently, both to dinner and casually, which was a pleasant variety to the small society of a Country ship. The band, which was a very good one, gave me great pleasure, and was a most marked contrast to the few musicians which I had been accustomed to in the *Marquis Camden*, who were not treated as bandsmen are in general, but made sweepers of in both watches for all time! If they did not play to please Tommy he would stop their grog for a month, and make them practice all their leisure hours besides. An old Scotchman, who played the clarinet, one day did not make his appearance very quickly when the sweepers were piped. When the chief officer found fault with him for it he said he 'did nae come abourd to soop the decks', he 'cam to play moosic!', for which he got one dozen lashes the next day when Tommy heard of it.

The frigate's lieutenants, four in number, were all 'acting' from other ships, but they were not quite so young as most of such rank are at the present time, the junior being certainly not less than 28 years of age. Captain Richardson had gone to Canton and all was very jolly, when one day we noticed a boat's crew sent on shore to wash clothes. At the same time the *Merope's* boat was getting water at the little stream to the right of the village, under the charge of Mr Grant, who had one Englishman and one sepoy with him, the rest were Lascars. Suddenly we saw a row commence between the Chinese and the frigate's crew, the midshipman running and hailing Grant to go and lend them a hand, which he speedily did. The sepoy fired his musket steadily till the only three cartridges he had were expended. The *Topaze's* men had no arms and were sore put to it, but the frigate immediately fired and hoisted the signal of recall. First Lieutenant Hamilton, as we learned afterwards, intended to batter the village down whenever he got the boat off but, seeing there was no time to lose, he manned and armed two boats and sent them to the

'European Factories, Canton', from George Newenham Wright, *China in a series of views*, 1843. (The Trustees of the National Library of Scotland.)

rescue. The natives were very numerous, but were a good deal kept at bay by Grant's pistol and the sepoy's three slowly delivered shots till, on the arrival of the boats, they soon took to their heels up the hill, but only to be brought down like pigeons by the marines and the guns of the frigate, which could now fire over the heads of her own men.

The recall was after a time again hoisted and when all were shoved off, after a very considerable slaughter of the Chinese, the great guns played on the village for some time till the damage was seen to be sufficient. This disturbance caused the trade to be stopped at Canton and Captain Richardson escaped from it just in time to save his life which, in the heat of the first account of the affair, was in considerable jeopardy from the Chinese authorities. He got on board the *Topaze*, I think, about three days afterwards.

Sir James Urmston,[9] the chief of the Company's factory, finding that the Viceroy of Canton was inexorable as to condemning the trade, ordered all the Company's ships to leave Whampoa and proceed through the 'Bogue' to Chuenpee on a certain day, and there to await further orders. On this day the *Topaze* got under way from Lintin, and the *Merope* also, and stood up the river to meet the fleet coming through the Bogue, which we did in the afternoon, remaining under way till all the ships had anchored. The Typan[10] and some others of the Company's civil servants were on board the *General Harris*,[11] the Commodore's ship, and the rest were on board some of the others, where they were to remain till matters could be brought to an amicable understanding with the Chinese Government.

As the *General Harris* neared the *Topaze* after passing the forts, the frigate began to salute, which we were anxiously waiting for, as Captain Parkyns had said that he would not be surprised if carelessness might cause a few shot to be in the guns! Sure enough the very first gun showed that he was right. The second gun sent a shot close over our forecastle and the fourth another between the main and the mizzenmasts, but the rest seemed to be blank. We were quite well pleased, however, when they ceased firing.

For six weeks after this, idleness reigned supreme in the fleet, and I occasionally went on board my own ship (*Marquis Camden*) to see how all was going on. Captain Tommy was always very kind to me and, one day, when I happened to be on board and the sails had been loosed to dry, the order was given to furl. I went aloft as formerly and furled the mizzen topsail which he did not seem to expect. He was very well pleased at my proceeding, expressing himself to that effect in some way or other, which was very gratifying to me.

I still retained my six men in the *Merope* and, at the end of the six weeks, the political affairs having come to a favourable conclusion,[12] all the fleet returned to Whampoa for tea, the *Topaze* and *Merope* alone being left outside of the Bogue forts. A day or two after this we resumed our former cruising, avoiding the Lintin anchorage for some time.

Some weeks afterwards, when lying in the Macao Roads, I was sent on shore in the jolly-boat, as was frequently the case, the distance being about three miles. Spring tides were running very strong indeed from late freshes in the river which, on returning to the ship, deceived me so much as to make me take in sail a few seconds too soon. We drifted past before a rope could be caught from the ship when alongside, and thence direct out to sea at a pace of at least five knots. We tried to pull in to an island, but it was all in vain and we could only do our best to hold our own till the ship should be under way and pick us up. We knew this would be the case soon because we heard the captain give the order to unmoor when we were not more than 50 yards astern.

It proved, however, a longer job than we expected although the ship's company mustered 50 Lascars and six Englishmen for a vessel of only 300 tons. It must have been nearly two hours afterwards e're we got on board, by which time we were at least ten miles out to sea in the Macao Channel, notwithstanding all our exertions at the oars. It took us nearly three days to get the ship back again to the Roads off the Nine Islands against both wind and a constant powerful tide. Fortunately, time was of no great value to us as we could deliver opium to the smuggling boats anywhere.

CHAPTER 5

My keepers put big knives to my neck

(1822–1823)

Youngsters are always fond of boating and I was no exception to the rule, which Captain Parkyns was well aware of, and in his kindness always employed me in that sort of duty to my heart's content, chiefly in the jolly-boat, which was a safe and stiff boat with two sliding gunter sails and a jib. But 'accidents will happen in the best regulated families', and the anchorage off the Nine Islands was the scene of two more of these warnings and teachings at separate times of no great distance.

It happened that the jolly boat was under repair when I was ordered one day to take the cutter, with as many small empty casks as she could carry, to get water at the largest of these nine islands, about two miles distant. Now this boat was a very crank one, and carried a large single sliding gunter sail with a boom on the foot which brailed up with the sail when temporarily required, leaving all the sail aloft. The wind was fair and blew rather fresh which, when we were leaving the ship's side, made the captain call out to me: 'For God's sake take care, mind, that boat is very crank'. I took all the care possible, with the wind right aft, till about half way, when the course had to be altered a little, and it was necessary to bring the wind on the other quarter. To affect this with safety, as I supposed, I brailed the sail up, boom and all, but the moment the wind took the other quarter the boat capsized! We were all instantaneously swimming about in the water, but soon managed to get on the bottom of the boat, the Lascars swimming like ducks picking up the casks and keeping them together the best way they could, till a Chinese fishing boat should come and take us in, she being only about a quarter of a mile off. But when she did come near us, they would not allow us to touch their boat, and kept at a respectful distance while a bargain was being made between them and me as to the number of dollars I would give them to take us in and tow our boat to the island. This was no easy matter as the demand was very heavy and, at one time, I thought they would have left us to perish, but after much trouble they agreed to take $20 and took us into their boat and towed ours to the island.

There we soon righted the boat and proceeded to fill the casks with water, when the natives said I must go in their boat to the ship and pay the $20, otherwise they would keep us all prisoners. So I sent one of the Lascars in the boat and told him to tell the captain that we were prisoners, and to come with an armed boat's crew and relieve us. This was soon done and after a pull of three hours against wind and tide in our wet clothes we reached the ship and there found the Chinese and their boat, but the Captain refused to pay a cent, as they had no business to keep us prisoners and doubt my word. Indeed, he was very near giving one of them a good flogging, so they were shoved off with a warning to trust to an officer's word another time. The people at the island were very numerous and we were totally unarmed; there was therefore no alternative left but to act as I did.

The next affair happened in the very same boat when I was coming off to the ship from Macao. It was evening when we shoved off, with darkness at hand and some very black looking clouds to seaward. But as it was quite calm and smooth water I thought we might reach the ship before the change should take place; in this I was sadly mistaken. After pulling out about a mile I found the wind set in dead foul, with thunder and lightening and rain. This made me step the mast and determine to run back to Macao and remain all night as we often did, but when we came to hoist the sail it was found that the halyards were jammed in the sheave. The order was given to take down the mast to clear them. Unfortunately, we had an American called Johnston in the boat who had been shipped only a very short time, and this man having got pretty well drunk, he persisted in shinning up the mast to clear the halyards, saying to me in answer to my repeated orders to stay down: 'You are not afraid of going to hell before your time are you?' The moment he was high enough to overbalance the boat the crew of four Lascars and myself instantaneously jumped to the higher side. By God's mercy we exactly counterbalanced this scoundrel's weight for a few seconds during which time he contrived to clear the halyards and slide down the mast into the boat. The relief of this to us all may be more easily imagined than expressed, and such was the impression made on my mind of the certainty of death during the whole drunken escapade, that I cannot even now think of it without a shudder. In the heat of battle it is easy for a man to forget death, but hardly when under such circumstances as I have just related.

The squall by this time had come on, and I was glad to unstep the mast and pull on shore with all speed which we reached in safety, putting up at Mr Matheson's house till next morning. Had Johnston belonged to the *Marquis Camden* he would certainly have got four dozen for disobedience of orders, and probably another for drunkenness, but in a Country ship flogging an American or a European would not have been tolerated, so he escaped with a lecture on his abominable conduct.

Not long after this occurrence the *Marquis Camden* and the *General Harris* were ordered to Penang[1] and to return to Whampoa in July to load with tea, there not being enough for all the ships belonging to the season of 1821. The *Merope* accordingly had to meet the *Marquis Camden* at Lintin some time in January, I think, where five of the men who were with me rejoined their own ship. The other, named Hood, was allowed to enter the *Merope* as gunner and I to remain as third officer till I should be wanted. This was a great favour and granted by Captain Tommy unasked by me, as I was receiving £8 per month pay besides that of midshipman in my own ship of 30*s*. per month. Captain Parkyns was my friend in this affair as in many others, wishing to benefit me in money matters as long as he could, and Captain Tommy seemed quite pleased to allow the same.

The opium fleet outside of the Bogue was now increased to four ships in all: *Samarang*, *Eugenia*, *Merope* and *General Quiroga*.[2] The last was a brig belonging to Macao, which shortly after the sailing of the *Marquis Camden* and *General Harris* being in want of a chief officer, Mr Lang was allowed to join her as such from the *Merope*, which gave me a step up to second officer and an increase of £2 per month in pay, besides a share of the cumshaw money from the opium delivered.

Captain Parkyns was always pleased to go to some new anchorage, and having heard of a very nice bay on the Macao side called Kumsingmoon, where good water was to be got, we went there a short time before the *Marquis Camden* was expected to return, finding the *Eugenia* and *General Quiroga* lying at anchor. The captains gave a most excellent account of the people on shore for quietness and civility, so we did not consider it necessary to go armed. For two or three times this good news proved true. But Chinamen are not to be trusted long, especially anywhere near Canton, as I very soon had the misfortune of proving in person (an account of which I published minutely in the January number of the *Leisure Hour* magazine for 1861).[3] I shall therefore only give a hasty sketch of it here, and refer my readers for all further particulars to the above publication.

Occupied watering on shore one morning, I thought that the Yankee, Johnston, who was in the boat, could manage that matter for a short time in my absence. Meeting the second officer of the *General Quiroga* on the same duty as myself, we thought that we might take a look at the country for a little distance, so we walked inland for about a quarter of an hour and then returned towards the shore. Before reaching it, which was hidden from our view by a small bluff, we were met by about 30 Chinamen, some of whom had hoes and sticks for carrying weights across the shoulders. They let us pass through them, but shortly after came up behind us and pulled us by the arms to stop, which caused my companion to bolt and trust to his legs which were good long ones. I may here state at once that he succeeded in getting into his boat and shoved off to his ship for assistance, while my man Johnston with the Lascar boat's crew, did their best to come to my rescue with oars and stretchers, till beaten back by showers of stones and other missiles into their boat. They also shoved off for the ship.

Almost at the same minute of my friend running away, I was knocked down and tied hands and feet on the ground, and kept in that humiliating position till the boats had shoved off to the ships. Then my feet were untied, and I was dragged along by the rope which bound my wrists by two men, two others following up behind with the heavy sticks before mentioned, which were occasionally used on my shins when I did not run fast enough (for some days afterwards I was quite lame). On we sped in the heat of a burning sun through paddy fields, then up a hill and down the other side of it, where we found the sea beach and a halt was called near a stream for a few minutes. Finding at this time that my wrists were beginning to swell, I showed them to the men and pointed to their taking off the ropes, which they did, leaving me for the rest of the journey tied by one only. Away we went again through heavy sand for nearly two miles more, when we reached a village of a tolerable size, and I was placed in a large open room of a house, where hundreds came to see me who had never seen a 'Fanquai' before.

My keepers put big knives to my neck and pretended to cut off my head, saying they only waited for the mandarin to come to put this into execution. The heat of the crowd was great and I begged that they would drive them away, which led them to place me in a very small room on the opposite side of the court, where I was shown only to a few. Amongst them was a man who could speak some English, who said that he had seen me at Macao. I got this man to agree to take a letter which I wrote with a paint brush and China ink to the captain, when I found that dollars would get me clear. Although the amount demanded was $2,000 the man lowered his price to $50 when he got to the beach at the watering place, where he found a formidable body of officers and men all armed and just consulting which direction to take in order to release me from durance vile.

I had not named any particular sum in my letter, so the captain went on board and brought the $50 in a bag, giving them to the man and telling him if I was not sent back immediately he would go and take me by force, cost what it would. In short, 'he would make a second Lintin business out of it!' He sent a Chinese carpenter of the *Eugenia* with him to transact the affair. In an hour or so I was let go with a precious growl at the small sum obtained, but I left the man to settle that the best way he could as he got all he asked, and the carpenter and I trod our weary way to the beach as best I could after such treatment. I found the captain and all from the three ships anxiously awaiting my return, by whom I was most cordially welcomed and congratulated on my escape.

A few days afterwards, a Chinese man-of-war junk came down from Chuenpee, having heard of the affair. The commander came on board the *Merope* at once, to make enquiries about the men who seized me. He said he would bring them on board and have them punished till I should tell them to stop. But next morning we saw the *Marquis Camden* at anchor off Lintin, distant about seven or eight miles, and we had to get under way immediately to join her there before starting, so I lost the opportunity of seeing the four men punished at my discretion! I was afterwards told that they gained nothing by my absence, and were well 'squeezed' into the bargain, i.e. made to pay a great many dollars.

Captain Tommy had a good laugh at my mishap, but at the same time said: 'It was no joke!' He told me he would send for me some day to rejoin my ship, and in the meantime to stay where I was. I was very well pleased, although I expected promotion to sixth officer, Mr Butler the chief having died at Penang.[4] Yet I knew that no one else would be preferred, and I could afford to wait and pocket a few more dollars in the shape of pay in the *Merope* as second officer, while enjoying the friendship of Captain Parkyns for some time longer to whom I felt deeply indebted for numerous kindnesses. Amongst the number I must not omit to mention the lessons which he constantly gave me in my profession by making me get the ship under way, work her and bring her to an anchor as chief executive, when only a lad of 18. Such practice I was not likely to have in a Company ship for some years, and when I did succeed to that mark which obliged me to act as number one, I felt that confidence which is only to be gained by practice. It would be well if captains in the Navy and merchant service would grant such experience to the young officers under them a little oftener than they do at present.

Towards the middle of September the *Marquis Camden*'s launch was sent down with a chain cable for the *Merope* in tow of some ship, with one man in charge, and I received orders through Captain Parkyns to ask the captain of the first Company's ship which should arrive to give me a passage up to Whampoa and tow the launch up at the same time. We had only a few days to wait when the *Sir David Scott*[5] arrived at Lintin where we were in the *Merope*. Captain Parkyns and I went on board, when we found she was commanded by Captain W. Hunter, who most politely granted our request and as usual gave us all the news in his power.[6]

Amongst the officers, I found a very intimate friend of my family in Doctor N. Grant,[7] from whom I heard of the death of my former shipmate in the *Castlereagh*, Patrick Lindesay, as already related. The following day I joined the *Sir David Scott* and made the launch fast to her for towing, having bade adieu to the *Merope*, her excellent captain and most agreeable officers with whom I had spent eleven months in the most 'jolly' manner, receiving such kindness from Captain Parkyns as have made the deepest impression on my mind both of gratitude and esteem.

Captain Hunter asked me to mess with him on the passage to Whampoa, and my friend the doctor gave me a couch in his cabin, so that for the term of four or five days I fared well and did duty as midshipman. Before leaving the ship at Whampoa, Captain Hunter very kindly offered me the berth of sixth officer which was vacant owing to the promotion made by Lindesay's death. He said he would ask Captain Tommy's permission, but I told him, with many thanks, that I expected to be promoted in my own ship, yet if any such should not take place I would gladly accept his kind offer. On rejoining my own ship, I found I was to belong to the officer's mess as sixth officer, which was at once followed up. The only occurrence worthy of remark before sailing was the great fire which took place in Canton of all the European factories, and a considerable part of the suburbs.[8] This gave us all more or less to do, first in assisting to put it out and save property and, second, in guarding the goods, etc., which were left open, till they could be placed in safety somewhere in the Chinese Hongs.

The delay in loading the ships, however, was not great and we sailed in the *Marquis Camden* for old England about the middle of November, arriving there early in April 1823. The general discipline of the ship was rigidly kept up to the last, and the vacancies filled up with 25 Chinamen with a boatswain of their own, all of whom turned out well and did their duty equally so.[9]

CHAPTER 6

Old Bloody Murder

(1823–1825)

After the continuous service afloat of the two years and six months just sketched, the enjoyment of shore was to one at my time of life great indeed. As the *Marquis Camden* did not sail again till the following winter, I had a delightful spell amongst family and friends in various parts of Scotland for fully six months, but especially during a short trip to Fife where I had never been previously. Yet this accidental visit, as I may call it, had in a few years afterwards a most preponderating effect on the whole proceedings of my future life. For the first time I saw as a very young girl, my future wife, who for the last 32 years has helped me to traverse this weary world in as much happiness and comfort as ever falls to the lot of man.[1]

'The longest lane must have a turning', and so had my cruise on shore, as in November 1823 I was once more called to join the *Marquis Camden* at Northfleet, near Gravesend, bound to Bombay and China. Along with my old friend Veitch, the assistant surgeon who had been again appointed to the ship, I started in a smack for the great city as before, steamers at that time of the year being then unknown.

Captain Larkins had promoted me to fifth officer, not having been able to get me fourth, as he wished. In a few days we got on board of old 'Bloody Murder', as the *Marquis Camden* was generally called by the seamen of the fleet. The officers' names were, in regular gradation: Morgan first;[2] Fox second; Sparrow third;[3] Forbes fourth;[4] myself fifth; and Storr sixth.[5] The doctor's name was Fowler,[6] the purser's was Collingwood[7] and the clerk's Pollhill, besides five midshipmen. All these officers, save Fox, were totally unknown to me and to each other when we first met on board the ship but, before many months elapsed, some of them had good reason to wish that their acquaintance had been of a much shorter duration than it turned out to be, and to regret the day which ever brought them under the command of such a man as Tommy.

As for myself, I knew 'my man', and hardly expected that we should get on so well as formerly, as I felt certain that he would some day attack me with his tongue in the same manner as he did others. I would not be inclined to put up with it quietly when, of course, a row would take place. He was very overbearing in his language to all, and found fault for the merest trifle, constantly trying the patience of the victims most severely. Hitherto, he had been my friend, and I had escaped all abuse, but such a state of things was not to last long as the sequel will prove.

We sailed about Christmas 1823,[8] and after a short stay at Cowes by foul winds,[9] we left the Channel with studding sails on both sides, made Madeira in six days and scarcely even took in a sail till getting into the variables near the Line. As formerly, men in irons and flogging were the rule, not the exception, and the ship's company was soon brought into capital order, as well as first rate discipline, without any rows as before. In short the *Marquis Camden* was the *Camden* of old, a very smart ship. The captain was also Captain Tommy of old and no mistake.

The third and fourth officers were frequently the victims of his attacks in a more violent style than to others, and I wondered how flesh and blood could stand it, and told them so. This I suspect had been overheard and told to Captain Tommy. There was a joiner who also played the French horn in the band and worked daily in one of the awning cabins with a turning lathe, where the captain amused himself very often, and through the windows of which he could see all that was going on on deck. This man was suspected of being a telltale, and was certainly a creature of Tommy's, so he may have told what he heard me say to the third and fourth officers. Be that as it may, before getting off the Cape of Good Hope, it fell to my lot to be put under arrest by the captain for what I and every one else considered was only doing my duty. The occurrence was as follows. We were in the act of trimming sails and shifting studding sails from one side to the other upon altering the course after noon in the third officer's watch with Captain Tommy on the poop. In short, he was in charge of the deck, according to one of his written orders stating that he was always so when he should be on deck at all.

The third officer, not seeing what I was doing in the opposite waist to where he was, told me to send the men to hoist some sail, to which I said I was getting the lower boom fore and aft. As the boom was in a critical position I asked: 'Should I knock them off or not?' On hearing this, Captain Tommy roared out to me by name, adding the word 'sir' to it:

'When an order is given, sir, by the officer of the deck it is to be obeyed immediately, sir, without any answer whatever, sir.' To which I replied: 'I must answer when it is necessary.'

'Hold your tongue, sir!' roared the Captain.

'I must answer, sir, when it is necessary,' was again my reply.

'Go to your cabin, sir, immediately!' roared the Captain.

'Aye aye, sir,' said I, and jumped down off the booms and bolted below.

In the evening he sent for me to his cabin and asked me to make an apology to him. I said I did not think that I had done anything which required an apology, nor would I make one. 'Go to your cabin, sir,' said Tommy, and off I hauled. Two or three days after this it was blowing hard and the chief officer (a most excellent, kind-hearted man) came to me and ordered me (from Captain Tommy) to attend the relieving tackles in the gun-room during the first and morning watches. This I refused by saying: 'If I am to resume my whole duty I shall obey the order, but not otherwise.' The Captain then sent the same in writing, with the addition of asking me if it was my determination to obey or disobey his order which required my attendance at 8 p.m. I wrote in reply that I could only repeat my words which were as above, writing the same by order, which I saw was with the intent of more easily proving my disobedience at a Court of Inquiry. He did not, after this, insist any more on my obeying the order. But about a fortnight afterwards he sent for me again and asked why I refused the advice of my superiors in years with regard to giving in to him and making an apology, saying he would give me one more opportunity of doing so. I told the captain if he referred to Mr Sparrow as my superior in years, he having been the only officer who had advised such a course, I begged to state that I considered I was old enough to judge for myself and I would make no apology.

The Captain then burst forth in a towering rage, saying to me: 'Now, sir, that you have refused my advice as your commander and your friend, I will bring all the charges against you with the utmost virulence!' I said: 'You are perfectly welcome,' and banged the cabin door to with some force. Now some people may say that I was very foolish in acting thus, but the result did not prove it so, and it was with a feeling of annoyance at the bullying and tyranny of Captain Tommy to others more than to myself that I was determined to have the matter tried at Bombay, and see who was to be master. I knew well at the same time that the rules of the service would not justify him in ordering me to do any particular duty when under arrest, and that the original charge was a piece of humbug.

After six weeks confinement below, we arrived in Bombay[10] and I requested Captain Tommy to call a Court of Inquiry, to which he said: 'If that's all you have got to say, sir, leave the cabin!'

'Certainly, sir,' I answered, and shut the door with a bang once more. Nearly a week elapsed and not hearing anything of the court, I wrote a letter to the Governor[11] and sent it to the captain to forward according to custom having left it open for his perusal. He at once sent it back to me with a message through the chief officer stating that he had already called a Court of Inquiry. But after three days lapse of time and still no information about it, I wrote to the Secretary to Government explaining the case and how Captain Tommy had refused to forward my letter to the Governor.

A court was then ordered by the Governor to sit at the Marine Office as soon as possible, and Captain Larkins got a severe reprimand from the Governor for not forwarding my letter. The court was composed of three captains and two chief officers, with the Superintendent of Marine as judge advocate, who patiently and justly heard the evidence for the prosecution. I then asked them for a few days leave on shore that I might get any assistance I thought necessary in making out my defence. To this Captain Tommy remarked that I seemed to think that I was not then under his command. I said to the court that I certainly did think so, and that I was under the command of the court.

'Of course,' said the President (Captain Hamilton of the *Dunira*).[12]

'Oh, I question it,' said Captain Tommy.

'Very well, clear the court,' said the President.

After a few minutes consultation we were again called in, and I was told by the President that the court allowed me to remain three days on shore to get the assistance which I might think necessary, and it would meet again on the fourth day at 10 a.m. So I went to the house of a friend in the Engineers, my brother having gone to the Cape on leave, and got a lawyer named Ayrton to make out my defence for me in case I should have expressed myself rather too strongly. On the appointed day I read the same to the court.

The decision of acquittal was soon given and I was ordered to return to my duty. The court, however, stated that some reply seemed to have been given by me which was not quite warranted by the customs of the service, but Captain Larkins had no right whatever to order me to do any particular duty when under arrest, and I was quite justified in refusing to obey it.

So far I had got windward of Captain Tommy in everything, and I had then time to take up the cudgels in favour of an old messmate of mine when a midshipman. He was still in that capacity on board, and had actually been punished by Captain Tommy with two dozen lashes a few weeks before our arrival in Bombay for slightly abusing the gunner who had called him a thief. He was a young man of 19 and of good family, but Captain Tommy, on hearing the gunner's charge against him, at once told him that he would be flogged on the following day. Sure enough at 10 a.m., in presence of his five messmates, he was tied up to a ring bolt in the cuddy, stripped and flogged by the master-at-arms to the extent of two dozen lashes, which was the more outrageous from its being without any Court of Inquiry or just cause whatever.

Poor Fowler (that was his name) knew nothing about writing official letters, so I took up his case and wrote a letter on his behalf to the Secretary to Government, signed by himself. This very soon called up an investigation by the Governor privately, and the result was that Fowler was ordered a free passage home if he chose to leave the *Marquis Camden*. Doubtless, Captain Tommy was once more severely reprimanded and reported to India House, but nothing of that sort came out publicly. Fowler left the ship, of course, and went home as a passenger in the *Cambridge*, a free trader commanded by Captain Barber.[13] I heard afterwards he went to America without suing Captain Tommy for damages or doing anything in the matter.

Shortly after my acquittal I breakfasted with the Governor at Government House, and was introduced to him specially by Captain Manson of the Artillery,[14] with whom I spent a week on shore by permission of Captain Tommy. He had not then found out that I had written the letter for Fowler to the Secretary to the Government which after we sailed from Bombay wound him up against me completely.

Forbes, the fourth officer, had long been so much annoyed by his abuse that he determined to run, and early on the morning of our sailing he left the ship in a shore boat, not being missed till we got under way. He then joined the Country service and died in China about two years afterwards from drink. He was an Irishman and the son of a colonel in the army, and certainly the treatment he met with from Captain Tommy had much to do with his melancholy end.

Two days after leaving Bombay, Forbes' cabin was ordered to be cleared out by Tommy, and when doing so Mr Sparrow, the third officer, took certain articles of furniture to himself, as he said to square up an account between him and Forbes at backgammon of £3. This I objected to and 'words' arose between us which made him run on deck and report me to the Captain as having struck him, which was grossly false. Tommy was delighted to have a charge against me, and sent for me on deck to tell me that he would try me in China. After such base conduct on the part of Sparrow it was not to be wondered at that we should have some more words when we sat down to dinner. He magnified this into my threatening to strike him again, going to the Captain with another false charge.

I was immediately sent for and, although I flatly denied both charges, he told me that if I repeated this threat he would put me in irons! I told him it was at his peril to do so. As he could not do without my services, and had been reprimanded enough for my former lengthened confinement, he did not venture to put me under arrest then. However, when we were mooring the ship at Whampoa in China six weeks afterwards,[15] he took offence at me not sending the men out of the cable tiers quick enough, he looking down the main hatchway at the time, and ordered me to my cabin once more.

When he left the ship for Canton he gave orders that I was to be kept under close arrest, and if I was seen outside of the cabin door, excepting to go to the quarter gallery, a sentry was to be placed there with a drawn cutlass to prevent my leaving it. It happened that the factory gentlemen were all at Macao, and I was to be kept in this close confinement until they should go to Canton, when a Court of Inquiry would be called. But I soon showed the doctor that he must apply for leave for me to walk the deck as boils were appearing on my body from the heat below. Tommy abused the doctor and told him that he was only siding with me, but he dared not refuse.

After a month spent in this way a court was called, consisting of three captains and two chief officers, who were also to try the second officer Fox for most gross and ungentlemanly language to the junior officers. As for the charges against me they were 13 in number, and all were so worded as to get any officer dismissed the service if proved. Some of them were for my language to Sparrow; one was for not leaving the boatswain's cabin when ordered by Tommy (which the sixth officer and I had purchased from him from Bombay to China); and another was for saying to myself on deck when Tommy came out of his cabin one day: 'Now we shall have it!' This was overhead, it appeared, by the steward, one of the telltales, but this meaning could never have been understood from the wording of the charge, which was strong enough to have hanged any man. It was so laughed at by the court when it was brought forth in its turn that the President (Captain Walker)[16] said to Tommy: 'Well, Larkins, what shall we have? A glass of wine?' Not one of the other charges do I recollect, but I know that there were none connected with what he put me under arrest for. To give an idea of the exaggeration of the whole, I may just state that the second charge was passed over, being a repetition of the first!

During the trial it was clearly shown that Tommy had made use of the second and third officers as telltales, as well as the gunner and ship's steward, making him lose caste afterwards very much amongst his brother captains. I shall only add one remark about the evidence given by Mr Fox, the second officer. He was in his cabin when the disagreement took place between Sparrow and myself and, of course, heard every word, which bulkhead information he wrote down and handed to the Captain as evidence against me. In my defence I took notice of this and said:

> The evidence of Mr Fox is totally unworthy of the consideration of this court. Had
> he done his duty, he would have used his authority as a superior officer when he
> heard the quarrelling between Mr Sparrow and I and come into our mess berth and
> put a stop to it, instead of writing down what he heard through the bulkhead for the
> purpose of handing it to his commander! I ask you all gentlemen if this is the conduct
> of a man of honour? If it is not, his evidence must be condemned.

Not a word was said by the court, and I went on with my defence to the end, under the evident satisfaction of the members, but not so of Tommy, who must then have begun to see his mistake. With less judgement than I gave him credit for, he remarked that I had 'again indulged in attacking my superior officer in a most unwarrantable manner'. I replied that I looked on Mr Fox as I conceived I had a right to do, solely as an evidence for the prosecution. 'Undoubtedly,' said the President, and Tommy had sense enough to say no more.

The decision of the court was not given in my case on that day at all, only the minutes of the trial sent to Sir James Urmston at Canton. In Fox's case they at once condemned and severely reprimanded him, ordering him to return to his duty, although Tommy had never put him under arrest at all. I think it was more than a fortnight afterwards when the court met again by order of Sir James to assign the punishment, having found me guilty only of one charge out of the 13, and that was 'improper language to my superior officer'. I was reprimanded accordingly without a single word of comment, and ordered to return to my duty.

This punishment it will be seen was merely nominal and Tommy, Fox and Sparrow had reason to repent of their conduct for many a day afterwards. A caricature was drawn by an officer of the *Macqueen*[17] and handed round all in Canton representing a fox being chased by a lot of officers and midshipmen with cobbing boards in their hands, two

Chinamen standing looking on with a sneer saying 'that have very quisei dog truly'. Captain Tommy also stood as a looker on, saying: 'Oh my poor fox!' This shows the feeling of the officers of the fleet exactly. On the other hand, I was asked on board of sundry ships by the senior officers to parties, where I had my health drunk along with 'the downfall of tyranny and oppression!' Mr Sparrow's turn was now about to begin, as in my defence I took condemnatory notice of his evidence as well as that of Fox, he having taken several gallons of the captain's brandy for his own use, 'for the trouble he had with the cask', as he repeatedly stated when I remonstrated with him in the mess. This was too great a crime for Tommy to pass over even in his coadjutor against me, and he called a Court of Inquiry upon him, which actually sat on the *Earl of Balcarras*.[18] The members seeing that there was nothing could save him from dismissal, they got Tommy to accept an apology and the charge was quashed.

About this time for weeks, indeed I may say months, there were continual courts on men or officers and floggings of men, which did not increase the popularity of the captain of the *Marquis Camden*. He, after worrying me so much as to sicken me of the ship, as he thought, got Mr Matheson and the captain of a small Country ship, a lieutenant RN whom I knew, to offer me chief officer's berth in her. But I knew that I must, according to the regulations of the service, be promoted to third officer in my own ship, the chief, Mr Morgan, having unfortunately been drowned at Whampoa, and Forbes, the fourth, having run. I had no idea of quitting her to be put down 'run' on the books, which Tommy must of necessity have done had I left the ship, so my answer to this was: 'I will accept your offer if Captain Larkins will give me a regular discharge.' This I hardly thought he would do, as he would have been fined by the Company I believe £200.

And so it turned out, leaving him in the quandary of promoting two steps the man whom he at that time, I think, could have seen drowned without much grief. He tried hard to get officers from other ships to join as third, but no one would accept. I said nothing as I intended to claim my right from Sir James Urmston, the chief of the Company's factory, e're it should be too late. However, this was rendered unnecessary by Tommy requesting Sir James to appoint an officer (since no one would accept his offer), or order one to join. To this, Sir James asked why I should not be promoted and if he thought me non-qualified. To the first he said I had done so and so and been tried by a Court of Inquiry, and to the second he said he had nothing to prefer against me as to qualifications. Then Sir James told him to order me up to be sworn in as third officer immediately which accordingly he did, with a very bad grace, along with a senior midshipman from the *Castle Huntley*[19] who thought he would run the risk of some bullying for the sake of three steps of promotion.

After Sir James had sworn us in at the factory in Canton, he said to me these memorable words:

> Now Miller, I should recommend you to put up with a great deal from Captain
> Larkins during the voyage home, rather than have any further words with him, as it

will be so much in your favour after arrival in England. We all know what Captain Larkins is, but neither the Company at home nor here will suffer him to twist and turn his officers about as he thinks proper, and his attempt to prevent your promotion was most unwarrantable and what I should never have allowed.

I thanked Sir James for his kind advice and promised to do as he wished.

Before sailing we had one more Court of Inquiry on Mr Storr, the sixth officer, but what the charges were I have no recollection. He was reprimanded, however, and made the number of four officers tried at Whampoa, one drowned and one run out of the whole six!

At last we sailed for home in company with the *Lady Melville*, Captain Clifford,[20] in the month of January 1825 and, extraordinary to tell, I was only once found fault with by Captain Tommy, and that arose from his supposing that I had heard him give a certain order on deck, when I had not, and he told me that he was not going to be laughed at by a boy like me on the quarterdeck. I said nothing. As third officer I had a great deal of duty and charge of a watch besides, but all went smoothly, although not very comfortably after all that had taken place. We touched at St Helena as usual, and also at Ascension for turtle, arriving at Gravesend some time in May.[21]

On getting the ship into the East India Docks, I found that Mr Fox had orders for the fourth officer to attend the ship there and not me, which was taking 10s. a day out of

'Gravesend' from William Westall and Samuel Owen, *Picturesque tour of the River Thames*, 1828. (The Trustees of the National Library of Scotland.)

my pocket. So finding out by inquiry at India House that as third officer I had the option of doing this duty, I told Mr Fox I certainly should remain, and did so without any further question till the ship was cleared.

Then came the certificate to be got and sent to the Committee of Shipping,[22] which Captain Tommy flatly refused when I asked him in the Jerusalem Coffee House,[23] telling me loudly that he wasn't going to be laughed at by me all the voyage and give me a certificate! I said I should write in to the Committee of Shipping and learn his reasons for the same. I did so and he was called before them and told that they were perfectly satisfied with my conduct from the minutes of the Courts of Inquiry, and since he objected to give me a certificate, they would not enforce it, but it should be entered in their minute book as dispensed with by the Committee of Shipping, which would suit me better when I should come to pass examination in future than the best he could give.

This was very satisfactory to me, but I was determined to have a private certificate of service from Tommy, and I got Doctor Kedslie of the *Dunira*[24] to go along with me to request it. At first, he got a flat refusal but, softening a little, he said: 'I assure you Kedslie it goes most dreadfully against the grain for me to give Miller a certificate as he is and has been my bitterest enemy, and is a person who has done me more harm in the world than any other man I ever met with.' I said I had no wish to have been his enemy, that he had driven me to act as I did in self defence and so far from being his enemy, I begged to thank him for all his former kindnesses to me, which even then I could not easily forget.

This had the desired effect and he gave me the certificate! After all this it will not be much wondered at that I should never again have sailed with Captain Tommy. Although extraordinary as it might appear, we lived to be very good friends a number of years afterwards in Tasmania and in Hong Kong, as may be noticed hereafter, abundantly proving that there was no want of kindly feeling in the man, notwithstanding his stern and violent demeanour in general when in command.

CHAPTER 7

My first really comfortable service

(1826–1827)

My next ship was the Honourable Company Ship *Asia*,[1] Captain T.F. Balderston,[2] bound to Madras and Calcutta in the spring of 1826,[3] after a long spell on shore of ten months spent most agreeably with my family in Edinburgh and moving about the country. Captain Balderston, a very different person from Tommy, plainly told me that he cared nothing for all the rows I had had with that well known severe disciplinarian, and got me appointed third officer of his ship, which proved to be the most comfortable in every way that I had yet belonged to.

H.M. Sterndale, the chief officer, was a most gentlemanly man and a friend of my own, remaining so not only to the end of the voyage, but to the end of his days.[4] All the others were very agreeable and good officers,[5] and the duties of the ship were uniformly carried on in a quiet, orderly style, very different from what I had yet seen in the service. The passengers were all most friendly and pleasant, and being in number about 38, both ladies and gentlemen, our society was quite as large as one generally meets with on shore in his own circle. Of course, various amusements were resorted to which made the time pass agreeably to all. We had 200 Company recruits, besides women and children, the whole being under the command of our own captain and officers.

This number of individuals with our own ship's company of 120, and the ship only 1,000 tons, made us rather crowded, but all went on well. We touched nowhere before arriving at Madras, I think some time in August, after the usual changes in what may be called a fine weather voyage.

During most of the time we had dancing in the evenings, having 15 young ladies and four elderly ones, and once a week there used to be cards in the cabins under the poop, followed on another evening by a musical party in the steerage. These, with a newspaper edited by a civilian named Wynch,[6] gave plenty of room for conversation and sometimes, no doubt, a little scandal. One match only was decidedly made up on board, between Mr Wynch and a Miss Maling who was with her stepmother, who certainly seemed to be agreeable to the whole affair. But alas, 'the current of true love never ran smooth', and on arrival at Calcutta the banns were forbidden by the father, the major at Fort William.[7]

A week or two afterwards, an hour before daylight, a carriage and four was seen at the fort gate where the major's house was, and Miss Maling, being in full expectation of the same, jumped into the arms of Mr Wynch. They started off for some church at Barrackpur where they were married, and 'done for', in spite of the crusty old major, who in this case was assuredly right.[8] He had some knowledge of family antecedents connected with the bridegroom which, had Miss Maling known, would have been to the good because a few years afterwards Mr Wynch became the inmate of an asylum.

I have said that only this match was got up on board, but there was another which was thought likely to come to something, between a young civilian Mr W.[9] and a Miss E.C. which met with a very sad and totally unexpected termination. After our arrival at Diamond Harbour in the Hooghly,[10] and all the passengers had left for Calcutta, we heard that the couple were often on 'the course' together. One evening Miss E.C., being in a carriage with her mother and two sisters, stopped to talk to Mr W. whom they met

'The East Indiaman Asia', by William John Huggins, 1836.
(National Maritime Museum, London.)

Calcutta: 'A view of the River, Shipping and Town from near Smith's
Dock', from James Baillie Fraser, *Views of India: Calcutta & its environs, 1824–26.*
(The Trustees of the National Library of Scotland.)

there, and whose horse was very restive and troublesome. On his leaving the ladies, Miss
E.C. said to him: 'Do take care of yourself with that horse.' Mr W. replied: 'Oh there is
no danger. I never was born to be killed by a fall from a horse!' Most memorable words,
when coupled with what immediately took place: they were hardly uttered when he was
thrown to the ground and killed on the spot before the eyes of all the four ladies he had
just left! His body was taken to his lodgings in the college and the carriage drove home
with the ladies, all more dead than alive.

I sincerely trust that the effect produced was a lasting and beneficial kind to all of
them as to the short-sightedness of the tempting of providence by man. I never heard
more of them than that, shortly afterwards they went up the country along with their
father, who was an 'old civilian'.

When it came to my turn for leave to Calcutta, I stayed with my friend Dr
Grierson,[11] the garrison surgeon at Fort William, who with his wife, let me see all that
was worth seeing in that city of palaces, and also a good deal of society both military and
civil. My 14 days were thus soon got through and there was nothing for it then but down
to the ship and stow saltpetre and silk, etc. in the hold of the good ship *Asia*, till, with a
fresh batch of passengers, we left Diamond Harbour for London in February 1827. We

sailed from Saugor under tow of a large tug steamer,[12] the wind being foul. In charge of the ship was Mr Clarke, a branch pilot whose brig the *Hattrass* had been sent on ahead some time before.[13] After getting down the Channel about five or six miles, the breeze freshened and the steamer, quite suddenly, let go the hawser and steered past us, hailing that he was going to Calcutta, receiving not a little abuse from our captain in reply. Immediately, orders were given to make sail with all smartness, there being no anchoring ground where we were and very little room between the shoals.

It was hooroosh and bear a hand every where on deck and aloft, and in an incredibly short space of time we had topsails, topgallant sails and courses set, in time to get way enough to tack before nearing the shoal on the starboard hand and all was right! The pilot said he never saw sail made on a ship so quickly, and had it not been so we must have gone on shore and most likely never come off again. We soon beat out to sea and, getting rid of Mr Clark, steered for the Cape.

I do not now recollect the passengers names,[14] but they were all very agreeable and no disturbances whatever took place either on the outward or homeward voyage, or anything which made discomfort in the ship. Sure enough the living at the captain's table was splendid and fit for any nobleman, including champagne every day and burgundy on Sundays along with an immense variety of other and more common kinds of wines. All, no doubt, had a very great effect in keeping up the general harmony which reigned during the whole of a four months voyage to England where we arrived some time in June.[15]

The only hitch in these truly pleasant 14 months was caused by Mr Pearce, the second officer, who was sometimes given to what is called 'lifting his little finger too often to his head' or, nautically, 'bousing up his jib stay'. Unfortunately for him, his habit showed itself on shore when at St Helena. The Captain, to his utter horror, was met with about half the ship's company on a cruise, which he soon found on inquiry was by permission of Mr Pearce, who had been left in charge by the chief officer when he had gone on leave for the day. As luck would have it, Captain Balderston soon found the chief officer in James Town, and ordered him to collect the men together at once and take them off to the ship and place Mr Pearce under arrest. Thus, he checked in the bud any chance of rows from the escapades of up to 50 seamen let loose in such a place as St Helena, where after getting drunk (an almost inevitable issue), some half dozen at least might have killed themselves by falling over cliffs or other dangerous places.

Mr Pearce did no more duty in the Company's ship *Asia*, and on arrival was reported to the Committee of Shipping at India House for trial by Court of Inquiry. On his assuring the captain that he intended to resign the service, the charges were temporarily withdrawn and, consequently, a vacancy made for me. Through Captain Balderston I was promoted accordingly and was told to be in readiness to join when the ship should 'come afloat' for the following voyage. After clearing the ship in the East India Docks, I left for Edinburgh by smack as usual, enjoying my holiday all the more from the fact of having obtained such timely promotion.

However, my return from this voyage was seriously dampened by a letter received in the Downs, informing me of the death of my worthy and beloved mother on 27 March, and that my father and eldest sister were waiting my arrival in London.[16] They had come up for the sake of a little change of scene for the good old man who had suffered much from nervous debility since the death of his dear wife. The meeting in London was of a very melancholy nature, of course, but I did what I could to amuse my father till he and my sister got tired of the great city and left for Edinburgh in a week. I followed them in about another fortnight to a sad, but still affectionate home, staying the whole of the autumn and following winter.

I found that my mother had been six months ill in bed with some internal disease, and had died most peacefully with her whole trust in a crucified Saviour, leaving all her five absent sons to the protection and care of our Heavenly Father. It is rather remarkable that on taking leave of my mother before joining the *Asia* for the late voyage, she called me back after I had descended some steps and kissed me a second time. It was the last I ever received from her.

Now that I have got to the end of this my first really comfortable service in a Company ship, and have time to look back quietly on days gone by, there is a remark that I heard made by one of the seamen of the *Asia* which has just occurred to my mind. At the time it struck me as somewhat worthy of notice coming from such a person and well knowing that 'Jacks' in general were not much given to express astonishment at anything or to moralise either on the work of God or man. The case was as follows. We had been at sea for upwards of three and a half months, had seen no land since leaving the Channel off the Lizard and we expected to sight the southern part of Ceylon at a certain hour. Accordingly, a topman was hailed and asked to look out sharp from the topgallant yard on the port bow for land. He had only been up about a quarter of an hour when he reported 'land in sight.' This immediately called forth from the man, who I happened to be standing near, this observation to his chum:

> Well, Bill, I have often heard of the cleverness of the officers of these ships in navigation, but it is wonderful when you see a fellow sent up to look for land after three and a half months out of sight of it and hear him sing out there it is, in almost the next minute after he has taken a squint!

The answer was full of expressions of approval and wonder also, and really gave rise to the remembrance of the words of 107th Psalm, verse 23:

> They that go down to the sea in ships, that do business in great waters, these see the works of the Lord and His wonders in the deep . . .

These very men had seen such wonders hundreds of times without causing a single thought in all probability, and yet they must marvel at the works of man. This arose entirely from their ignorance on the subject of navigation that certainly, to the untutored mind, looks very mysterious especially when such perfect accuracy is the result.

No doubt the sciences of astronomy and navigation are very wonderful and striking to the mind of anyone, but the latter has been so simplified during the last 60 or 70 years as to render it a comparatively easy matter to take a ship with accuracy all over the world. This is done by 'inspection' or by certain forms and tables of various kinds in figures educed from the theory, which is founded entirely on spherical trigonometry. Although passed over altogether by a great many for the more easy and simple method of inspection it is essential to the thorough understanding of navigation.

A good navigator must be a correct observer with the sextant and other instruments, and consider himself independent of chronometers entirely, trusting to the sun, moon, planets and stars for his guidance. Chronometers should be left for such times as when distances, and so forth, of the heavenly bodies cannot be obtained because the best of them are liable to error. You can always find the error of the sextant before or after observing. The shorter method will, however, always be in general use as despatch is too often of the most material consequence at sea, both in navigation and everything else.

While on this subject I shall mention a circumstance that happened to me a few years after the date I have now arrived at which will show the necessity of a commander of a ship being so far skilled in navigation as to be independent of chronometers, and more especially when there may be only one in the ship.

The case was on a passage to Mauritius Island. Coming from the Cape of Good Hope it is necessary to run down the longitude before entering the south-east trade winds, and then steer nearly due north till the island be sighted. Consequently, it is essential that the longitude should be quite correct otherwise the ship may get to leeward of the island and cause either a dead beat up against the trade wind or a run to the leeward until the easting should be run down as before. Either causes a loss of perhaps three or four weeks in time.

Now it so happened that I had observed the longitude by chronometer to gradually differ from that by lunar observations during the whole voyage from England, making the total when entering the trade wind before steering for the island as much as 60 miles, or one degree. I had to choose between my lunars and the chronometer. Of course, I considered the former correct and the chronometer wrong, and steered accordingly, making the island to a nicety! Had I trusted to the chronometer I should have been 60 miles to leeward and not seen it at all! The rate had been wrong or changed, from the difference of being placed in a ship instead of the shore. Even in the best instrument this will always make a small difference, and I had had no opportunity of rerating it after first placing it on board.

CHAPTER 8

Passengers we had plenty

(1828–1830)

Months rolled on in the pleasures and society of friends and home, but the spring of 1828 found me again bound for London in a Leith smack. These vessels were not only remarkable craft of their day, well commanded and sailed in every way, but a mode of conveyance to a sailor which gave him frequently much amusement from the people met with on board as cabin passengers. We had, in general, plenty of time to decipher their characters, being occasionally a week or even 10 to 12 days on a voyage due to foul winds and putting into Bridlington, Harwich or other ports to escape them, and to buy fresh grub. Indeed, I have seen after an 11 days passage everyone more sorry than another at parting. The steamers, when they took heart to sail during both winter and summer and reduced their fares, soon drove the far famed smacks into a corner. They were re-rigged as schooners so they might be sailed with fewer men, having fewer passengers and less able to afford expense.

This last trip in the *Eagle*[1] was rendered famous by our having a very distinguished French officer on board, a Colonel Millard, formerly ADC to Napoleon I during most of the Peninsular War. He had been banished by the Bourbons, of course, and had been supported in England and Scotland for several years by Masonic Lodges. He was then going to London to try to steal over to his beloved France. We could make out his meaning by signs and gestures, although he could not speak a word of English, and had an infinite deal of fun with him. One day at dinner he sat next to me and I had been making some remark about Napoleon at St Helena, thinking he did not understand it, but he fired up at once, and seizing a knife, he pointed it to my breast, singing out in a most determined manner: 'Qu'est-ce que vous dites?' [What are you saying?]. I soon found it was all in play and he really did not know what I had said.

'Setting in of the Monsoon, Madras', by William Danniel, from *Oriental Annual*, 1834.
(The Trustees of the National Library of Scotland.)

That trip came to an end in eight days, and I soon found myself ensconced on board the old *Asia* once more, as second officer, which made me a messmate of the captain, along with the chief, Mr Pitcher,[2] the doctor, Mr Renwick,[3] and the purser, Mr Irwin,[4] who, with all the other officers and midshipmen, were what may be termed 'well met'.[5] Passengers we had plenty of both sexes, including nine officers and 200 men of HM 26th Regiment for Madras, commanded by Lieutenant Colonel Campbell, besides women and children belonging to the regiment.[6] We were rather crowded, but all went well and comfortably during the voyage, touching nowhere till arrival at Madras where we landed the troops and remained a week.

The amusements of the passengers were much the same as before: dancing in the evenings and occasional parties for cards and music. Colonel Campbell was a hater of pork in all shapes, and used frequently to say that no one could deceive him with it. However, Captain Balderston one day told the steward to cook a piece of pork, and make it appear as a fillet of veal. Now, the cook was one from the 'City of London Tavern', and knew his business well. No one at the table was aware of the intended deception when the 'fillet of veal' was uncovered before me for carving. I very innocently asked the colonel to take some supposing it had been 'preserved', he partaking of it twice and praising it up as most excellent. Some of the others, however, were not to be so easily gulled and, remembering

[49]

the repeated declarations of the colonel, took great pleasure in declaring the meat to be pork, and appealing to the steward, and even the captain, for the truth of it. Neither denied that it was veritable pork. The colonel looked daggers at the captain and from that day to his quitting the ship he never spoke to him again, but no words passed, or anything to make things uncomfortable. It was a good lesson to the colonel against boasting of his knowledge of pork and I believe he was more vexed at himself than the captain.

Amongst the 'soldier officers' was a Lieutenant Kelly, a very fine looking, dashing and agreeable Irishman. This unfortunate man, not long after leaving the ship, got irritated with a young cadet in a billiard room and struck him. He was tried by court-martial and dismissed the service, which I regretted very much, both for his own sake and that of the regiment with which he was a most deserved favourite.[7] Another officer 'of ours', I may say, was also dismissed by sentence of court-martial for some improprieties in barracks. He was the son of Colonel Campbell and an ensign.[8] I met him about three years afterwards at Mauritius where he was teaching English: such are the changes in this world, and I could not help thinking 'tempora mutantur, nos et mutamur in illis' [times change and we change with them].

It has often been remarked that passengers on board of ship have uncommonly good appetites, and I have had opportunities of proving the truth of this beyond the possibility of doubt. This was especially so on this voyage, in the person of a Mr Paxton of the civil service who had been home on sick leave, and was returning to Bengal with his wife,[9] who was also rather famous for her 'twist'.[10] Her husband, however, beat her and every one else at knife and fork work, and enjoyed the good living at Captain Balderston's table amazingly, so much so that at dinner he never ate less than four plates of meat, three of puddings and tarts, besides dessert and a full quantum of beer and wine. His only difficulty at first was to get through this quantity within the same or nearly the same time as others who ate about half as much, but he soon found a plan which answered admirably. While despatching one plateful he kept his eye all over the table to see what he should chose next and, having a servant well up to his requirements, he at once gave the empty plate to him over his left shoulder, with the single word 'mutton', 'fowl' or anything else wanted. 'Black Tom' was off in a moment and served both liberally and quickly, as all carvers knew well whose plate it was when he shoved it in. He was a spare, lean man notwithstanding all he ate, and never 'turned out' to breakfast which both he and his wife always took in bed trusting to the purveying qualities of Black Tom, as well they might, as he would seize on the steaks, chops, hot rolls, butter, coffee and a four pound pot of jam the moment after the captain had taken his seat. He used to say that it was 'very ungentlemanly to turn out before the world was well aired' and, when off the Cape where the Pintados or pigeons[11] were very numerous, that he could 'conceive nothing more delightful than their life, always hunting after food'! In fact, his only pleasure was in eating and drinking, but he never indulged too much in the latter. This extraordinary man only lived about a year after landing at Calcutta, which was not much to be wondered at.

It is a very difficult thing to please a number of passengers on board ship, and one would have thought it impossible that any could have a single fault to find with Captain Balderston's viands and liquors. Yet even ladies cannot prevent themselves acting foolishly in this way sometimes. We had an instance of it in the wife of a colonel of cavalry, who used to have mutton chops sent into her cabin for lunch daily at noon, for herself and daughter, a girl of 16. Because pork chops had been sent on two occasions she returned them, and told the servant to say to the steward that her daughter could not eat pork chops every day. The steward reported the same to the Captain who ordered the chops to be stopped entirely, which gave the lady time for reflection, and she was soon glad to sing to a different tune.[12]

On arrival in the Hooghly in October 1828[13] we soon had a clear ship to ourselves. The usual harbour duties were carried on with great peace and comfort, officers relieving each other on leave to the Captain's house at Calcutta for a fortnight or three weeks at a time. There we were always most hospitably and kindly treated, as on the former occasion. I could not but wonder at the difference between the Captains Larkins and Balderston, the former scarcely ever asking an officer to his house at all, either in India or China.

I was much pleased one day to see my old ship the *Merope* coming in from the sea, and Captain Parkyns, knowing I belonged to the *Asia*, hove to till I went on board to call for him. He was from China and going to Calcutta for more opium, with which he told me he had done very well, and only intended to make one trip more. His liver was affected and when we met in Calcutta a few weeks afterwards I seriously advised him to go home with what he had got. He did not till two years later when, after succeeding to the title of baronet through the death of some relative, he died, unmarried, with little enjoyment of the fortune he had made.

Early in March 1829 we left the Hooghly for London with a full complement of passengers of the true upper class Indian type amongst whom, and at the top of the tree, was the Honourable Andrew Ramsay, a judge, a brother to the Earl of Dalhousie and one of the pleasantest and kindest of men.[14] I soon found out from him that he had been a class fellow of an uncle of mine at the High School of Edinburgh in his young days, and he used to go over the recital of the master's (Cruikshank) tyranny in the way of punishments, with great gusto, of which I had often previously heard my uncle speak also. Indeed, this monster had been repeatedly brought before the courts in Edinburgh by the parents of the boys of his class, and fined only, I am sorry to say, but never dismissed from the school, extraordinary to relate. Mr Ramsay told me that it fell to his lot to be nearly killed by him in this way. He was playing with a good sized piece of Niggerhead tobacco when he was observed by Cruikshank, who at once forced the whole of the tobacco down his throat! This of course soon made him very ill, and he was confined to bed and the house for three weeks by it, in a very dangerous state. Yet the Earl, his father, sent him back to the same class when well enough to go, which seemed to me equally extraordinary as the punishment and, so far as Mr Ramsay knew, there was no notice taken of it in any way.

Another cruelty commonly practised by this wretch on the boys, but especially the fat ones, was to place them with their backs close to the large fire of the class room till nearly roasted! Constant thrashing with the tawse was not thought to be sufficiently lasting on the memory by this teacher of youth, who assuredly ought to have been served like Roderick Random's schoolmaster by Lieutenant Bowling.[15] Fortunately, these days are now gone by, but it makes one's blood boil to think that such a fellow should get off from the hands of the jailer so many times in those days. This man and his brother teacher, William Nicol, 'par nobile fratrum' [a well matched pair], were the chosen friends and cronies of the great poet Robert Burns in many a drinking bout in Edinburgh! In fact, the last man named was the 'Willie' mentioned in the first line of the famous drinking song of Burns: 'O Willie brew'd a peck o'maut, And Rob [Burns] and Allan [Allan Ramsay] cam to see'.[16]

But this is a digression and I must back to my old ship *Asia* again homeward bound from Bengal. Mr Ramsay proved a very kind friend to me during the whole of the passage, frequently playing chess together in his cabin in the evenings, with a glass of hot whisky toddy at our elbows, and having many a pleasant yarn during my watch on deck in fine weather. After getting to north of the line on the Atlantic side Mr Ramsay and the captain took a bet of £10 that the ship would not go 200 miles in 24 hours before reaching the Lizard Point, the captain not being in favour of the ship! About a fortnight afterwards the ship did go 200 miles, as was put down on the log board. Mr Ramsay had thus won his bet and the captain paid it, but at the same time said that he did not think the ship had gone the distance, the board having been over marked by me. This so annoyed Mr Ramsay that he cut the captain from that day, ever after messing in his own cabin. He went over the gangway when off Plymouth into a pilot cutter without taking the least notice of him. Captain Balderston, however, did not at any time show me any ill will whatever on account of this vexatious occurrence, nor did he think for a moment that I had done it on purpose to make him lose his bet of £10, as was amply proved on the ship being cleared in the docks,[17] when he told me that I should go with him as chief officer if the *Asia* should be again placed under his command.

This much to be desired change never took place as the *Asia* was not destined ever again to be commanded by T.F. Balderston, which was not decided till the spring of 1830. I had been thereby detained at home under false expectations, but it was no fault of the captain who never went to sea more in any ship, retiring to his place in Essex for the rest of his life.

CHAPTER 9

The Scotch frigate

(1830–1831)

By this time I was too late to apply for any Company ship of that season, and hearing of a vacant command in the Ship *Portland*[1] at Leith, belonging to the Australian Company there, I lost no time in making my bow to the directors.[2] Several of them were well known to my father and, after a very short canvas, I was unanimously appointed commander, taking charge of the ship immediately as she was due to sail for Calcutta in, I think, about six weeks. Captain Balderston's certificate did the business, only one solitary director objecting to me on the score of my being a *gentleman*, 'mirabile dictu'! [amazing to say]. He was soon silenced by my friends, 11 out of 12 directors, and made the vote unanimous. This was not then and may not be now a very uncommon objection to commanders by shipowners who assume that gentlemen are 'extravagant' in the expenditure of stores. I lived to be rejected for the same reason at Liverpool only 15 months afterwards by a man of a similar stamp to the Leith merchant.

The manager of the Australian Company was a most troublesome individual, and brother-in-law to the solitary opposing director.[3] I was told that he could agree with nobody especially the commanders of their ships, some of whom had been and were Royal Navy lieutenants and masters, and had given rise to the idea of extravagance in the mind of Mr Solitary. The 11 majority were, I suppose, too heavy metal for the old manager and his relative, and I was not only allowed to have all my own way in the fitting out of the ship, but occasionally asked to dine with both! One day, however, the manager lost his temper and behaved very rudely to a lady and her two daughters who had come to see the ship and were friends of mine. I was obliged to remind him that I was in command of the ship and answerable for the work being done in a proper manner and in good time. I suggested it would be better for him to attend to the business of the office and not behave rudely to my lady friends by telling them that they were stopping the work of the ship! To this he said nothing and very soon took my hint by taking himself off.

I was then only 27 years of age and, not being a large person, looked rather young. Many old sailors on the quay, when the ship was being towed out of the harbour, observed that a mere boy had got hold of the command of the ship, and he 'would be knocking her brains out before he got out of the Firth!' When the boatswain used his 'call' to hoist the jib, they sung out that there would be 'bloody murder in that ship', boatswain's calls not being very general in Leith ships. All these predictions, which were told to me afterwards, by those who heard them, were only like so much smoke, and I never spent a more pleasant time at sea than in command of the *Portland* (400 tons). We had ten passengers in the ship, three of whom were surgeons in the EIC Service, besides one belonging to the ship, and two ladies. Our crew numbered 30 in all, which was then considered ample, although it looked to me very small. However, they were of the right sort, and I never had to find fault with a single man during the whole voyage.

We left Leith Roads with a fair wind early in May 1830 and, after clearing the Isle of May, stood to the southward.[4] Off Flamborough Head the wind got round to the south-east and blew a gale for some days which obliged me on the fourth day to bear up for the Firth of Forth again, finding that we had driven to the northward so much as to be in danger of getting on the Farne Islands if we continued to be hove too much longer. We ran up the Firth during the night and anchored in Leith Roads about two in the morning of the sixth day after leaving them. The gale soon began to abate and some of the passengers and myself went ashore on the second day for a few hours. Being anxious to get to sea again as soon as possible I got under way as soon as it was moderate weather, beating down the Firth out to sea. We were more fortunate this time, getting off Deal[5] and down Channel in a reasonable length of time, all being most comfortable on board, and passengers enjoying themselves very much in various ways. Chess was a great favourite with many of them and the board was seldom off the table, Doctors Handyside[6] and Cumming[7] being the leaders in almost everything, two very fine and clever young men.

The old manager had allowed me to order what mess stores and stock I thought proper, and sent a most liberal supply of wine and beer on board. So, with a capital fellow as steward who had been my servant in the *Asia*, we enjoyed the good things of the table with a proper regard to our health and stomachs.

When near the Line in a calm, or very light breeze, we fell in with a ship homeward bound. The doctors were all anxious to board this ship for the sake of variety, and I took three of them with me in the boat. The ship proved to be a French one from Valparaiso to Bordeaux. On board were two passengers, a Spanish lady and a priest, with whom we had some conversation through the captain in French, the priest only being able to speak Spanish. The captain asked me if we had a doctor on board, I pointed to the three. He then said that he wished them to look at a boy who had fallen from the mainyard two months before, and hurt himself severely. We all went to the steerage where the lad lay in his hammock and found that his leg had been so torn to pieces that the flesh had all sloughed off nearly up to the knee, leaving nothing but the bare bones of the leg and foot. The leg was also broken above the knee. The doctors saw they must amputate so Dr Handyside came back with me for his instruments, returning with our own doctor, making four of them. They took off the leg, instructed the mate (the captain's son) how to dress it daily and then returned to the *Portland*. The French captain wished to pay the doctor for operating, but he would take nothing. However, on going into the boat, they found a case of champagne there, which they did not like to insult the captain by refusing. This was a famous bit of practice and pastime for the four doctors who were very lucky in the weather remaining quite moderate all the time. Of course, we did not forget to drink better health to their patient in champagne that day, and every Sunday for the rest of the voyage while the case held out.

We made the Island of Trinidad off the coast of Brazil near Rio de Janeiro, and passed between it and the Martin Vaz Rocks. It was on a fine day and moderate breeze which gave great pleasure and excitement to the passengers. After this no more land was seen till arrival at the mouth of the Hooghly, having previously got a pilot off the Sand Heads,[8] a Mr Hand, who was then in rank a 'mate'.[9] Before getting up to Calcutta, being aware that it was customary to fee these men to some extent, I took an opportunity of asking him plainly to tell me what he considered would be a fair sum to give for such a ship as the *Portland*, being unwilling to err on either side of what might be customary, however questionable that custom might be. He answered, since I had put the question to him so distinctly, he would tell me that, if I should be pleased with his services on getting to Calcutta, he would expect me to apply to the Superintendent for him to take the ship to sea again, and then to give him 100 rupees (or £10), which I did not consider to be very exorbitant! But the system is a bad one and makes these men not only greedy, but sometimes run too great risks with ships of a heavy draught of water. They will allow them to load far beyond the regulation depth before leaving Calcutta, instead of completing their loading at Diamond Harbour or Kedgeree, beyond the dangers of certain shoals. When I say that I have known pilots bargain for and receive £100 extra fee in such cases, it will be seen that it is high time these practices should be stopped, if indeed they are still carried on, which I am not at the present time aware of.

The pay of the pilots in the East India Company's day was very good, a branch receiving £70 per month besides the chance of sick officers living in his brig for their health at the Sand Heads. All the others were paid in the same ratio according to rank and seniority. They are, in general, men of great respectability, and very smart officers. It is a pity that such paltry customs about fees should prevent them being looked upon as gentlemen, although they are not the only class in this world who have fallen into this great mistake.

On arrival at Calcutta I lived with an old friend in the EIC Service named W.W.R. and also received much attention from Mr Henry McKenzie,[10] the agent for the ship, as well as from other acquaintances in the city of palaces. All going on satisfactorily on board, three months soon fled past, and the time of sailing for London drew nigh.

Before this took place, however, I was one day much gratified by the receipt of a gift from the passengers as a mark of respect for the kind and considerate treatment they had received from me during the voyage from Leith to Calcutta. It was a very massive, inscribed silver cup with cover. From this I was truly glad to find that they were all satisfied and pleased which was not, and probably is not, always the case, more especially in ships from the outports of England or Scotland, those from London having a very considerable preference. St Andrew's Day occurring while at Calcutta,[11] I went to the dinner at the Town Hall along with Dr Handyside. We were regaled with 'all the delicacies of the season' under the chairmanship of Sir John P. Grant,[12] with many other celebrities of the grand city, in all 150 of the small and great which, leaving out the viands, was a sight worth seeing.

We were also regaled by the band of the 14th Regiment[13] during dinner and between the toasts with songs. At such a dinner I was quite aware that the latter were sometimes called for, and I had seen Sir John stand up twice requesting Mr So and So to favour the company with a song and duly responded to. I had not the most distant idea that such an insignificant individual as myself could have been known in any way to the worthy chairman when, lo and behold, he stood up and sung out my name most lustily and begged me of all men to favour the company with a song. I sat on the opposite side of the table to him, a little on his right, and thunder struck as I was I saw it was better to sing at once than make a long speech of apology, so I sang 'Bonny Jean' to the best of my ability, which was received with loud applause, to my no small satisfaction. Immediately after the next toast, Dr Handyside was called and I told him to sing something to which I could join a 'second', having been in the habit of singing together on board the Portland. He then struck up 'The Light Guitar', and we acquitted ourselves so well as to bring forth thunders of applause. Without even a toast intervening we were called on by Sir John to give them another duet, which we did, with the very same effect. I think it was 'The Merry Swiss Boy'. The chairman soon after vacated the chair, and then the mirth became fast and furious till the small hours began to appear and an end came to this, as to all other temporal things in this fluctuating world.

There was one poor fellow who would have been delighted to have been there, a most thorough Scotchman in all his ideas. Dr McIsaac was one of our four doctors who, although I never knew it when on board the ship, proved after getting on shore and away from example or check, a most determined drinker of spirits.[14] He had been so both when in India previously and at home, conducting himself so badly when in barracks at Fort William that a court-martial had been ordered to try him: he only escaped dismissal by death! For six weeks after leaving us, he had never been sober so it was not to be wondered at that death closed the scene in such a climate as that of Calcutta. He was a good natured and inoffensive man and was never drunk while on board the Portland, nor any other person so far as I ever knew.

The *Portland* was a very nice looking ship and I had taken care when fitting out to make her appear to the best advantage especially in the way of paint, by which I managed to rake the ports in such a manner as to look like the tumblehome side[15] of a 26-gun frigate at a little distance. I learned afterwards that she was taken for the *Alligator* frigate of that class[16] by a revenue cruiser which we met when beating down the Firth of Forth and reported accordingly!

The ship's company liked their ship and took a pride in her being called at Calcutta the 'Scotch frigate', as also in doing their duty highly to my satisfaction at all times and on Sundays especially. Regularly during the whole of our stay in that port, one watch marched to the Scotch church under the chief officer one week, and the other under the second officer on the next. They got great and well-deserved praise from the clergyman and the Reverend Dr Duff[17] with whom I was then acquainted to command such men was a great pleasure to me, but infinitely so when I found one forenoon on going to the riverside that the ship was 'all-a-taunt-o'[18] with topgallant yards across having only given the order the previous evening at which time the three topmasts and jib boom were housed, and the yards in the tops. This was done and every rope taut by 10.30 a.m. by only 27 men! The pilot had called on board a week previously and said that it was time we began to get our topmasts on end, expecting like other ships that it would take at least a fortnight. He was indeed surprised when he saw the ship nearly ready for sea in one day! The crew were determined to show those of other ships what they could do, and sure enough they gained the 'éclat' which was their due.

For the homeward voyage we had only four passengers, Captain Le Strange and his son, Lieutenant Higginbottom and Ensign Campbell of HM 14th Regiment,[19] with whom the time was spent very agreeably after sailing from Calcutta in February 1831.[20] Save occasional gales of wind nothing worthy of notice occurred till towards our making the Island of St Helena, when Captain Le Strange showed great anxiety on the matter, he being particularly desirous of visiting Napoleon's tomb, whose great deeds were his constant theme of admiration. On seeing the island look a mere speck on the chart, he felt great doubt of our ever seeing it at all notwithstanding all I could say to the contrary. When about 60 miles off it was cloudy about darkness setting in, and nothing was to be seen of the island. I assured the Captain that we should be all right and stood on till within about 20 miles of it, and hove the ship to for the night, telling him that he should see the island large enough at daylight next morning at which he was very sceptical. Some time before sun rise there stood St Helena towering up to the clouds in all its majesty, and the Captain was astonished at the wonders of navigation! We were just about 18 or 20 miles from it and got in early in the forenoon, passing and being hailed by the forts under the lee of the island much to the delight of the soldier officers.[21]

We found the Honourable Company Ship *Reliance* at anchor, she having got in on the previous evening only, having outsailed us a few hours after speaking to her about a week before.[22] An old Edinburgh friend of mine was the surgeon of her and he very soon came on board to see me, and have a talk about family and other matters.[23] I got a letter here from my very worthy father enclosing an introduction to Governor Dallas from his brother, but little did I know or think then while reading it that the hand which wrote it was by that time cold in the grave. General Dallas was at his country house[24] all the time I was in James Town, and not being able to find leisure to go so far I sent it sealed to him before leaving the island.

The morning after our arrival Captain Le Strange, with his son, made a walking trip to Napoleon's tomb and house at Longwood, spending not only the whole day there but the night also, sleeping in the very room in which the great man had died, which had been turned into a barn by that time. Such was his reverence for the memory of that despot, although an Englishman and belonging to the British army. He very nearly lost his passage by it as he only got on board half an hour before we got under way, very much delighted with all he had seen and heard at Longwood.

The voyage from St Helena to the Downs was made with the usual changes of weather, not omitting gales and their disagreeables off the western islands. But the ship was a first rate sea boat and although hove to by gales six different times during this voyage, yet we never lost a spar nor strained a rope yarn! On arriving in the Downs[25] I got the information of the death of my father which had taken place in January 1831, and also of an uncle in Edinburgh about two months later.[26] I need hardly say that such a loss as that of a father made a great change in our family affairs, and I felt then that I was really to be dependent on myself alone for the future. He died from inflammation of the lungs in a most peaceful state of mind, and much beloved by all who had ever known him, as a truly honest and upright Christian.

Shortly after getting the ship into the East India Docks Mr Brown, the manager of the Australian Company, came to London from Leith and told me that the *Portland* was to be sold when cleared, which was under all circumstances a great blow to me. I was not surprised at it, however, as I had been told by one of the leading directors before sailing from Leith that the company would certainly be broken up before I should get home if Mr Brown remained as manager. He had great interest in the company through his two brothers-in-law, and it was seen that he could not easily be turned out. Thus, they had determined to sell their ships as opportunity might offer.

The *Portland* was too good a ship to be long in the market, and she was very soon sold and fitted out as a convict ship.[27] I was left to find another as best I could, not a very easy matter with the small interest I possessed in the commercial world.

CHAPTER 10

Dull solitude

(1831–1832)

After a few months stay with my sisters in Edinburgh I returned to London, as being the best mart for everything. In a short time I succeeded in getting the command of a brig called the *Countess Dunmore* belonging to a Mr Scott of Scotland who, having commanded a ship himself previously, was not the best man to serve in that capacity.[1] 'Beggars, however, mustn't be choosers', so I took what I could get and, in three weeks time, I was off to the Mauritius, chartered by a London mercantile house. It was the dead of winter, I recollect, but I do not know whether it was before or after Christmas 1831.[2]

I thought I was fortunate in getting my late chief officer, Mr Charles, to go with me again, and the second was a very good man who had lately belonged to the East India Company Service as a gunner. Whether it was that the brig was not thought worthy of the same attention to duty as the *Portland* I don't know, yet Mr Charles was at no time the same officer he had proved himself to be previously. His being my only messmate made the sea going part of this voyage not a little uncomfortable, and threw me almost entirely on my own resources. The brig was nominally 230 tons burden, but when I state that the owner told me she had just delivered 390 tons of sugar from Mauritius, her build may be guessed at, especially her depth of hold, which I was not a little surprised to find was 17 feet 2 inches, or just two inches less than that of the *Marquis Camden*, a 1,400 ton ship. Certainly, the latter had three decks above that, but such was the actual depth of hold. The consequence was that the brig was no clipper although she sailed much better than any one would have supposed possible and, being short, she worked like a top.

We were very fortunate in getting clear of the Channel without a gale of wind, and soon afterwards ran into the north-east trade, then across the Line, and all through the south-east trade in fine weather. Off the Cape the customary westerly gales soon took us

'Port Louis', from T. Bradshaw, *Views in the Mauritius*, 1832.
The peak of Peter Botte Mountain can the seen on the right of the picture.
(The Trustees of the National Library of Scotland.)

into the longitude of the Mauritius which I made afterwards by my lunar observations as stated before. On arrival at Port Louis, I found Messrs Thomson and Co., the agents for the brig, very kind and attentive.[3] I went to live with an old friend, a former purser in the EIC Service, who had then become a partner in the house of Sampson and Ainslie, with whom I enjoyed myself very much during the whole of my stay at the island. The Colonel of the 99th Regiment and a Captain Weir of the 29th were also old friends, occasionally asking me to their different messes.[4] The officers of the *Talbot* frigate[5] I likewise became acquainted with, so the days passed along very agreeably, of course always attending to the duties of the brig at the same time. The island is very pretty and the mountains are all of a most picturesque peaked nature, forming a very marked feature over the whole of it.

The tombs of Paul and Virginia were duly visited,[6] and one or two sugar plantations to see the process of sugar making. What I wished most to see, however, was the old man who could distinctly observe in the sky, by a sort of reflection there, dismasted ships, sometimes 200 miles off, which were sure to come to the island for repairs in a few days afterwards. This curious old Frenchman I found had died a short time before I arrived, and left a name for this peculiar sight universally believed.[7] One grand proof of the reality of his gift of second sight took place about a year before he died. It was this: he had been up the mountain where he always went to look out for these things somewhat longer than usual, as he had seen a four-masted vessel, a very uncommon kind of ship in those days. When it first appeared to him he said to the person who had gone up with him: 'I see two brigs very close together, indeed, so much so that I would call it a four-masted ship if I thought there was such a thing in the world.' After looking again and again he said: 'I am satisfied that it is a four-masted ship, and not two brigs.' Sure enough a four-masted ship came into Port Louis two days afterwards. She, like most of the others seen by him, had lost her topmasts in a hurricane, and was at the time of observation about 100 miles off.

The Peter Botte mountain is the most remarkable in the island, as the peak is finished by a huge rock shaped like an egg stuck on a sort of neck the sharp end downward. This makes it quite impossible to scramble up excepting by a rope ladder, which has been used effectually in several instances, including by Lieutenant Taylor, first officer of the *Talbot*, shortly before I was on the island.[8] The plan of the procedure was to fly a rope over the top by a kite, and then haul the ladder up by one or two ropes as may be, making them fast to the neck of the rock to hang the ladder by. The British flag was flown from the top, held by Lt Taylor; it was a great and most dangerous feat.

About the middle of May 1832 the brig was loaded with 360 tons of sugar, which I thought as much as she ought to carry in going round the Cape in the dead of winter, more especially as she had damaged some of the 390 which she took home on her former voyage. To be on the safe side with the owner, I had her surveyed and a certificate given by the harbour master that she was fully and sufficiently loaded, considering the time of the year in which she must go round the Cape. It was well I did this, as the owner found fault with me for not bringing more cargo when I got to London, and probably would have charged me with the 'lost freight', had I not at once stopped his mouth by producing the certificate.

We left Mauritius about 20th May,[9] and soon got towards that dreaded promontory, the Cape, where for three weeks I had constant north-westerly gales, being obliged to keep as close to the land as I could to escape the very heavy sea which is created by the strong current which always runs to the south-west and north-west along the edge of Agulhas Bank. The gales were so frequent that I had scarcely time to run in shore from where I had been driven off e're another commenced, and I was again hove to under a close reefed main topsail. At last, however, I weathered Cape Point, and away we ran for St Helena, where I only remained to fill up our water, sailing again immediately.

The same dull solitude prevailed in the cabin as when outward bound, and I was not a little pleased to get to London again some time in August[10] where, after clearing out the sugar, the brig was put into a dock at Millwall. All her planking was renewed, a poop put on and her rigging changed to that of a barque. On completing repairs the ship was taken to the St Katherine's Dock to load with a general cargo for Launceston in Tasmania, a place I had never so much as heard of before. The island on which it is situated I had only a small knowledge of being tailed on to the great one of New Holland, as it was then generally called. However, I lived to have that knowledge a good deal enlarged before many years had gone over my head, and to see huge numbers of the human race spread over large portions of the surface of both, in what are now divided into some of the largest and richest colonies of Great Britain.

CHAPTER 11

On first arrival at a penal colony

(1833)

From the day the *Countess Dunmore* came out of the dry dock she began to make water. Every inch of submersion increased it, making me recommend the owner to throw the ship on the carpenter's hands and have the leak stopped. But he only said: 'I dare say you will go to sea with a leaky ship, but she will soon take up.' This was a poor look forward to me. Obtaining a cargo for so new a place as Launceston then was took a very long time, and I think we were six months e're the ship was fully loaded. Although the brokers Buckles, Bagster and Co. were considered a first rate house,[1] this was very tiresome work, and the owner at the same time, I may say, almost living on board, having nothing else to do in London. He had told me some time previously that he intended to send his son with me as an apprentice. He was to have a cabin and mess with me, which was to be paid for by the handsome sum of £1 per month in addition to my own mess allowance!

The day of sailing came at last, about the end of June 1833, and I left England with the ship making two inches of water per hour in smooth water![2] I was glad enough to get away even with that fact fully demonstrated, and the expectation of an increase at least of as much again in blowing weather. We had six or eight second class passengers, three of whom were females, all of a highly respectable nature, but who of course messed by themselves.[3] One of them (a girl of 23) was going out to be married to a bookseller and newspaper editor;[4] so there was always someone to talk to when inclined, and I occupied myself for a short time daily teaching the owner's son navigation. Thus, and with books, etc., the weeks rolled on, till we approached the southern boundary of the south-east trade, when I thought it was necessary to consult with the two officers and carpenter touching the leak. We found it had increased in blowing weather to six inches per hour; we could not say where it was, or how caused, but we came to the decision that it would be better to put into Rio de Janeiro and caulk the ship's upperworks than to round the Cape as we were. We steered for that port, then not more than two or three days sail distant, and in due time Cape Frio hove in sight. Next morning we passed the forts at the entrance to the harbour after being hailed by that on the starboard side, which has a double tier of guns. We stood on to the anchorage, about three miles inside of the most magnificent bay in the world, and about three-quarters of a mile off the city of St Sebastian. We found lying here HMS *Spartiate*, 74 guns,[5] with Rear Admiral Sir Michael Seymour's flag flying,[6] and a considerable number of merchant ships of various nations.

I soon found respectable agents in the firm of Hudson, Wuegledon and Co. who at once set about getting caulkers for the ship. But in foreign Roman Catholic ports matters are carried on with deliberation, and a due respect to the rights of religion so far as holidays are concerned. It took a whole fortnight to effect what in England would have been done in three days at most. However, 'it is an ill wind which blows nobody good', and I had by their delays all the better opportunity of seeing the place and its environs, which were very beautiful. Amongst other things I saw the young emperor in his carriage one day, being then only six years old. He has since that time shown himself well worthy of being placed in so high a position, and I believe is still much beloved and admired by his people.[7]

The city is large and in a fine position, with monasteries and nunneries on all the heights round about, as also lots of churches and spires and plenty of fine public buildings, quays, markets and warehouses. The mountains in the background and all round the large bay are very fine and mostly covered with wood. I took the two young girls, my passengers, over to the north side of the bay one evening in the boat to see an orange grove. When I asked the proprietor for leave to take a few oranges, he said that I might load the boat if I chose, and helped me to do so with a large quantity of very fine ones, which lasted the whole ship's company for several days.

I visited the theatre or rather 'Opera House' by name, although it was a play which was acted on two occasions when I was present. It was a very large and fine house, but wretchedly lighted. I think there were few or no lights, save on the stage, which I thought must have made it very disgusting to the ladies who wished to show themselves off to the public. This may have altered now, but such was the case in August 1833.

Having completed caulking, filled water and also drawn a bill on the owner for £150 to pay expenses, which I thought he might have saved had he taken my earlier advice, we got under way early one morning and, after passing the forts, got well out to sea with the land breeze. A few days before this, I was much pleased to see the *Samarang*, 26-gun frigate, come in from sea with the wind right aft and all sail set: lower, fore and main topmast, and topgallant studding sails on both sides (strength of breeze five).[8] When she got within 100 yards of the Admiral's outside bow 'in came everything, to the topsails', booms and all. When on the Admiral's quarter down went fore and main tacks, up jib and spanker, sheet home topgallant sails (which in this short time had been furled), braced up sharp on the port tack, luffed round the Admiral's stern, stood inshore for five minutes,

'Entrance to the Bay of Rio de Janeiro', by Leon Sabatier, from Hyacinthe de Bougainville,
Journal de la navigation autour du globe de la fregate la Thetis et de la corvette l'Esperance, 1837.
(National Library of Australia; PIC S11040 /30.)

then tacked and crossed the Admiral's bow, and stood on for a few minutes on the
starboard tack, 'bout ship again, crossed the Admiral's bow a second time, 'in everything',
luffed up, squared yards, and let go the anchor about 250 yards on the Admiral's starboard
bow! All the manoeuvres were beautifully done without a single hitch.

Captain Paget came on board of the *Countess Dunmore* the next day with the first
lieutenant to look at two whale boats I had, and I could not help telling him how much I
admired the manner in which he brought his ship to an anchor on the previous day.[9] He said:
'Oh, I have a capital set of officers, and we all mess together in the gunroom (officers' mess
so called then). I have only a couch on the after part of the main deck, with all bulkheads
down, and we get on famously.' This certainly showed where he got room to bundle the
studding sails to when taken in, and thereby leave room for working ship immediately. The
next time I saw the *Samarang* she was in very different kelter, lying as guard ship at Gibraltar
in 1848 where I believe she lies still. So much for her being a teak ship.

While on the subject of naval officers I shall mention an occurrence which took place
when lying at Rio a few days before the arrival of the *Samarang*, which will show the nature
of the discipline on board the flag ship *Spartiate* at that time. One evening when I was on

shore, two of my men came aft and demanded grog from the chief officer. Of course, he would not give it to them so they then took possession of the cuddy, refusing for a considerable time to quit it till their demand should be complied with, and were very insolent. Eventually, however, they were induced to go forward, and next morning this mutinous conduct was reported to me on going on board. I instantly ordered the two men into the boat, and pulled on board of the *Spartiate* to have them punished or exchanged. But when I had made my request to the first lieutenant, Mr Grant,[10] he plainly told me that by the Admiral's order they were not allowed to punish their own men (with the cat) and, if it were not for the large number of officers and petty officers on board, they could not keep the ship's company in anything like tolerable order. He said he would ask the Captain,[11] who was then on the poop, to see what could be done for me. Captain Tait's answer was that he was sorry he could do nothing to assist me either in exchanging or punishing the men, and that I must go to the consul who would give me two other men in exchange from the jail. I did not think it worth my while to bring myself to the notice of Captain Tait after this message, as I saw that he had not the power to do anything. I recollected him very well as a visitor at my father's house when a lieutenant on half pay, and I a very small boy. He was the son of the factor to the Duke of Buccleuch. I got an exchange from the consul, and made the best of a bad bargain, but I thought we could, in the Company's service, have shown the officers of the *Spartiate* a somewhat better state of discipline than reigned on board of that ship. There was little use for men-of-war in peacetime if they could not assist the merchant service in punishing or exchanging two mutinous seamen.

Poor Admiral Seymour did not live long after the time I mention, and I learned from a mate who belonged to the *Spartiate* then, and who I met at Hong Kong some years afterwards, that the Admiral was no sooner in his grave than Captain Tait turned the hands up and warned them all that he was determined to have the discipline of the service properly carried out, and he should flog all and everyone of the crew who from that hour he should consider deserved it. He did it too, till he had the ship in that order in which a man-of-war ought to be, for the comfort of all, and the benefit of the service.

I must now proceed with the barque *Countess Dunmore* towards the Cape during which time, from leaving Rio, we had moderate breezes and fine weather. When in the colder latitudes of 38 degrees and 39 degrees south, the gales kept pretty frequent while running down our easting till nearing Bass Strait in the month of September. I was told before leaving England by a man who had been to Launceston that the mouth of the River Tamar was not easy to discover, as an island just inside of the mouth of it filled up the space, giving a complete sameness to the coast. Fortunately, however, a lighthouse had been built on Low Head since that report,[12] and I twigged it at once as the spot. I soon found a pilot boat coming off when I got near enough. The weather was beautiful, and we got in quite safely, although the current of tide amongst the narrows round the island was very alarming to the uninitiated.

'Tamar River, Launceston', by Frederick Strange, *c.* 1840. The town of Launceston is just
out of view to the right. The river winds into the distance towards the sea some 60 km distant.
(State Library of Tasmania.)

After getting through these narrows which are close to George Town, we opened a
large bay, or arm of the river, and turned sharp to the left for some miles amidst the most
beautiful scenery of wooded hills close down to the river. After six miles more it turns
pretty quickly to the right, amidst primeval forests everywhere, and the most perfect
silence for ten miles more, when we came to a settler's house named Reid.[13] After this
there is a narrow reach called Whirlpool, from a rock rising to nearly low water mark right
in the centre of it, and causing such an eddy as in light winds makes ships whirl round and
round, sometimes throwing them on the rock itself. I believe it has now been blown up,
and the passage cleared entirely; at least it was long spoken of being about to be done even
23 years ago. I therefore presume that it really is so, being an essential to the safe navigation
of the river. The whole scenery right up to the town of Launceston, 40 miles, is splendid,
and is even likely to strike the mind with awe at the unparalleled works of God.

The first day we got to within ten miles of Launceston before dark. The pilot offered
me his boat to go on which I accepted, arriving at the Commercial Hotel near the wharf
about 9 p.m. The boat's crew consisted of four prisoners, or convicts as they are called in
England, but this name being offensive to these unfortunates, the former has been

uniformly adopted in the penal colonies. When the pilot first came on board I noticed one of his men as a very bad looking fellow, and I asked him if that man was a 'convict'.

'Oh yes,' he said, 'they are all prisoners we call them here.'

'What was he sent out for?' was my next query.

The answer was: 'I don't know, and we never think of asking them, as they will all tell you the same thing, that they were wronged entirely and it was not their fault at all which got them punished.'

My queries were what every stranger feels a wish to ask on first arrival at a penal colony, but a very short time suffices to do away with all disagreeable feeling from the contiguity of these men or women, and they are treated in the same way as any others of the lower classes. While in the boat on the river in a dark night I could not help thinking several times that these four men, who might have been the companions of murderers at least, could easily heave me overboard and run away into the bush. But when I came to know what the bush was, and how few bushrangers ever made their escape from the island, I saw that it was not worth a moment's consideration and very far from being so easy as I thought it.

After getting to the hotel I had a word or two with the buxom landlady while the cloth was being laid for supper by a very smart and good looking lad about 18 years old, whose antecedents I immediately felt inclined to be acquainted with as before. Having asked the question of the landlady, she told me that the lad was the son of a lieutenant RN, and had been sent out for picking pockets. Melancholy indeed thought I, but have we not seen of late years much greater robbers of the mercantile world calling themselves gentlemen, banished for misdeeds of a far more infamous nature?

Be that as it may, this youngster very soon placed before me an excellent supper of beef steaks and a glass of grog. Almost immediately after my conversation with the landlady a gentleman came in and began to talk to me, giving me all the information about the town and country that I desired. I very soon found that he was nautical, and he told me that he was a settler. His name was Lieutenant Pearson Foote, RN, who I am glad to see, by that name being still on the Navy List as retired commander, must be alive, whether in Tasmania or elsewhere.[14] I visited him afterwards at his farm more than once, and I have every reason to suppose that he was a successful man in his new calling.

CHAPTER 12

In and around Launceston

(1833–1834)

Next morning I appointed Mr P.W. Welsh agent for the ship, having that power to confer on anyone who could give me good hopes of a homeward freight. He was a bustling, active Irishman and a great hand for speculation, but seemed to be in a fair way of business, living moderately though in one of the best houses in the town. He introduced me to his wife and her two younger sisters, who were living with her at the time, and for a reason which I was not made aware of till three years afterwards.[1]

The ship soon got up to the Bar and, about a fortnight later, to the quay, which was most convenient for discharging cargo.[2] Meantime, I had been invited by Mr Welsh to become one of his family, and was soon introduced to his father-in-law, who had a very nice property down the river about four miles. Through these people I soon became acquainted with many others both in town and country, and passed my time very agreeably in various ways, such as picnics, riding about seeing what was worth inspection and private parties.

At the billiard room of the Commercial Hotel one day I was not a little surprised to find the marker had been a brother officer in the Company Service, whom I had often heard of by name, which was Sam Dugdale.[3] Indeed, it was hearing him called such that made me ask him if he was the Sam Dugdale of singing and jocular notoriety in the Service, and he told me he was the same individual. He had been brought to his then low degree by drink, which I readily foretold from the whole appearance of things, certainly not much to the credit of his former rank in his profession, but such are the changes in life! Another old officer of the Service I found in a very different state, living on his own property called 'Trafalgar' in comfort and opulence, about ten miles from Launceston. His name was Barclay, and he was at least 20 years my senior.[4]

Having got well acquainted with the family of Mr Allan at Allan Vale (the father-in-law of my agent) I occasionally used to go down to his place by boat. I observed he was always very kind to the boys who formed my boat's crew, of whom the owner's son was one, but it never struck me that anything sinister was meant by the same, although they were several times asked to go there by themselves to shoot parakeets and other birds, to which I gave my consent, of course. Meantime, I had been informed by Mrs Allan that they had a young man named George Haig as an 'assigned servant'[5] who was related to herself distantly and, having been convicted of forgery, had been sentenced to 14 years' banishment. He was a clever fellow and had got a first rate education, both in England and Paris, and he had been the teacher of her two youngest girls and three boys, since they had been at Allan Vale, about one year and a half. The girls were then to be sent to a boarding school, and the two eldest boys had gone to their brother-in-law's store to learn business.

When the ship was nearly ready for cargo, I paid a visit to a Mr Ashburner at Silwood Park, who was a friend of my brother, the major at Bombay, when Mr Ashburner was partner in the House of Forbes and Co. there.[6] He had now a very fine property about 20 miles from Launceston, where he always treated me most hospitably. The first time was along with Mr Welsh, when the bushrangers were supposed to be somewhere near to his house, so we took care to be armed in case of a visit from these daring robbers, but were not disturbed by them at any time. There were four of them then out and had been so for about two years, much to the dread and loss of the settlers. Their day, however, was not far from being closed and, being very hard up, they had courage enough to commit four different robberies of plate, etc., even within and close to Launceston.

One of these was from the house of the Rev. Dr Browne within a quarter of a mile from the police office. About 11 p.m. they knocked at the door quite softly. The doctor himself opened it, found four double barrels presented at his body, and was plainly told that if he made the least noise they would fire. They also said that they knew Mrs Browne had been confined a few days before, but they would not disturb her. Two of the bushrangers went in and made the doctor show them where the plate was, and other valuables, to which they helped themselves. They took also his gold watch from him which, on their leaving, he begged hard to have restored, as it was a gift from his father, and they at last gave it back to him. They said to take care he did not make a noise about them for some hours, otherwise they would return another time and blow his brains out. After this, they left with their booty and Mrs Browne never knew of their presence till some time after their departure, so quietly did they go about their work.[7]

The last of their attacks was on the house of a surgeon right in the town, and still with perfect success. But a £100 reward was offered to any man who should secure these four men and, if a prisoner, he was to have also a free pardon and passage to England. This had the desired effect in the course of a single week, and they were all four taken by one man, a prisoner constable, in the following manner. He had heard of their being near a country public house about 50 miles from Launceston, and he went there shortly after it was dark, when the man of the house told him outside that there were four men unarmed in the parlour who he supposed were the bushrangers (they had 'planted' their arms in the bush). The constable took a look at them through a crack in the shutters, and saw two of the men sitting at the table and the other two in bed, all of whom he knew to be the men he wanted. Immediately, laying hold of one of his pistols by the muzzle and keeping the other ready in his belt, he burst open the door quickly, knocking the two men who were at the table senseless with the butt of his pistol, one after the other. Turning instantly to the bed, he did the same to each of the others as they were coming out of it, and before they reached the floor. He thus had them all four senseless on the floor, and succeeded in putting on the handcuffs and tying their arms behind before one of them could resist. He then called assistance and marched them right into the town as fast as he could. I need not say that such conduct was very highly applauded by everyone, not excepting the prisoners themselves, whom I saw in their cells in jail just three days afterwards, and had some conversation with each and all of them.

They told me how very hard up they had been frequently in the bush, even to eating their dogs, and that they had to rob the settlers of flour and provisions to save them from starvation. They knew they would all be hanged, but they had never committed murder during all the two years they had been out. Whatever should be their fate they all declared, but especially a short man called Buchan who had been a sailor and belonged to Greenock, that the greatest credit was due to the constable who took them, which was wonderfully well done. Everyone of the men bore the fresh mark of the blow from the butt of the pistol on his forehead, almost exactly in the middle of the brow of all, showing the skill with which the business was done. I forget the names of the other men now, but one of them escaped death and was sent to Norfolk Island for life. The three were not hanged till after I had sailed for England.[8]

I had not been long in Launceston before I heard of the loss of my old ship the *Portland*, within 12 miles of Low Head. On going to the Lloyd's agent's store one day, I was astonished to see several parts of her which had been brought from the wreck, particularly a drumhead for the capstan which the carpenter had made on board on my own plan.[9] Dr Inches, RN, who was in her when she got on shore, and also had been in charge of the convicts from England to Sydney, agreed to go home with me, and do the duty of surgeon. I was delighted with his society during the whole passage. He was a man of congenial ideas with myself, and of the most kindly and gentlemanly disposition. I have never ceased to regret that he should have quitted this world without our ever having met after arrival in London. He died I think about ten years ago.[10]

The time for the sailing of the *Countess Dunmore* put an end to a very happy period spent in and around Launceston of three and a half months, exclusive of three weeks more detention in getting down the river, and waiting for a wind to take us out. The pilots were then afraid to beat a ship out through the narrows off George Town, and no steam tugs had yet begun to ply. We lay two days near Allan Vale on the passage down, when Dr

Inches and I went on shore to bid farewell to Mr and Mrs Allan and their two fair daughters with whom we had both spent a goodly number of very pleasant days.

At last, however, we started, having bullied Mr Ward, the pilot, into beating out after all.[11] Fortunately, the ship was one that never missed stays, otherwise, according to the pilot's ejaculations, we should have been lost to a certainty. He was in such a funk every tack as to jump about on his stocking soles, like a paper man. He had taken off his shoes to give him some good footing on the poop, as the ship lay over a good deal in a fresh breeze. We cleared the Heads in safety in February 1834, and steered for King's Island Strait, determined to go by Cape Lewin, and not by Cape Horn.

I think it was the second day after passing King's Island that the chief officer came to me on the poop and asked me if I knew that George Haig was on board. He had just seen him and found that he had secreted himself for the whole three weeks during which we had been in the river, evading the searchers at George Town, where every ship was overhauled to prevent the escape of prisoners. This was a blow to me I did not expect, but I was not then going to put back for the sake of this rascal. On sending for him, I told him that he must do his duty before the mast; if he did not behave himself well I would give him up to the Government at the first port we might touch at. It never occurred to me for a moment that Mr Allan had done all he could to effect this escape, to suit his own purposes, and thereby make me run the risk of being fined in London £500 if I did not give him up, or should the fellow complete his escape on shore. But such was the fact and I did not wonder at Mr Allan's conduct after I came to learn the real state of the case, which I did not do till about three years afterwards on my return to Launceston in another vessel.

I shall give the story now in as few words as possible, as I got it from a person who had the most undoubted right to know the truth of the whole. I have said that this young man George Haig was the teacher of Mr Allan's two daughters at home for some time, which of course gave him opportunities of lovemaking, and the scoundrel had attempted an assault upon the younger, when he was detected. The girls were then sent to live with their married sister, and the boys to learn business. Rather than publish the affair by handing the fellow over to the Government, he was kept till an opportunity occurred of his making his escape from the colony. This was easily done by getting him acquainted with my apprentices, who assisted him in every way to secrete himself on board the *Countess Dunmore*, which they did not deny when taxed with it.

On nearing St Helena, this young man wrote to me a most pathetic letter, appealing to my feelings in every way not to give him up on arrival there, but I made no promises. I told him it would still depend upon his good conduct, both there and until we should reach London. But I did not give him up at either place, as he had uniformly done his duty well, and behaved with the greatest propriety during the whole four months passage.

On arrival at Gravesend, however, after he had decamped, I thought it would be well to inform the Bow Street magistrate that a prisoner named G. Haig had been found secreted on board after sailing, but had absconded from the ship on the previous day, giving the necessary description of his having only one eye, the left one being closed. This I never doubted, having always seen him so, as well as everyone else in the ship, not excepting his friends the apprentices. However, on my return to Launceston, and casually mentioning the circumstance to Mrs Welsh, I found that he had two eyes, but had a trick of shutting one sometimes. This at once showed me the complete deception he had played during the whole five months he had spent on board the ship, and to what good purpose too. I have no doubt he would have been laid hold of by the police if I had described him as having two eyes. For his cunning and persistency I could not help thinking he almost deserved his liberty. Had I known that I was liable to a fine of £500 for not securing him that liberty he certainly should not have had.

On arrival at the docks, I was very soon enlightened on this subject by two Bow Street officers coming on board and telling me plainly my liability to the above amount. I pleaded ignorance and, on leaving me, they said they would report all to the magistrate, but I never heard more of the matter, or whether the prisoner was ever caught or not. I knew he had a brother, a wharfinger in London, who no doubt would help him to get off to Paris with very little delay.

Our arrival in London was I think early in July 1834,[12] and Mr Scott the owner was not long of making his appearance on the scene. He soon began to find fault with me for going into Rio de Janeiro, and also about my treatment of his son. To the first of these charges, I told him I had only done my duty to the ship's company, passengers and myself, in trying to stop the leak, with which he ought never to have allowed the ship to go to sea. I did not succeed in stopping it till we got to Launceston when we found a whole butt seam without a particle of oakum in it, which no doubt had been done intentionally by the carpenters who had been heard by an apprentice to say that they would serve the owner out yet for looking after them so sharp and boring them with his presence.

To the second charge I merely observed that I had treated his son far too well as he was a lazy, good-for-nothing fellow, and if he had belonged to anyone else save himself, I would have rope's-ended him every day he had been on board the ship. I begged to tell him that I should no longer have anything to do either with him or his ship from that hour. To this matter of fact language he replied that I should never have gone the last voyage at all had he not thought I was the best person he could get to instruct his son in his duties. I thanked him for the compliment and we parted, never to meet again.

CHAPTER 13

No sinecure

(1834–1836)

After my arrival in London I immediately went to Edinburgh, having learned that my eldest and youngest sisters were both dangerously ill, the one with a complication of complaints, and the other with consumption. I found them, for a change of air, at Lasswade about six miles south of Edinburgh where they remained till within three or four weeks of their deaths, when they were brought back to their home in Edinburgh. My brother William (the major) who, with his wife and child, I had met in London, had then just sailed for Bombay, so I was the only brother left at home to attend to the dying girls, along with my second sister, and to administer to their comforts so far as human aid could do. It was not for long as it soon pleased God to take them to himself, the elder dying only six days before the younger, and both in a truly Christian state of mind in the month of October 1834.[1]

While at home in Edinburgh I had the satisfaction of learning that I was henceforth to receive a pension as compensation for the EIC Service having been broken up.[2] The sum of £112 per annum would always 'keep the wolf from the door', and I have lived to know the real benefit of such a standby. The Company's China charter having expired, it was thought better for the country that it should not be renewed by the Government, and to ensure the trade being on a fair basis, they purchased the Company's right to trade for £300,000 (if I mistake not), which of course did away with the 'maritime service'. Hence the pensions allowed by Parliament.

In November 1834 I went to London to see what was to be done for the future in the way of employment. Hearing soon after that Captain Scott (late of the *Vansittart*)[3] was to command and partly own the *Abercrombie Robinson* to Madras, Bengal and China, and being heartily sick of little-minded shipowners as my superiors, I applied for the appointment of chief officer, as the pay of that rank in such a ship was better than I had got in my late commands. Captain Scott was an old school fellow of mine and, although we had never sailed together in the Company's service, yet we had always kept up our acquaintance. Having satisfied himself about all things, he at once gave me the berth. The *Abercrombie Robinson* was a 1,400 ton ship and, like several others about to sail, had been sold out of the Company's service, the captain being owner of one-half of her.[4]

I joined her at Blackwall immediately, I think in December, and began to fit out, the time for sailing from Gravesend being the 23 February 1835.[5] In due time the ship was towed to Northfleet, where we took in the remainder of the cargo and prepared to receive 34 first-class passengers. To accommodate them cabins were built a good way forward on the gun or main deck, which was now without any guns, having only six 32-pounders on the quarterdeck, with a ship's company reduced to 120 in all. The number of officers was six, as before, and six midshipmen, but I am sorry to state that the quality of the former in some cases was not of the best, although all had belonged to the Company's service previously. The discipline and organisation was the same in all respects, and the uniform also. The warrant officers, petty officers and seamen were quite equal to former times. We had one surgeon only with no assistant and a purser who, when in the Company's service used to go by the soubriquet of 'the Prince of Pursers', being a good deal inclined to assume 'the great man'.

Of passengers we had six married ladies and one single, with 27 gentlemen, all belonging to the Company's military and civil services, or royal army. On the 24th or 25th February we sailed from Gravesend and got down channel and out to sea, so far as I can recollect, without a check, all going on comfortably, save finding the third officer quite unfit to be trusted with a watch. The fourth was too inexperienced also, so the second officer and I had to keep 'watch and watch' during nearly the whole 18 months spent in that ship when at sea which, with the chief executive duties of every day, made my position no sinecure.

The captain was in weak health generally, and frequently told me that he regretted not being able to relieve me a little by keeping part of or a whole watch at night, but he was not able, and at one time for three weeks together was so ill as to oblige me to navigate the ship and take temporary command. The amusements of the passengers were pretty much the same as I have previously related, with one little exception, the getting up of a play on the quarterdeck one evening in a very artistic manner, in the shape of 'new music, scenery and decorations'. The name of the play I forget, but the farce was 'Bombastes Furioso', in which Lieutenant Pattle (the late colonel of the 1st Dragoon Guards), and Mr Grey (the former Lieutenant-Governor of Bengal) shone out in great lustre till, towards the end, the champagne behind the scenes began to show a little![6] But the whole went off admirably, and with thunders of applause from the ship's company whom we placed on the poop, that they might see and be amused.

In mentioning the crew, I may as well add that they were remarkably well behaved, and we had only occasion to flog twice during the whole 18 months: on both occasions it was for theft. There was neither tyranny nor oppression, and I took especial care that the comforts of all should be attended to, working always to regular hours (unless on special emergencies). I also ensured that the young officers should give their orders to the men in a gentlemanly and not irritating style, having seen too often the evil effects of that foolish conduct.

After rounding the Cape a rather remarkable affair took place from a very slight cause, creating much sickness, two deaths and several men paralysed for life, some in legs and others in arms. It was this: one of the water cisterns on the poop not being used, I thought it would do well to keep the rum in for daily use, and filled it with the same, in quantity about 60 gallons, never for a moment thinking that the cistern, being lead, would extract the poisonous acetic acid and mix with the rum. Although the doctor saw the steward serve it out from thence to the crew almost daily, yet he never took any notice of its probable bad effects, not even when many of the men were ill with 'painter's cholic'. He was dosing them with calomel and castor oil in any quantities. Twice I had refilled the cistern before arriving at Madras, where we lost the boatswain and another man from this horrible rum. On arrival at Kedgeree in the Hooghly[7] we had actually 50 men ill of cholic, and still the doctor never thought of the lead cistern, although he was nearly worked to death himself.

About a fortnight after this, a gentleman from Calcutta came down to spend some days with me, and when showing him the cistern with rum in it, he at once said he did not think it was 'very good' to keep rum there as it would extract acetic acid from the lead! I immediately saw my mistake, and sent for the doctor, asking him if that was not the cause of all the cholic sickness of the crew. He said, certainly it was. He had supposed that the cistern was lined with tin all the time! Of course no more rum was served out from that quarter, and when a man got out of the doctor's list he did not go back again the next day after he had got his grog. It showed me that the doctor was anything save a man of observation, or a student of causes and effects. Two men went on shore at London who had never recovered from the paralysis of the arms and legs, and several others were long ill with the same before recovery. At one time and another I believe there was hardly a man in the ship who had not been ill from this trifling and ignorant act of mine, though the doctor was assuredly much more to blame than I.

I saw nothing of Calcutta this time, as my duties kept me closely on board of the ship during the whole period of our stay at Kedgeree. The second officer also, I think, never quitted the ship, having the responsibility of the hold. The third left us there, having done no duty after sailing from England, and his successor was almost as useless, so was discharged in China a few months after. Leaving the Hooghly early in September with a full cargo of cotton, we arrived at Singapore about the end of that month,[8] where we found the *George the Fourth*, Captain Waugh,[9] and in a few days sailed for Whampoa under agreement to keep company with that ship through the Palawan Passage, the southwesterly monsoon being all but blown out.

For the first week the winds were light and variable, with fine weather, and we progressed quietly and smoothly amongst the numerous reefs which abound in that part of the China Sea, till one Sunday forenoon, when we were at prayers in the cuddy. The officer who was looking out on deck suddenly reported seeing a reef right under the ship's bottom, causing a break up of the church in a moment, and 'turn the hands out 'bout ship', which was done with great smartness, everyone knowing well what depended on his exertions. We had no sooner trimmed on the other tack than I pointed out to the captain the sharp top of a rock just about six inches above the water on the weather bow, distant only a few yards. By this time we saw our consort 'wearing ship', and most fortunately both of us escaped touching the reef, which some current had set us a good deal nearer to than either we expected or was at all agreeable.

Another day shortly after this the Captain said to me that he would stand on towards a certain reef, which we should soon see, till within a mile or two, that the men might see what they really had to look out for, and the danger thereof. I observed that such would be all very well so long as we carried the breeze we then had, but in the event of it falling calm when we got near the reef it would certainly be a very dangerous experiment. However, he determined to try it, and in a very short time we saw the surf breaking on the reef which we were looking for, just on the verge of the horizon. On we sailed till about 5 p.m. when we were within five miles of the breakers. It then very quickly fell dead calm, the very thing I had feared would happen! The ship was quite unmanageable and driving fast towards the reef, so we had to bend cables and unstow the anchors. For nearly two hours almost within hearing of the breakers, we drove about with no soundings and night setting in, in a very pretty state of anxiety, when at last a breeze sprung up, and we made our escape as fast as we could, very nearly getting foul of the *George the Fourth* which had gone about a short time before. When we had time to breathe freely, the Captain wished heartily that he had taken my advice, although no damage had been done.

Another time, in this same passage, we really did get foul of a French ship called the *Courier de Manill*, who kept so bad a look out as to be within a few seconds of running right into our gangway when at last he heard our roaring. But it was so late that he could not clear us entirely and, his anchor catching our quarter gallery, tore it away a bit, carrying away his jib boom and fore-topgallant mast. There is many a slip between the cup and the lip, especially at sea, and this little Frenchman was within an ace of sending his ship to the bottom merely from the want of a proper look out, or rather a look out at all, as our ship being 1,400 tons was not a mere speck on the ocean when under all sail, even in the dark. Had he struck us right at the gangway as we expected he must have gone down at once, and probably done us a great deal of damage as well. But 'there's a sweet little cherub that sits up aloft, who takes care of the life of poor Jack'.

It must have been about the end of November 1835 when we reached Whampoa[10] and, having a full cargo of cotton to take out and another of tea to take in, as well as paint ship and refit the rigging within the space of six weeks, it was quite clear that no man would eat the bread of idleness in the *Abercrombie Robinson*! Nevertheless, this was done, although I never worked later than 6 p.m. on any day, each 'watch' of the men having a day's liberty at Canton, and always the Sundays to themselves. I was short of a third officer the whole time, as well as all the rest of the voyage home. As for myself, I spent two days in Canton, the Captain relieving me on board, which were the only days I ever spent out of the ship from first to last. Yet I did not wish it otherwise, as everything went on agreeably and comfortably. The second officer was an excellent one, and did all the hold duty, having no third, but for a chief officer to be in watch and watch with a ship's company of 120 men to look after during the whole day is very hard work. Yet I never had a day's illness during the whole time I belonged to that ship, save in coming up Channel for a short time.

We sailed from Whampoa within the six weeks,[11] and as only the usual routine of nautical duties were gone through daily, with the change of a gale or two off the Cape, there is nothing to relate further concerning my service in this ship, excepting our arrival in the West India Dock Basin about the beginning of June 1836.[12] She was the largest ship that had ever entered this basin, and the gates were only ten inches broader than the ship's beam, so the wooden fenders had all to be taken up before she was hauled in, in safety, but no farther than the basin, as the other gates were too small.

When the ship was cleared in the course of a fortnight, I asked Captain Scott if he had any objections to me sailing with him again in winter to which he replied: 'Certainly not, as I never spent a pleasanter or more comfortable voyage at sea than this last, and I shall be very glad that we sail together again.' With this I was satisfied, and never thought of saying anything about pay which he had promised me before joining the ship at all should, if I went with him a second voyage, be as much as any other of those late Company ships' chief officers got. If he had meditated any alteration of this promise, I thought he would then have told me so.

My mind being at rest as to future employment, I left the great city for Edinburgh once more, but with a very different prospect before me, to any of those on former occasions, being nothing less than that of marriage with the individual 'young girl' whom I mentioned having met in Fife in 1823. Since then I had found sundry opportunities of observing that she was all I could wish as a wife, and we had been engaged for some time previous to this. But I have no intention of writing a love story, and will cut all this matter short by at once stating that we were married on the 22nd August 1836,[13] and, after a fortnight's trip to the Highlands, we took up house with my sister in Edinburgh where we remained for some months, till summoned to London by Captain Scott to join the *Abercrombie Robinson* once more. In this letter, however, he distinctly told me that he could not perform his promise as to pay, the ship not having done so well as was anticipated.

Of course, my wife and I lost no time in getting to London after such an intimation and, on a personal conference after getting there, I found that Captain Scott even went so far as to tell me that he must take £50 off the pay I had during the last voyage which,

'Mrs Miller', by John Adamson, undated. This image of Jessie Miller is
from an album by her brother, John, a pioneer of the calotype process in Scotland.
(The Trustees of the National Museums of Scotland.)

considering all the hard work I had done for him during that 18 months was anything but liberal. Although he afterwards withdrew this reduction, I considered he was bound to perform his promise and claimed the same, which still having been refused, I declined sailing with him again, but parted very good friends. In this matter I could not help telling Captain Scott that he seemed determined, for the sake of a few pounds, to risk the truth of the saying of old Shakespeare: 'T'were better to bear the ills we have, than fly to others that we know not of'.

CHAPTER 14

If any craft could do it, the Black Joke was she

(1836–1837)

It was then the month of November 1836, and I was a married man without employment which would never do to last long although, with the assistance of the purser, I had made a few hundreds by trading when in the *Abercrombie Robinson*. So, having heard from my old messmate T. Hutchinson[1] that there was a chance of getting the command of a steamer at Antwerp, I thought it a good opportunity of seeing that city, and went there with my wife for ten days, sightseeing and trying what was to be done in the way of the command just mentioned. The former we enjoyed much, both at Antwerp and Brussels, but with the latter I found nothing could be done. We returned to London and resided for a week or two with my brother James and his wife at Islington, quietly watching both men and things. My old friend and agent P.W. Welsh and his wife had arrived from Launceston by this time, having made money enough to allow a few months cruise at home. On falling in with them, we consulted together as to what might be done for the good of both parties.

I knew he was a very speculative character and that it was necessary to be cautious in my transactions with him. He suggested purchasing a small vessel and taking her out to the colonies to trade with stock from port to port, and we soon found a very nice brig exactly fitted for this purpose, having been a slaver. She was called the *Black Joke* and had great beam, as also a very fine bottom, and consequently a very fast sailer. Built in the West Indies, her tonnage was 209 tons old measure and only 113 new, with very raking masts, stern and sternpost.[2]

The price asked was £1,000, stores included of course, and I agreed to pay £600 down and £400 in 14 days, Welsh agreeing with me to take the half. A few days after concluding the bargain, I found that his funds were not forthcoming, putting me to great inconvenience as I had to borrow the money to complete the bargain, as well as build a raised deck aft to give some necessary cabin accommodation, and fit her out completely. In short, I was brought into a very heavy expenditure of at least double the amount calculated on. In the course of time I effected the whole by one good friend and another, but chiefly through my agent Mr E. Luskins[3] who behaved most liberally.

At last the time came when we were loaded for Algoa Bay, and had got cabins and everything very comfortable for my wife, myself and two sons of a missionary as passengers. We left London on 25th August 1837, taking in 200 barrels of gunpowder at Gravesend, and getting down Channel and half way across the Bay of Biscay before meeting with any bad weather.[4] Here the wind got into the south-west and soon blew a gale, which continued for three days, during which time we were hove to under a close reefed main topsail, and pumping continually. Indeed, the brig made so much water that I frequently felt that I ought to run back to some port which, with the debt I had already incurred, I knew would be total ruin. I held on till at length the gale ceased, and so did the leak in a great measure. We pursued our voyage in comfort, reaching the Line on the 20th day from the Lizard. I can never forget the anxiety I felt in that gale of wind with such a leak in the brig, and my young wife on board. We had a capital crew, however, of 16 in all, and the little craft herself was faultless in everything save the leak, a first rate sea boat, dancing over the seas like a duck. Her sailing properties were also splendid: ten knots on a wind and 12 off the wind. The leak was in the forefoot, we found out afterwards, caused by the working of the raking stern.

In some of the thunder and lightning squalls in the variables, the idea of being struck by the electric fluid was not very pleasant, having so much powder on board, and no conductor, but we were mercifully spared. Unfortunately, we did not fall in with any homeward bound ships near the Line, but we overhauled several outward-bounders, who I saw clearly would gladly have dispensed with our company, at least until I had hailed them, as they always cracked on every stitch of sail that would draw whenever they sighted us, no doubt under the idea of our being a pirate from the fast-sailing and rakish appearance of the brig. Indeed, I frequently gave chase to strange sails for the fun of frightening them! We were always quite sure of coming up with them very quickly, but, as already stated, none were homeward bound so we had no opportunity of sending letters till off the Cape, which I determined to pass pretty close for that purpose.

Sure enough one morning about six o'clock we saw a large ship coming down upon us from the eastward with studding sails on both sides while the brig was close hauled, standing off shore near Cape Hangklip. I thought now was our chance for letters at last, and I kept the brig shaking right in the course of the stranger till she came up, giving her no more than room to pass under our stern, when I hailed her, and found that she was the *Adelaide* from Calcutta.[5] Immediately, I fancied that I knew the voice, and sang out: 'How are you, Guthrie?'[6] causing him to take the glass and make sure of me because, I learnt shortly, he took us for something very suspicious, more particularly as we had a black burgee flying at the main, with the brig's name in white letters which he did not see very well! The moment he made out my person (intimately known to him from our very school days), he sang out for me to run abreast of him till he shortened sail, and he would come on board. All this being done both of us hove to, and he stepped on board of the *Black Joke* about a quarter to eight by which time my wife had got up and was ready to do the honours of the breakfast table. His passengers were expecting him back to that meal on board the *Adelaide*, so after introducing him to the lady of the pirate, and a hasty 'crack' about old times for a quarter of an hour he left a couple of jars of China ginger and shoved off, all parties much delighted with this very pleasing little episode to their voyage.

Two days after the above meeting we arrived at Algoa Bay,[7] having had a dead beat up to the anchorage from Cape Recife, which gave a good opportunity of showing the people of Port Elizabeth what the *Black Joke* could do. The harbour master came on board in his whaleboat whenever the anchor was let go, and I learned not long afterwards that his boat's crew had reported on shore the inevitable wreck of the brig in the first south-easter coming to blow, and this judgement and comfortable prognostication was made from the apparent small size of our cables. The wiseacres had no idea that the build of such a vessel as the *Black Joke* would enable her to ride out a gale of wind with twice as much ease as the generality of the clumbungy merchant ships which came to that open port. I was made acquainted with the reason for this information having been given: that buying wrecks had been so profitable a venture as to cause some men, calling themselves gentlemen, even to go so far as get boatmen to knock one or two pins out of the shackles of some ships' cables that they might work adrift, and the vessel become a wreck, by being driven on shore!

The surf is always considerable at Port Elizabeth, and whaleboats only are considered safe to land in, yet I was not told so by the harbour master, or that many people had been drowned by the capsizing of ships' boats, although he took me in his whaleboat the first time I visited the agent for the brig. On this occasion I took a room at Story's Hotel for my wife and self and, next day, seeing nothing impossible for a punt to go through, my wife and I left the brig in her with two boys to pull. This being seen by the people on shore, a crowd soon gathered there to enjoy, as I soon learned, the anticipated spill or drowning as the case might be. But having been accustomed to the surf at Madras, I watched my opportunities and, by pulling hard and slacking up when necessary, I managed to get my wife safely on shore without even a drop of water touching her or any in the boat, no doubt much to the vexation of the lookers-on who, although quite aware of our danger, not one of them had the heart to warn us to go back and wait for a whaleboat.[8] Such was our landing at this port of wreckers, where the little *Black Joke* during three weeks stay rode out at least three southeasterly gales with the greatest possible ease, with one anchor only down, while all the other vessels were pitching bows and jib booms under, with two anchors ahead.

We met here with two or three military officers from Grahamstown, and the time passed away very agreeably. The only place within a reasonable distance from Port

Elizabeth worth seeing is Uitenhage, about 20 miles off, where we went one day and returned the next in a horse wagon, a rather primitive sort of conveyance, but very well adapted to the country.[9] It has four wheels and a canvas cover all over, is very strong and light for six horses to drag. They go at a hand gallop the whole way, one man holding the reins and another the whip, which is long enough to reach the leaders with good execution. The village is a tolerable size with two or three broad streets with beautiful trees on each side, in common with all towns in the Cape Colony. The scenery was not very remarkable, and the land seemed to be very poor the whole way, at one part being covered with a crust of salt like the debris of a lake for several miles. We were not sorry to get back to Port Elizabeth on the following day, and thereby get clear of the jolting and dust of the wagon. The horses were capital, and did their work with great ease over the natural plane, no roads having then been made anywhere between Grahamstown and that port, 100 miles distant.

The delays in getting cargo out and in at Port Elizabeth were very great, the barges being quite a monopoly, and the men taking a holiday on the slightest ripple of the sea, so we were three weeks in clearing and taking in some ballast to take us to Table Bay for wine to Sydney. Before leaving I had found it necessary to discharge the chief officer for neglect of duty, and was fortunate enough to get another on the spot, although the change was not quite such as I could have wished as to gentlemanly bearing, but otherwise it was a gain.

A few days only were expended in going round to Table Bay, another 'terra incognita' to me then and, from its being so, very nearly the cause of the loss of the brig. It was dark before I got round abreast of the Whale Rock,[10] and the wind fell very light, but continued

View of Cape Town and Table Mountain, from Felix Achille Saint-Aulaire, *Voyage de la corvette l'Astrolabe*, 1833. (National Library of Australia; PIC U1939 NK3340.)

quite fair for the anchorage. The sound of the surf on the beach was distinctly heard all the way in, but I wondered that I could never see the ships at anchor, and stood on with a light air. Nothing was visible under the shade of the mountain, and the low sandy land at the head of the bay to the eastward looked exactly like the sea, till our soundings came to seven fathoms, which made me let go the anchor for the night, or rather morning, as it was then about 12 midnight. When the officer called me at daylight he said: 'It was well that we did not stand on any farther as we are now only about a quarter of a mile from the shore.' This was very comforting certainly, but there was still a light breeze blowing dead on shore, and we were close to the breakers, so no time was to be lost in getting under way, if such could be done with safety. I knew well if any craft could do it, the *Black Joke* was she, and we hove short and made sail, all ready for a run with the anchor the moment the breeze should give us a favourable chance. To cant the wrong way was certain destruction, but the order was given, and away they ran with the tackle (we had no windlass). Up came the anchor, filled the head yards, and the brig shot ahead instantly. Then, down fore and main tacks, and in five minutes more we were safe! A few tacks brought us up to Cape Town, where we anchored about breakfast time, not a little pleased, when we came to know that the brig had been thought to be on shore and irretrievably lost.

It is rather curious that my old ship the *Abercrombie Robinson* was lost a very few years afterwards, and left her bones on that very spot so nearly fatal to the *Black Joke*. As a transport filled with troops, she drove from her anchor in a north-westerly gale, I think without losing a man as she was strong enough to hold out, not only till all got on shore by some means or another, but for many a day afterwards till broken up.[11] A convict ship which drove on shore quite close to her in the same gale broke up at once, and nearly the whole of the poor prisoners were drowned.[12] I mention this to show the difference between the strength of a late Company ship, and merchant ships generally, notwithstanding all the boasted precautions of what is called 'Lloyd's', a society with every good intention, but too often frustrated in its endeavours to benefit the public by the sheer want of honesty of self-interested men.

It has often been a subject of astonishment to me that the whole shipping and mercantile people of England, Scotland and Ireland should quietly submit to be ruled by a private company of merchants or others, as to how they shall build and repair all ships belonging to the whole of these realms, and that the mercantile world should be so completely governed by the opinions and rules of the said association, as to make them look upon all ships which are not on their list as interlopers and intruders, and unworthy of being employed. Although for the purpose of an excuse for shortness of hands and stinginess in stores I have constantly heard owners bring forward the argument that foreign ships could be employed much more cheaply than English ones. My own opinion of the matter is that the whole system of Lloyd's is a thraldom totally unworthy of being submitted to by a great naval and mercantile nation. The sooner such a state of things shall be altered, either by opposition or Act of Parliament, the better. If no man can, with any hope of success, build a ship for the carrying trade without conforming to certain rules of a private company, those rules ought to issue from the government of the country from whom we might expect justice and uprightness, without favour or affection, especially if the present Admiralty system should be carried out as to fees to officials. I should strongly recommend the whole matter to the serious consideration of the united shipowning and mercantile community.

CHAPTER 15

This little paradise

1837–1838

My agents at Cape Town received us most kindly during a fortnight's stay there, and we were much pleased with the sights, mountain and country round about. All have been so often described by travellers that it would be superfluous to add anything here. I was not a little surprised when my wife and I were walking through the town one day to meet a former very intimate class fellow at the Edinburgh High School in Captain Edward M. Orr who, with his wife, was going to Edinburgh for the purpose of succeeding to his late father's property of £30,000, being twice as much as he ever expected.[1]

This and a subsequent one were very happy meetings, having a great deal of talk about days gone by, not omitting our last appearance at school which was an escape from 'the prison'. Defaulters used to be locked up there for one, two or three hours, by the order of our friend and master Pillans, but we defied him by scrambling up on other boys' backs to the top of the door where a good sized broken pane of glass allowed a passage through. From thence we climbed over the back wall of the yard, down some back stairs to the Cowgate to clear the janitor and goodbye to 'paltry Pillans' forever, neither of us having returned to his dominion from that truly memorable day.

We left Cape Town with a full cargo of wine for Sydney some time in November 1837, and after sundry fair gales as well as light foul winds, we arrived in the following month of December or early in January.[2] My agents there were Messrs Lamb and Parbury, who were most attentive to us in every way. I must not omit to take notice of the day of our arrival which happened to be very fine for yacht racing and boat racing so that the whole bay was filled with small craft under sail and boats of all descriptions, a very animated scene adding much to that natural beauty of the bay and harbour for which Sydney has always been so famous. The pilot was delighted to show off the sailing qualities

Sydney Harbour, from Charles Rodius, *Views of Sydney and Parramatta*, 1833.
(Mitchell Library, State Library of New South Wales.)

of the little *Black Joke*, and we ran through the 'muskitto fleet' at a rapid rate under all plain sail, till so near the wharf off which we were to anchor that there was hardly time to take in sail. After letting go the anchor we were very nearly foul of the wharf before the brig was brought up, then we had time to survey the whole panorama before us which was truly beautiful, and of course much enhanced by the newness of everything, never having been in these waters before.

The entrance to the bay is only about half a mile broad, between stony cliffs of a considerable height for about one and a half miles, when the bay opens up sharp to the left for nearly two miles, and then to the right for about three more till the city is reached. Altogether the distance is six miles from the Heads, where there is a lighthouse and pilots' houses. It is not a place where anyone should come in during the night, unless well acquainted with it previously, although there is no want of water in mid-channel. The city in 1837 was even then a large place, carrying on a great deal of trade, and had been settled exactly 50 years on the day of our entrance, which was the cause of its being held as a jubilee.[3] At a little distance off the Heads the passage is hardly observed, and looks only like an indent of the coast, the land filling up the inner background where it is necessary to turn sharp to the left.

When Captain Cook was passing on one of his voyages to this coast the lookout man at the masthead reported a harbour, but so doubtfully that the great discoverer said: 'Very well, I'll put it down and call it Port Jackson in case it should turn out anything by and by, but we have no time to look into it just now.' He afterwards, when the first batch of convicts were being sent to Botany Bay, told the Admiralty to order the captain to examine this supposed harbour. This was accordingly done after arrival at Botany Bay by the first

Black Joke advertised in the *Sydney Gazette*, 24 March 1838.
(State Reference Library, State Library of New South Wales.)

Governor, from the top of the hills between the then infant colony there and Sydney, from whence he saw the splendid harbour which he shortly after called by that name, and removed the camp and prisoners there forthwith: thus originated the capital of the eastern colonies. The name of the man who discovered this beautiful bay from the masthead of the old *Discovery* was Jackson, Captain Cook calling it after him.[4]

Our time was fully occupied here taking out one cargo and getting in another for Launceston, Tasmania, where I intended to pitch my headquarters for some time to come.[5] After a very pleasant fortnight had been spent in this lovely place, and frequently enjoying the society of the families of both Captain Lamb and Mr Parbury (who had married two sisters), we sailed for Bass Strait one beautiful morning,[6] and beat out through the Heads in company with HMS *Conway*, 26 guns,[7] Captain Drinkwater Bethune.[8] The breeze was quite light most of the day, but freshened up in the afternoon when we passed the *Conway*. In four hours we had run her down astern to her topgallant sails only above water, so in the morning nothing of her was to be seen; she was bound for Hobart Town. On the third day after leaving Sydney we passed Cape Howe, and next morning took on board a pilot, Mr Waterland,[9] off Low Head, and stood up the River Tamar, my wife quite delighted with the very picturesque and lovely scenery.

'Launceston, V.D.L., from the Westbury Road', from John Skinner Prout,
Tasmania illustrated, c.1844. (State Library of Tasmania.)

On arrival at Launceston the following day[10] we found that Mr Welsh and family had preceded us by a month, having touched nowhere on the passage. At their invitation my wife and I took up our abode with them for the time being, in a large and handsome house in the principal part of the town. It was now Welsh's turn to do something to help me with the brig, and he did so to some advantage for a time, till I could manage for myself as agent. I had a heavy debt of £1,100 to pay my London agent, and I set to work at once. In a very few days I started for Adelaide with a full cargo and passengers,[11] one of whom was a Captain Hurst who had commanded a vessel which had formerly been a Royal Navy 10-gun brig.[12] He considered her a very fast sailer and everything that was good, till we came to clear the Heads in the *Black Joke* when, with a fresh breeze and a heavy head sea, she went nine knots clean, close hauled, and never shipped a drop of water, which caused the said captain to confess that he had certainly never seen anything like that before in any ship!

This was a most agreeable trip, saving that I had left my wife with Mrs Welsh, she having had sailing enough for a time, as may be supposed. We soon got to our destination,[13] and found the creek and port a very shabby concern. The place had not been colonised more than one and a half years, and all was in the rough in the truest sense of the word.[14] A small canal had been cut for ships' longboats to land cargo, and there let it lie exposed to the weather till the owners or agents could contrive to cart it up to the town of Adelaide. Unfortunately, this canal was cut so narrow that two boats could not pass. Consequently the boat which came first had to wait till the others were cleared before she could get out. These are mistakes which new colonies are subject to very often, and they only learn what is best by experience and time. The town, if such it could be called, consisted of a few houses of wood and thatched huts of all sorts, and the bare ground for a floor. The best hotel in the place was one of the latter, having a small deal board table in the middle, with some trunks or chests all round it for chairs, and two or three stretchers at the sides for beds. You could wash if you could find a bucket of water and, if not, leave it alone.

The distance from the port to the town is about five miles, on a beautiful plain, and the park about it is like that of a wealthy lord in England, and timbered lightly. Government House was a very small wooden cottage with a ground floor only, where Captain Hindmarsh RN received me very kindly, and conversed for half an hour.[15] I did not envy him his billet, nor anyone there at that period, but it is wonderful what time, and a short time too, will do in a new colony, and what millions of money are made there, even without a single gold field. Yet the first settlers have hard work indeed, and deserve to make money, if that is their only aim.

At the port there were only two pilots and a harbour master, namely Commander Lipson RN[16] who had formerly sailed with Captain Hindmarsh, and was a most obliging man, but the state of things in his department was such as to try all his good nature and temper to the utmost. However, every day made some improvement in all matters, and in those of the worthy harbour master there was I presume no exception, and he lived there for many years in great comfort with his family under a variety of regimes, dying there an old and highly respected individual. After all sorts of bother with the cargo we got off within about ten days for Launceston.[17] The pilot, taking the brig across the bar of the creek before breakfast, expected his boat to come off for him from the shore abreast of the head of the creek. I hove to and waited half an hour. Not seeing any boat I made sail and stood out to sea, pilot and all, whom I sent back from Launceston in another vessel, with an order to my agent to make Captain Lipson pay his £6 passage to Adelaide. I believe it had the desired effect of having the boat sent off for the pilots a little more correctly ever after, rather than trusting to the ships sending them in their boats, which I did not do as it was not my business to let a boat's crew go away nobody knew where, or for how long, merely because the harbour master neglected his duty.

In three or four days we arrived at Launceston[18] where I found all right as to my wife, and every prospect of a cargo for the brig to Sydney. So, after laying her on the hard, and trying to stop the leak by securing the forefoot more effectually and refitting the rigging, while the cargo was being taken on board, I put the chief officer[19] in command and sent her off to Sydney. During her absence of three weeks[20] I purchased a cottage with three acres of land about a mile out of town, and furnished it as economically as possible with the view of remaining on the island for some years, but this plan was not thoroughly carried out.[21] Meanwhile, we made some very agreeable acquaintances, especially those of a wealthy family who were our nearest neighbours and had a beautiful property there. Some of this family remain in friendly correspondence with my wife to this time.[22]

The view from our cottage, which stood on the face of a hill, was magnificent, comprising three separate tiers of mountains, most of them wooded nearly to the top. One, called 'Arthur's Seat' from its great likeness to the hill of that name close to Holyrood Palace near Edinburgh, was the most remarkable. We felt the change from a sea life to this little paradise to be very delightful, and the climate certainly the finest in the world. The cottage had been inhabited only for a short time, and the garden was in tolerable cultivation, but there was plenty of occupation in bringing the whole place into a proper state of dress and effect as to plants, shrubs and flowers which continued to the end of our sojourn there.

In a few weeks the brig returned from Sydney after a very successful voyage, but during her absence I had made arrangements with a party to let him the vessel for some months at a certain sum per trip to Port Phillip or Adelaide. Not being very well pleased with the man I had made commander, I appointed another, who managed matters much better.[23] I paid him £20 per month, and with the chief mate and crew they mustered 15 in all. I fitted her to carry sheep with expedition, and paid them all well, as I was so myself by the charterer. So we started fair, making generally two voyages in the month.

About this time a very curious occurrence took place with a man who had previously come as a passenger with us from Sydney and called himself Collier, also claiming that he was the brother of the MP for Plymouth. Professing to be a surgeon he was what might be termed a smart, rattling kind of fellow. He used to joke our doctor of the brig (who left us on first arrival at Launceston) for his quietness and gravity, saying he would never get on without a little more impudence. He plainly told him how he acted when he went to strange hospitals with his 'hah hahs', and learned medical questions which he seemed quite qualified to carry out to advantage, and did so at the hospital in Launceston very shortly afterwards.

This clever individual was, however, very soon found behind the counter of Mr Bates,[24] the first chemist of the place, where he remained for some time unnoticed generally, till we heard that he had gone to Portland Bay to attend on a Mrs Henty there, the wife of a settler who was expecting to be confined.[25] A week or two elapsed while Mr Collier was in waiting, during which time Mr Henty found that he had lost some silver spoons and other things under such circumstances as to throw some suspicion on the doctor as the thief. He considered himself quite justified in opening his bag one day in his absence when he not only found the spoons but the 'free pardon' of this man from Sydney where it showed that he had been the 'assigned servant' of a surgeon for several years, the date of the same being a little previous to his sailing in the *Black Joke* as passenger. Mr Henty immediately told him to be off, and think himself very lucky in not being handed over to the police.

The next thing heard of him was that he had gone down to join the ship *Henry* as surgeon, bound to England.[26] But Captain Walmsley in a very short time after the appointment heard of the Henty robbery, and who he was, from Mr Henty's brother in Launceston. Not being able to get another surgeon, and Collier having certainly a smattering of that profession, he was obliged to content himself with turning the fellow out of the cabin and making him mess with the second mate in the steerage. Thus did this late prisoner and thief obtain a free passage to England, and a small sum as pay also, if I recollect rightly. This impudent rogue after returning from Portland Bay, and before his appointment to the *Henry*, came out to our cottage two or three times to call. Although I did not then know of his true character, I was so much annoyed by his impudent, forward manners that I ordered him out of the house, and never saw him more.[27]

While on the subject of prisoners, I shall add one more story to those of George Haig and 'Dr' Collier as an example of what may be done by a man who fell from the rank of a gentleman and manager of a bank in England to that of a convict in Tasmania while I was there. Although many even of the lowest rank have risen to be very wealthy men, one in particular, who was well known in Sydney, died leaving about £300,000. The manager was transported for forgery and, at the time of his arrival at Hobart Town, it was customary for anyone who required an assigned servant to go on board of the convict ship on arrival, and choose from the number any of such trade or profession as might suit him, all of course being in the same grey dress and leather cap. Mr R. was picked out by a Launceston merchant as a clerk, in which capacity I first saw him, and used to wonder what portly gentleman he was, going about the wharfs and Customs. I got a little acquainted with him before knowing his position, from having business to transact with the office to which he belonged, and found him all that his appearance portrayed, that is a pleasant agreeable gentleman.

I learned afterwards that he had more than once told a brother clerk how deeply he felt his punishment in every way, but chiefly in having been subjected to the society of such a villainous set as he had to herd with while on board the ship, and always to muster with them at the police office once every month for several years. Mr R., however, was at no time in the least contaminated by such society; and after serving a certain number of years with the very best character he got his freedom, beginning business as an agent in company with another freed person at Melbourne. This connection did not last long, and the colony of Hong Kong in China having just been established, Mr R. went there, beginning a boarding house in which he was so successful that in three years or less he sold the business, and commenced as an agent and general store keeper. I found him in this position there in 1848, doing an excellent business, and afterwards met him in England in 1856 where, I am glad to say, he was once more highly respected by all his former friends. He told me that he had left a partner carrying on the business, but he intended to return to China shortly after I met him, to arrange matters finally. Since that time I have heard nothing of him.

CHAPTER 16

I held the rascal of a pilot by his pigtail

1839

The little *Black Joke* continued to perform her voyages with sheep to Port Phillip with great rapidity, and I took care she should never be more than three days at Launceston. Everything was going on well and I was in a fair way to be able to clear off my debt to my London agent very soon. To add to this comfortable state of matters my wife presented me with a son on the 21st March 1839,[1] shortly after which, the sheep carrying coming to a close for the season, and the brig continuing to leak, I saw that I should soon be obliged to give her some repairs. I therefore came to the decision of going to China in the month of July, and there sell the vessel and go home for another. In the intervening months I sent her to Adelaide instead of Port Phillip, which paid very well. On winding up previously to starting for China via Sydney I found that I had paid all my debts in London and elsewhere, lived comfortably on shore ourselves for 16 months and had £300 in my pocket to fill up with some trading goods at Singapore, besides the freight to Sydney.

When nearly ready to sail we sold off furniture and let the cottage, leaving the Controller of Customs to manage for us till our return.[2] In the first week of July we bid adieu to Launceston,[3] having two passengers for Singapore: Mr George Ashburner, a cadet for the army of Bombay,[4] and Mr Carr, the son of the then Bishop of Bombay,[5] on his way to his family there, as well a female servant for our baby. In a few days we once more visited Sydney where we remained a week, but alas had to sail without any female servant, who thought proper to bolt on the evening before we were to leave.[6] As I had agreed to keep company with a certain ship through the Torres Strait[7] there was no time to look after another.

I trusted to getting charts of these straits on a large scale at Sydney, but I found there were none to be got, and was therefore obliged to go by a large outline chart which had

Captain Cook's track pricked off on it, although on so small a scale that I could with some difficulty lay down the course to be steered. Still, I expected to have another ship in company, and there could not be much to be feared in the matter. We had only been three days at sea from Sydney when we lost sight of our friend in a gale of wind, and never saw him again, or any other ship till close to Timor Island. After entering the 'Inshore Passage' at Breaksea Spit, we continued to run day and night for several days amongst sundry groups of islands, till reefs, sands and islands became so thick that we were obliged to anchor every evening at sunset, and get under way at daylight next day.

At Whitsunday Passage[8] we were chased by half a dozen canoes filled with natives hallooing to stop us, but I had no idea of being troubled with these savages, soon making them turn tail by out sailing them, but they pulled most desperately for a time. The scenery was truly beautiful all through, being chiefly mountainous on the mainland and covered with wood almost everywhere. At one place on the side of a hill we got a capital view of a large number of natives holding a corroboree, and dancing round numerous fires nearly all night.

During the whole passage I kept the second mate looking out from the masthead as it is much better to have one person to trust to than many, he getting so well accustomed to everything in a day or two as not to make mistakes, the most trifling of which might be ruinous to the ship and lives of all. We had often to steer entirely by the directions of this man. At one place in particular, where Cook had gone between two sands which were so close that we could have thrown a biscuit on shore at either side, yet we had from five to seven fathoms water for the whole distance of about two miles. At another place his track ran between two small islands, which of course I trusted to being alright, but just as we had entered the passage the second mate sung out from the masthead 'no passage!' a most ominous sound indeed. I instantly sent the chief officer up, and he repeated the same. I told them to look well out, as I felt sure there was a passage. The brig was then going about seven knots, there was no room either to tack or wear and the wind was then dead aft. So I must have let fly everything, and then the anchor as fast as possible, if the same report should have again come from the two officers, but I trusted in Cook having found a passage, and after a few more minutes they sung out that all was right, as they saw there was a passage now! Joyful indeed was this sound, after which we breakfasted in peace, and stood on as before under all plain sail, ready for any emergency.

On coming to an anchor that evening Mr Ashburner remarked to me the great smartness of the ship's company in shortening and furling sails, and said he would time the proceedings the next day, which he did. We found that only 13 minutes elapsed from the order being given to take in the royals and topgallant sails to the anchor being down with 40 fathoms of chain out, all sails furled and the whole of the men down from aloft. Not one of them had the least idea of having been timed, or anything extraordinary being looked for. They were stationed to work one watch up forward and the other aft, under their respective officers, which of course caused a little emulation between them, but the whole number was only 15. The average of five or six more trials was 14 minutes, which was very good practice for a small merchant craft.

On the 12th day after passing Breaksea Spit, in latitude I think about 23½ degrees south, we passed Cape York, the most northerly point of 'New Holland', or more properly 'Australia'. It is a small island very close to the mainland, where there is now I believe a small detachment of marines to keep possession of this part of the great island and be in the way to assist ships which may happen to get on shore in the Torres Strait, no very uncommon occurrence. Possession Island is very near to this Cape to the westward, and it was up one of its hills that Captain Cook climbed to look out for the open sea after having traversed nearly the whole round of Australia from North West Cape, and his eyes were regaled with a sight of what he had so justly calculated on, the Timor Sea. His track on my chart was laid down from Cape York as having passed close round Possession Island in a very narrow passage between it and a small rocky island in a south-south-westerly direction, which course I followed in preference to going round by Booby Island to the north-west. I found the passage so narrow for about one and a half miles that, being close hauled with a fresh breeze, it placed me in a very dangerous position in the event of the wind heading us by a single point, as I should then have been obliged to get out the way I came in, by sternboards only. I knew the *Black Joke* could go five knots with everything shaking excepting her fore and aft sails in such a breeze as then blew, so we carried on in good hope of all being right. In a very short time we cleared the little island and its outlying rocks, and then squared away through Endeavour Strait into the open sea, although for some time in only three fathoms water.

When clear of Princes Island, however, we had nothing to fear, and cracked on both by night and day once more. In a few days we passed through the Strait of Samao in the dark, where we saw a barque a short distance ahead tearing away under all possible sail to get into Timor before us where the captain supposed we were going for ponies as well as himself. He had refused to keep company through the Strait so we let him enjoy his suspicions, as also his victory which he would next morning suppose he had gained when he did not find us there. We carried on for Lombock, where we soon after arrived and found the *Royal Saxon* lying waiting for rice.⁹ My wife was delighted with the scenery all round this beautiful island as well as the splendid fruits, eggs and fowls, all of which were to us dirt cheap. We laid in a store sufficient to last for some days till we should arrive at Singapore. Finding that nothing was to be done in rice we sailed the next afternoon, and soon got into the Java Sea, never ceasing to admire the truly splendid sight of the peaks of Lombock and Bali till they sank in the receding distance astern.

During the south-east monsoon the weather amongst all the islands in the Java Sea is beautiful, and the sailing past Hog Island, Madura, Lubec and through the Carimata Passage is very fine, every inch of the ground of all, apparently, being covered with wood. We arrived at Singapore about the end of August 1839,¹⁰ where we were most kindly treated by Mr Johnston, to whom I had an introduction from Mr Ashburner. This is also a delightful place to arrive at after a two months spell at sea, and my wife was enchanted with everything. Mr Johnston soon procured a Malay nurse for the baby, who had thriven well during the voyage in his little cot slung under the main boom nearly all the day, and dandled by one or two Lascars who were on board. He only required the sybelle to whom he was now handed over to allow his mother a little relief, and see what was to be seen. I here filled up with rattans and ten chests of opium, the value of the latter being £800 which Mr Johnston let me have hypothecation.[11] After a week most delightfully spent in all the luxuries of the east (so my wife thought), we started for China having, of course, left our two young gentlemen passengers to find a passage to Bombay from Singapore.

The monsoon was nearly done in the China Sea, and only light winds prevailed, so that our passage to Macao extended to nearly three weeks. The last few days were very typhoonish indeed in appearance, and we were very glad to get to Macao Roads without encountering such an unwelcome visitor. The pilot we got there seemed determined to take us by the Capsingmoon Passage, instead of the outside one to Hong Kong, which I agreed to, not knowing the state of matters with the Chinese sufficiently to cause suspicion of foul play.[12] After anchoring for one night at Lintin, and getting under way in the morning, he persisted in passing between a rocky island and another large rock, where he said there was plenty of water. When right in the middle the brig touched the ground and hung for a

'Harbour of Hong Kong', from George Newenham Wright, *China in a Series of Views*, 1843.
(The Trustees of the National Library of Scotland.)

minute till I sent all hands chock forward which made her lift and stumble over it. I held the rascal of a pilot by his pigtail all this little time, promising him faithfully to cut it off if the brig should stick fast. However, this was not the case, and he escaped this capital punishment.

A large mandarin boat was lying at the Capsingmoon, and I have no doubt that he had expected it to attack us on the previous night, to take the ten chests of opium. Getting us on shore, he must have thought, would place us in a still better position for attack on the following night, but such was not to be, as I terrified the fellow into doing his duty. We beat through the passage and into Hong Kong Bay about 11 a.m.[13] when I dismissed him with only four dollars instead of ten as payment for pilotage, but he should have had nothing, and certainly been handed over to the superintendent of trade (Captain Elliot) had I known the state of things and the occurrences which had a very short time previous taken place.[14] One of them was that a small schooner of the same name as my brig had been boarded off Lintin, and everyone murdered, including a lady and child, and the vessel plundered. The news of this getting home before our letters caused great anxiety to our families there for some time, the brig's name and a lady and child corresponding with us so well. In fact, all sorts of robberies and murders in vessels had been rife for some time before our arrival.[15]

Immediately after anchoring I went on board of the *Scaleby Castle* (an old Company ship)[16] and had a very pleasant conference with Mr Matheson, and handed over the brig and my affairs to his agency. In answer to my query of: 'Do you wish to purchase the vessel?', the answer was: 'No.' But he purchased my opium at a 100 per cent profit to me exactly, thereby putting £800 in my pocket without any trouble whatever. On the second day after this it blew a heavy gale which lasted for two days and prevented any communication from ship to ship. The whole of the British community of Macao and Canton was at that time (at the end of September 1839) on board one ship or other at Hong Kong, as also all the offices and staff of every mercantile firm. The fleet consisted of upwards of 70 ships of all kinds, our Government being at loggerheads with the Chinamen about the opium trade, and a war actually looming in the future, the commencement of which we very soon afterwards saw. The only men-of-war in the bay were the *Volage*, 26 guns, and *Hyacinth*, 18, and a small cutter for the use of Captain Elliot, the Superintendent of Trade.[17]

All the commerce was carried on through the Americans, and consequently ships had to suffer great delays. In short everything was in a state of derangement which was not very encouraging to me as to my prospects in selling the *Black Joke*. The gale had scarcely died away, however, when a Parsee merchant called Dadabhoy Rustomjee[18] came on board with one of his captains, asking if the brig was for sale and, if so, at what price. After a very trifling examination of her by the captain, he seemed quite willing to come to my terms. When I told him that I must see my agents before concluding any bargain he said he must either have it decided at once or not at all. Not being willing to lose a certainty for what I then considered a great uncertainty, I struck the bargain with him for $9,000, including all the rattans on board, which was not a bad bargain, considering that I had already paid every shilling the brig had cost, stores and all, besides my profit on the opium. The exchange at five shillings made the sum about £2,250, but when Mr Matheson knew what I had done he said that he would rather have given me $12,000 and burn the brig next day than that Dadabhoy should have had her! If I had known this I might have done pretty well with one or other of them, yet I was very contented. Mr Matheson had himself only to blame having told me that he did not wish to purchase.

After giving up the brig having had her exactly two years, my wife, child and I took up our abode on board the *General Wood*,[19] a Country ship commanded by an old Company officer named Rickett,[20] who very kindly offered this hospitality in our extremity until we could get a passage in some ship bound for England, which were then very rarely to be got. Mrs Rickett and four children, as also her mother, lived on board at the same time. Although still cooped up in a ship, yet the weeks passed away very agreeably with visitors and visiting during the day, and a walk on shore in the evening occasionally, where the city of Hong Kong now stands.

Our programme was more than once varied by a ball on board of some ship. The first of these entertainments was given by Captain Parry in the *Hercules*, the opium receiving ship of Jardine, Matheson and Company.[21] It was on the first anniversary of the worthy old captain's marriage, his 'cara sposa' [dear wife] being somewhat younger than himself. It was a very well got up affair and the supper was elegant, being on the upper deck of an old clipper brig made fast alongside, with a proper accommodation ladder to descend by when the order was given. The whole number present was 50, out of which I think only ten were ladies.

The next ball was given by Captain Wills of the *Charles Forbes*[22] who had at one time preceded me as midshipman of the *Marquis Camden*. It had blown pretty fresh all the day, and the weather looked very squally when we went on board to this ball. Both Mrs Rickett and my wife were nursing babies so we took care to order the boat to remain alongside in case of its coming to blow hard, but to keep out of the way of others till wanted. This was very soon found to be an excellent precaution, as we had hardly got on board when it began to blow and rain furiously, but chiefly in squalls. The dancing, however, was well kept up for about two hours when the captain, seeing the rain coming through the awning on to the supper table on the quarterdeck, gave the order for supper while it was possible to sit there, the dancing having been on the poop, under double, sloped awnings. The supper was got through in a very hurried manner, the rain in many places pouring through on everybody and everything, but the dancing was recommenced. Both rain and wind continuing, I watched for a lull, when both Rickett and I dragged our wives from the centre of a quadrille, got them into the boat and pulled as hard as we could to the *General Wood*, which we reached just in time to escape a tremendous squall. From that time the gale increased so much that upwards of 30 people were detained on board the *Charles Forbes* for the whole of the next day and night, much to the horror no doubt of poor Captain Wills, though outwardly appearing highly pleased with his guests. The end of these things showed that the change of the monsoon was not the time for balls and parties on board ship.

CHAPTER 17

We were not likely to go the same road again

1840

After a sojourn of six weeks in the *General Wood*, we shifted to the *Fort William* (an old Company ship) commanded by Captain Hogg.[1] Our intention was to take passage in her for Bombay when she could get away, and to proceed home by the overland route from thence, having made money enough to allow of this, as we might never have the opportunity again of seeing Egypt. We had not been more than a few days on board when the Kowloon forts began to fire on the fleet over the point of land intervening. On the second evening of this game two of the shot fell close alongside of our quarter when the ladies were sitting within three yards of them on the poop. This caused Captain Hogg to move the ship farther down the harbour next day, and Captain Elliot seeing that mischief might happen to some ships, under this daily or evening cannonade, ordered the whole fleet to remove to Toong Koo at the back of Lintin Island, where we lay till the middle of January 1840, when the old *Fort William* made a start for Bombay.[2]

After touching at Singapore and Tellicherry on the coast of the Indian peninsular, we arrived at Bombay alright,[3] having spent about three months altogether with Captain Hogg and his most agreeable passengers, Mr and Mrs McLean and Mr Daniel of the Bombay Civil Service. As the *Berenice*, a Company sloop-of-war,[4] was to sail for Suez in six days, we did not remove on shore to reside, but only occasionally to let my wife see the place. My brother, then Judge Advocate General of the army, had died at Ahmedabad in September 1836, and I did not care to hunt up his former friends at this Presidency for so short a time.

The mail service was at this date carried on by the Company war vessels, and the charge for passengers was very high, the greater part going into the pockets of the captains. Each one, male or female, had to pay £80 to Suez, and babies under two years £20, which

I thought quite outrageous, telling the Paymaster so when he asked it, our baby being only 11 months old. He said that he had no doubt it would be remitted by application to Colonel Wood, the Secretary to Government, so I went to him and asked this favour. He objected, telling me that the charge was made as a compensation to passengers for the noise and disturbance created by these little darlings. Then I said:

'I ought to pay the money to the passengers, and not to the Government.'

'Impossible, sir.'

'It is clear to demonstration that such should be the case, according to the reason given by you.'

'Well, the Governor-in-Council sit tomorrow and, if you like to write your request, I shall be happy to lay it before them.'

So I left him and did write, but the answer was truly official: the charge was according to the regulations, and could not be remitted. Had I known at that time that Colonel Wood had been a great friend of my late brother and introduced myself to him in this relation, I have no doubt that I should have had nothing to pay for the baby, which the Paymaster said was the youngest that had ever crossed the desert.

On the sixth day after arrival, I think about the 20th February 1840, we left Bombay in the *Berenice*, Commander Low, HCS, a most agreeable man, as also all his officers.[5] There were a considerable number of passengers and, amongst others, a Mr and Mrs Warden of the Company Service. Indeed, I beg his pardon, he was a member of Council who, be it known to all men, ranks in India next to the Governor, and precedes all military officers whatever. Now this rank was especially pleasing to Mrs Warden, but we had also a lady by title, the daughter of an earl, the wife of a major of cavalry, and one of the most accomplished and pleasing of women in every way who cared little for empty titles and grandeur.[6] On the first day at dinner the captain placed the name of Lady Elizabeth on the plate to his right and that of Mrs Warden to his left, according as he and everyone else knew was proper. But Mrs Warden looked unspeakable things when she saw this arrangement, although she was obliged to sit there for that dinner, yet she would not do so a second time, and ever after sat alongside and to the right of her husband, no doubt under the idea if she could not be first, she would not be second. Lady Elizabeth only laughed at her and, on speaking to me on the subject a few days afterwards, said she had often known similar ideas in the ladies of India, and they preferred to herself in rank, although she knew that as the daughter of an earl she could, if she chose, precede any commoner either in India or elsewhere. She always let these things pass without remark.

Mrs Warden showed her folly one evening on deck when a country dance was being formed, by taking the head of the dance, and on Lady Elizabeth coming to take her place anywhere, being my partner at the time, Mrs Warden begged her to come up next to her, and put my wife down lower, who was then the next in order. Lady Elizabeth would not do so, making my wife stand where she was and giving way to nobody, which seemed to be anything but agreeable to this 'Dame of the Council'. Such are the follies of little-minded women who sometimes meet with their match and look like fools.

A circumstance something similar to this took place at Bombay when my old ship the *Marquis Camden* was lying there in 1819, almost a year before I joined her. The second officer when at a large ball on shore stood up with a lady partner to dance a country dance, the custom of standing according to rank being then quite general.[7] The officers of the Company Maritime Service, having no comparative rank assigned to them, this officer found himself pushed down in the order of the dance so much, as to apparently annoy his partner a good deal. As it happened he had a lieutenant's commission in the Royal Navy before entering the Company's service, and his naval uniform and epaulette were in a house almost next door. He begged his partner to be seated for a few minutes, and he would quickly put all this descending to rights. She did so and he ran off, very shortly afterwards returning in his naval uniform, took up his partner again and, beginning at the bottom of the dance, asked every officer separately what rank he held in the army. To all who answered that of ensign or lieutenant he walked up above him in the dance, and when he came to a captain at last, he said: 'Oh, very well, we shall not quarrel about the dates of our commissions, so I shall stop here,' much to the delight of his partner. The captains in the Company's Maritime Service held comparative rank with the army and civil service and, for many years when at the Presidencies in India, used to sit as members of Council, but the officers do not appear ever to have asked that boon. Notwithstanding the absurdities of Mrs Warden, she never succeeded in 'kicking up a row', and the trip from Bombay to Suez was passed most comfortably and agreeably.

When at Aden we were met by a Captain H., whom we had been acquainted with at Tasmania, but who was now with his regiment at the camp on that miserable spot. He brought a tonjon[8] for my wife and a horse for me, and off we went up the rocky hills to the top till we reached his hut, where we were most kindly received by Mrs H. whom he had married before leaving Tasmania.[9] The camp was right in the hollow of what was once a crater of a volcano. In the evening we returned to the ship by the same mode of conveyance as we had come, next morning sailing for Suez where we arrived in six or seven days more. It is a wretched place in every way, saving the hotel, which had been built only a very short time. We soon procured a donkey chair for my wife and baby, a horse for myself, and a donkey for our black Portuguese servant, and off we started along the desert. Some of the passengers went in one-horsed, covered carts, which they regretted much afterwards, as they got knocked about so much. The donkey chair was something like a sedan chair with the upper half cut off and open in front, a donkey being harnessed into the shafts in front and another into those behind, with its head pretty close to the person inside. They went about five miles an hour and were managed by the native who owned them, the horses and other donkeys having their owners also along with them, besides there being a head servant who ruled the whole, and spoke English.

At that time there were stations every ten miles.[10] At every second one a person might by some means get a few hours sleep, but the centre one was a good sized, two storied building, with very tolerable accommodation. In this way we slept three nights, or part of them, on the desert, getting to Cairo in 56 hours altogether. The great sameness of brown desert with a constant mirage was very tiresome to the eyes, the relief to which was truly delightful on coming in sight of the beautiful green fields of the Land of Goshen, and in entering the city of Cairo we almost felt that we could eat the splendid green clover on the backs of numerous camels which were carrying it to market. I forget the name of the hotel at which we put up, and where we spent three days 'doing' Cairo and the Pyramids, which created our wonder and surprise as much as that of the 'world' in general. Lady Elizabeth was 'trump' enough not only to go inside, but to the top of the Great Pyramid, a work of no little exertion, and more than either my wife or self could do having been so completely choked before getting to the centre chamber of the inside. We had been obliged to return and get out to the fresh air as quickly as possible: the highly pulverised dust of 3,000 years, with the stifling heat, were indeed quite overpowering.

These pyramids are most stupendous buildings, especially when it is considered that about one-third of the height is taken off by the accumulation of the debris of lime, etc., having either fallen or been dug out of the great steps, as they may be termed, and which now forms an immense raised foundation, as it were, for a very large space all round. The whole of the outsides have been evidently made perfectly smooth from the bottom to the top at one time or other, as it is still seen on about 20 or 30 feet of the top of the second one, which is quite smooth and pointed. Never was anything more greedily seized than the bottles of water which the native children offered on our emerging from the dismal bowels of the Great Pyramid: it felt as if it were the saving of our lives entirely. A substantial luncheon in one of the native houses hewn out of the solid rock, like those of Petra in Idumaea, wound up our visit. We then trotted back to Cairo on our donkeys, which certainly are the best in the world.

In March 1840 there were no railways in Egypt, so we had all to hire boats with raised cabins at the after end, to go down the Nile to Alexandria, which after three days torment of fleas we duly reached. There we waited for the sailing of the French packet to Malta which we preferred, for the sake of variety, to the English one, as well as from a wish to see how French men-of-war were managed by their officers, these packets forming a part of that navy. We had not to wait more than two days, when we started in the *Rhamses* to Syria in the archipelago, where we met the ship from Constantinople, to which we were turned over. We got to Malta on the fourth day, after a very pleasant passage with the Frenchmen, all of whom were most attentive and obliging. One of our fellow passengers was Horace Vernet, the great painter, who had been taking drawings of some battles in Turkey for the French Government.[11]

On arrival at Malta we were all put into Fort Manuel for 20 days quarantine, a most horrible nuisance and expense for no purpose that we could see. However, it was got through, and after a week's spell in the town seeing all the wonders of the place and island, which have been so often related by travellers, we sailed for Marseilles in another French steamer of the then Republican navy. We touched at Civitavecchia and Leghorn, giving us a peep of Italy for a few hours at each of these places.

At Marseilles we remained a few days and then hired a carriage, posting to Paris in the usual way, which I think occupied about five days in such a manner as allowed us to see what was worthy of inspection very comfortably. At Paris we did not 'do' a great deal, but visited an aunt and two cousins of mine there, whom I had not seen for nearly 22 years. Three days were all we could spare in Paris before starting for London via Boulogne. From thence, in another week, we went to Dundee by steamer where we arrived about the middle of May 1840, our whole passage from China having cost £420, including everything, a very large sum compared with what the same could be done for now. But we were not likely to go the same road again, and we comforted ourselves with the idea that we had got a good deal for our money, although not the full value.

The next question was: what was the best thing to do? For a couple of months I thought of taking a farm, and even looked at one with that intention, but it was too small and a cold situation. My relatives advised me against doing anything of the kind, so I turned my attention towards building a vessel like the little *Black Joke* on an improved scale, and try my luck again as before at Tasmania.

CHAPTER 18

Cheated by all and sundry people

1841–1842

Meantime we took a house at Portobello for six months, being near to my only remaining sister in Edinburgh where, on the 23rd January 1841, I was presented by my wife with another son.[1] Two or three months later we moved up the Firth of Forth to a place called Brucehaven, where I had agreed with a shipbuilder to build me a vessel on my own model, of about 150 tons new measure, and to complete and launch her within three months from the time of signing the contract.

The bargain was very favourable for me since the builder did not care about making money on the job: all he wanted was not to lose by it, as he would be satisfied with the credit that the building of such a fine clipper brig would give him. With this he set to work with between 50 and 60 men daily, under my own constant inspection, completing the whole, even to coppering, the lower masts in and rigged, painting outside and in, and two boats, in exactly three months and ten days. I then took her to Leith for a cargo to Port Phillip, intending to sail early in October 1841 which was also accomplished within the time. This brig was a very handsome craft, measuring $142\frac{1}{2}$ tons new measure, but 236 old measure, being exactly the size of the old 10-gun brigs of the Navy, from which scale I masted, sparred and rigged her, reducing the yards only by two feet.

The cabin was fitted entirely for our own accommodation in the most comfortable style which the size of the vessel would admit, and the 'tout ensemble' [general effect] was that of a large roomy yacht, with four carronades with elevating screws on the quarterdeck. She was much admired in Leith and I could have manned her there with 100 men if I had wished, so much did she please the eye and ideas of the 'Jacks'. There was a young lad wished very much to go with me, the son of a Landing Waiter of Customs. His father had taken it into his head that we were going 'a-pirating' and, to the last, would not allow his

'Phantom', by Frederick Garling, 1847. The portrait shows the vessel
at this date when registered in Sydney in the ownership of Thomas Woolley.
(Australian National Maritime Museum, Sydney.)

son to join the brig, which I have omitted to state, I had named the *Phantom* as sure
enough she proved to be.[2]

We left Leith about the middle of October 1841,[3] passing in the Roads my old ship
the *Abercrombie Robinson* which had been sent for troops from Edinburgh Castle, having
changed hands to Mr Somes,[4] the great shipowner, and turned into a 'transport'. She was
admirably adapted for this service, and altogether superior to any other of that gentleman's
ships, who for many years had made so much money by Government charters for his
vessels that, after he died, a cheque was found in his desk for £30,000 in favour of Mr
Meek, the head of the Transport Department at the Admiralty,[5] with a note attached
addressed to his executors stating that no questions were to be asked on the subject. On
their refusing to pay it, the matter was taken before the Government of the day, and at once
canvassed before the House of Commons. The end of it was that Mr Meek got his money,
and resigned HM Service as well he might, with such a sum in his pocket, besides what
other trifles may have previously stuck to his fingers. There is too much reason to suppose
that Mr Meek has not been the only high official who has become rich by douceurs,
although Messrs Gambier and Rumble[6] are the only two unfortunates, since the above

PHANTOM, 141, *Miller*, to Port Philip, &c.—37 casks ale, 1 cask spirits, 13 casks 2 cases wine, 2 casks brandy, 2 cases geneva, by J. Anderson —10 hams, 16 casks wine, by C. Cowan and Company—1 cask honey, 2 bales sacks, by Taylor, Bruce, and Company—9 bales 1 box paper, by C. Cowan—28 casks ale, by D. Henderson—45 boxes soap, 26 kegs sheep's salve, by W. Taylor and Co.—25 casks wine, by W. Kay—1 carriage, 28 coils cordage, 38 casks salt, by J. Broadfoot and Son—8 pianofortes, by Adamson and Co.—30 casks herrings, 12 bags corks, by D. Robertson and Son—800 boards, 29 cases cheese, 2 cases cordials, 20 casks pork 10 casks beef, 4 bales 6 boxes books, &c., 60 casks ale, 30 tons pig iron, 2 bales cotton wick, 6 bales 2 boxes canvass, linen, &c., 2 cases 4 bales linen, 4 boxes stationery, 2 cases hats, 6 boxes 6 trusses apparel, 1 box cheese, 1 cask meal, 3 bales linen bags, 3 carriages, 42 casks pease, 11 casks barley, 15 casks herrings, 6 bxs confectionery, 1 box books, 10 casks meal, 1 box sulphur, 1 box boots and shoes, 14 cases woollen maufactures, 1 case linen thread, 8 pkgs furniture, by Wm Allan and Co.

Manifest of Phantom published in the *Leith Commercial List*, 19 October 1841.
(By courtesy of Edinburgh City Libraries.)

occurrence took place, who have been legally detected. I myself know of one instance of a Captain Superintendent of a dockyard refusing to try an invention though ordered by letter from the Secretary of the Admiralty to do so unless the account was to be sent in with £35 tailed on to it beyond the price agreed to. For ought that I know the invention remains in the Superintendent Office to this day. These are disgraceful proceedings, and I am glad that the present Government have determined to put them down with a strong hand.

We ran down the Firth of Forth with a fine fair north-westerly wind, having one passenger, Mr A. Allan, my wife, two very young children, a servant girl of great respectability, and a ship's company of 15, including the first and second officers and carpenter. The brig sailed beautifully, and was quite equal to the *Black Joke* in this respect, and superior in many others. I had rigged her with wire rope, which after passing the North Sands Head off Deal, we had some reason to regret, although it had stood out a gale off the Sunk Light vessel very well.[7] When off Dungeness the breeze freshened considerably north-east and, the compasses having taken it into their heads to fly about at a great rate, the men at the helm got confused, bringing the vessel sharply round to the wind twice without damage, but the third time the two topmasts instantaneously went over

'Falmouth', from William Clarkson Stanfield, *Coast Scenery*, 1836.
(The Trustees of the National Library of Scotland.)

the side. I was at that minute about to order a reef to be taken in, yet it might have happened at a worse time of the voyage, but we made the best of it, although obliged to cut everything adrift to save the wreck from damaging the side.

This being done we stood down Channel, intending to go into Spithead, but the wind was too much to the northward when we came abreast of it, so we ran on under our courses till the next evening. We hove to about 8 p.m. off the Eddystone under a reefed mainsail till daylight, when a pilot cutter bore down to us, asking if he should tow us into Falmouth, the wind being then dead out of Plymouth Sound. I told him that we required no towing as long as our lower masts should stand, but he might come on board and take us into Falmouth, which he did. In a couple of hours we beat into that harbour under courses and boom mainsail in capital style, to the admiration of all the nautical world at least, as I very soon learned.

On anchoring, I went on shore and arranged with Messrs Fox[8] to transact my business, and gave the orders for new topmasts, rigging and sails to be got ready as quickly as possible. I found a Mr Teague[9] there who had come from a Captain Tilly[10] who wished to send some packages to their son at Melbourne, and to offer their hospitality to my wife and children while the brig should be in harbour. Mr Teague, a master RN, was in raptures with the brig, and made me promise that I should let him take the helm of her when we should sail from the port. The kind offer of Captain and Mrs Tilly was at once accepted and my wife, bairns and servant went on shore with Mr Teague and took up their quarters with the worthy couple. I slept on board, going occasionally to the Captain's house. Poor man, he had been struck with paralysis about a year before, and was confined to the house entirely, but Mrs Tilly did the honours most delightfully, driving my family about wherever there was anything worth seeing, and sometimes spending a day at their country house at Tremough, a beautiful old place. In short, they were kindness itself, and the remembrance of our fortnight's stay with these worthy people has ever since that time formed the most pleasing theme for our conversation wherever we went.

We were fully supplied with vegetables of all sorts, not only for the ship's company in harbour, but in such a quantity when about to sail as to last nearly to the Cape of Good Hope. The good lady persisted in paying freight for the packages sent to her son, as also passage for a stag-hound which we took for him. Captain Tilly had commanded an Admiralty packet, and Mr Teague had been a messmate of his at some former time, hence the intimacy and good feeling which existed between them. When the day came for sailing, Mr Teague was at the helm and, the wind being easterly, we had to work out under topsails and courses only, not having had time to get the topgallant masts up before starting.[11] Yet we beat one of the packets all to nothing, although she had all plain sail set, which greatly pleased Mr Teague who declared, before leaving us, that he had never seen a finer vessel in his life. On the pilot leaving we soon got the topgallant sails and royals set, and squared away in passing the Lizard to a fine fresh north-easterly breeze under all sail we could set, which to the best of my recollection was but little altered till near the Line.

The incidents of this voyage were nil, until arrival at Table Bay,[12] which we hailed with great pleasure, enjoying the society of our old friends very much for a few days. We could not afford to stay long, having only put in for refreshments, before encountering the gales to the east. So at the end of four days we were again passing round the 'Lion's Rump', and off for Port Phillip. On the run from this to Cape Otway we had much light weather, with a few westerly gales of course, in which the *Phantom* showed many good qualities. Our passage was a long one, being 100 days from Falmouth, including those spent at the Cape.[13] It was my first appearance at Port Phillip, and I knew nothing about the customs of the place, or the kind of men I should have to deal with as officials, but 'experientia docet' [experience teaches], and I paid for my lesson.

When the anchor was let go off Williamstown I was visited by the Superintendent of the Water Police and his chief constable, the former presenting me with two printed forms to be filled up with the names of the crew and passengers respectively, and to be delivered at the office 'over there' (pointing to the opposite side to Williamstown) when finished. I was led to suppose that some Custom House official would be there to receive them, but, on going to the place next day, I could not find either an office or man, and went on to Melbourne to deliver the lists there to the Collector of Customs who, I presumed, was the proper person to receive them either first or last. I thought no more of the matter till four days afterwards, when the captain of a Leith ship[14] came to pay us a visit along with his wife, who was well acquainted with mine before marriage. He asked me if I had sent in my two lists to Captain Gordon, the magistrate at Williamstown, telling me at the same time that this gentleman was in the habit of not only fining captains of merchant ships when such were omitted, but of dragging them into error by deception.[15] He wondered that I had not been summoned to account for my very great neglect e're that time. It was also hinted to me that the two officials who first came on board went snacks with the worthy magistrate in sharing the fines.

I thought it was full time for me to pay my respects to this paragon of justice, going on shore for that purpose about 5 p.m., being quite ignorant of the place. I was shown to a small wooden hut for the police office (not court), and had no idea of finding the magistrate there at all. I had hardly entered this paltry place when a common looking man at the back of a counter sung out to me with the voice of a Stentor, 'Take your hat off, Sir! Take your hat off, Sir! This is the Queen's Court, Sir!'

'I wasn't aware of it, Sir,' said I, doffing my cap, and proceeded to tell him that I had left the lists at the Custom House. He wouldn't allow me to say a word, and kept roaring out to the Chief Constable: 'Give him the summons, give him the summons!' which doubtless he had been just about to send on board. The man tried to thrust it into my hand, which made me say to Captain Gordon: 'If you will hear what I have got to tell you, it will be seen that there is no need for a summons.' But he kept roaring out: 'Give him the summons,' till the constable succeeded in getting it into my cap, when he roared out: 'Clear the Court! Clear the Court!' and still would not listen to one word from me. At the third burst of 'Clear the Court!' the constable took me by the shoulders and shoved me out at the door of this said 'court' in the most ignominious manner. I then turned round, and seeing this drunken commander RN at the door, I plainly told him that I should report his outrageous conduct forthwith to the Governor, and he would find that he had got hold of the wrong man for once to play his pranks upon. He never replied, and I returned on board to concoct matters for his destruction.

It so happened that nine of the crew refused to do duty on the second day after this 'fracas', being the day prior to my appearance before the police magistrate according to summons. The ostensible reason for these men behaving in this manner was the bread being bad, but this was grossly false. The true one was to get more pay in a colonial vessel as was too much the custom of crews of merchant ships, and which the magistrates everywhere ought to have put down as much as possible. Of course, I complained to the worthy Captain Gordon, RN, and he summoned them all to the police court for the next day, my day for trial also. When it came he never asked for a sample of the bread said to be bad, and merely fined them 5*s.* each, with orders that they were to be discharged from the brig! This was exactly what they wanted, and a most illegal punishment to me only.

Then came my case which he read out as being 'neglect of the rules and regulations of the port' and, in the same breath, added: '. . . for which he is hereby fined £20.' The only people in this said court were the magistrate's two myrmidons and sharers of all fines. When I attempted to speak I was immediately stopped, as before, with: 'Clear the Court!', to which I said: 'Do you condemn me, Sir, to pay £20 without hearing me say one word in my defence?' The answer was simply another roar of: 'Clear the Court!' I was shoved out by the shoulders as before by the Chief Constable. Again I opened fire upon him when outside, told him that he should have reason to repent of this abominable conduct and that I should not rest till I had got him dismissed from his office.

I wrote immediately a full statement of the whole proceedings to Mr La Trobe,[16] and did not forget to point out the great damage which such a man as Gordon must do to a young colony. I requested at the same time that a copy of my letter might at once be forwarded to the Governor at Sydney[17] for his deep consideration, and not to forget also to take notice of all I had heard of the disposal of the fines. I had also a long conference with Mr La Trobe before appealing to the Court of Quarter Sessions against this iniquitous fine. I am sorry to relate that they confirmed it,[18] which I attributed to my stupid attorney with whom I had to leave the case when I sailed for Launceston. But, three months afterwards, this decision, as well as the whole of those of Captain Gordon, were not only condemned by the Governor at Sydney, but he himself dismissed from his office of magistrate,[19] as also the Chief Constable, and the Superintendent of Water Police was told that he had better resign, which he did. Thus ended the official career of all those three worthies.

I must not, however, omit to state that when I asked all the captains of the 30 ships then lying at Williamstown to sign the letter which I wrote to the Governor, not one of them would do so. Further, when I asked the Melbourne public, both nautical and civil, to assist me in the expenses which I had incurred (£60) through the newspapers, not one shilling was ever offered in response, nor did I ever get a penny of the £20 fine returned by the Government which I look upon as quite inconsistent with their otherwise just decision. I cared little for the money then, and was in all other respects well satisfied with the result of my endeavours to free the place from an iniquitous trio.

The Superintendent of Police (who I am sorry to add was a master RN) got the command of an honourable's yacht at Melbourne, and went up to China in her with his wife, where he succeeded, by some means unmentionable, to be appointed Consul at one of the trading ports, dying there about ten or eleven years afterwards. The honourable owner of the yacht went to Borneo in her where he and all hands were massacred. As for old Commander Gordon, I believe he went to Sydney and died there a couple of years after, having 'lifted his little finger' rather too often.

Finishing our business at Melbourne, we started for Launceston, Tasmania, once more, which we reached in 36 hours in March 1842.[20] Again we enjoyed the splendid scenery of that beautiful River Tamar, and in a few days we took possession of our cottage a second time, renewing our acquaintance with our excellent neighbours, as well as sundry others both in and out of town. I found the sheep trade was done and, as I could not afford to keep the brig idle, I sent her in a week or two to the Isle of France for sugar, being chartered, and put the chief officer in her as captain 'pro tempore' [for the time being]. I intended to resume command myself on her return and go up to Calcutta to lay a train for future business.

She sailed with a full cargo and several passengers.[21] One person of a rather quisquis character I refused as a passenger, merely not to annoy the others, and thereby lost £40 and the poor fellow his life, as he immediately took his passage to England in a whaler called the *Noormuhul* which has not since been heard of.[22] I found that people generally thought I was foolish in refusing a passage to anyone: so much for consulting the comfort of others. But I had always found that the 'golden rule' had very little to do with the proceedings of colonists of any trade or profession, a discovery not made without paying for my knowledge on that head. On one occasion I required a bank draft for £200 from my agent to send to the Cape, before leaving for India, and I was most particular in telling Mr Connolly[23] and his head clerk that I would not take a private bill. He put me off for three days with the excuse of forgetfulness, till it came to the very last half hour, when it was said that being Saturday, the bank would be closed before they could send there. A letter was written to the party for me to sign to be sent after my departure in which it was stated after the word draft, 'as per note at foot'. Being so pushed I signed it, never supposing it possible that a private bill would be sent, but such was the case and it came back dishonoured.

In a previous transaction by the same house I had put ten kegs of tobacco into their hands for sale. After the account sales were rendered, stating that so many had been sold to three different individuals at a certain price each, I found that the whole had been placed in the bonded warehouse in the name of my agents Messrs Connolly and Co., and they had sold the kegs at a much higher price, and to other people from those stated to me in their account sales. Yet when spoken to about such conduct, they held out to me that it was quite a mercantile transaction!

Again, after the failure of this house, their second clerk, who had been retained to work along with the official assignee, came to me one day and said that Mr Connolly was due him privately £100, which he saw now that he had no chance of ever getting from him. He asked me to allow him to add that sum to my account, with £30 more, which should be given to me when he should settle the other sum for himself. To this impudent request, I replied that I would let him know my decision next day, going at once to relate the whole story to the official assignee, who had the good sense to dismiss him forthwith. In short, uprightness and honesty were quite at a discount in Tasmania and other eastern colonies, and it required a very bright lookout indeed to be kept at all times to save oneself from being cheated by all and sundry people. Not having been accustomed to that sort of thing, I could not help cutting several persons for misdemeanours of the above kind. When on mentioning the subject to a mercantile gentleman he said: 'I'll tell you what it is, if you cut everyone who tries to cheat you, you may just as well at once cut the whole island.' I mention these things as a warning to others, although I hope sincerely that morality has improved along with other things since the days about which I write.

CHAPTER 19

The consequences of this conduct were ruinous to me

1842–1845

During the absence of the *Phantom* at the Isle of France, a third son had been added to our family,[1] and all was going well with us when she arrived after a very quick voyage.[2] After a few weeks I resumed the command and sailed for Singapore early in August with 400 sheep,[3] a joint speculation between a farmer and myself, leaving my wife, children and servant girl to the care of our good neighbours at Elphin, and other friends.

I pursued the same route as before through the inshore passage of Torres Strait, but I had the charts on the large scale, and got on much more comfortably. Even so I followed Cook's track in all parts excepting that where 'no passage' was reported, going through Endeavour Strait after passing Cape York, between Possession Island and the little rocky islands with the same fresh breeze from the south-east and, close hauled as on the former occasion, with the same success into the open Timor Sea. We then sailed through the Strait of Samao, Lombock and Carimata Passage to Singapore, by which time we had lost a great number of sheep by the heat of the weather, and the sale of the remainder did not pay expenses. In a few days I pushed on for Penang,[4] arriving five days later. I went on shore to see my friends the Browns for a short spell and, finding that they were not inclined to entertain my proposition of sugar on hypothecation, I left for Calcutta arriving there towards the end of September 1842.

We had no pilot from the Sand Heads to Saugor, all being employed. I was therefore obliged to steer in the wake of a brig which had a pilot. The difficulty was to keep astern even with nothing but the two topsails on the caps and the other vessel with all studding sails set. At length we rounded the Gaspar Buoy, when the pilot hailed me to say I might go on by myself, and steer so and so for Saugor Roads. The moment we hoisted our topsail we passed this brig, the *Vanguard*,[5] as if she had been at anchor, running up to Saugor where we got a pilot next morning for Calcutta, which we reached in two days more.[6]

My agents were Colvin, Ainslie and Co.,[7] but I lived with my old friend W.W.R. at Garden Reach. I tried to sell the brig privately but, not succeeding in obtaining my price, I filled up with some cargo on freight, the rest for myself, with borrowed money, in sugar. I had also some cargo for Madras and one passenger to Launceston. About the end of January 1843 I left Calcutta,[8] and in a few days got to Madras, where I lived with Mr James Ainslie of Beeby and Co. There I met my former shipmate Jaques of the *Marquis Camden*, then in command of a regular passenger ship to London.[9] We enjoyed a week together very much.

Nothing worth mentioning occurred on the passage from Madras to Tasmania, and we arrived in the Tamar in due course early in April.[10] The Customs Landing Waiter at George Town came off to inform me of the death of our last baby, about three weeks previously, and of my wife having been very ill.[11] This melancholy news made me hasten to Launceston as fast as possible, where I found her still in a very weak state from diarrhoea, but convalescent, the baby having died from the same complaint. She owed her life to the unremitted attentions of our kind neighbour Miss Dry.

My attention was now directed to becoming a partner of a very steady young man as general agents, he having been some time in business for himself in that line. I thought I would send the brig back to Calcutta for sale, via the Isle of France, turning the proceeds to good account in trade, but 'man proposeth and God disposeth'. Sugar was low in price and, being obliged to sell to meet my bills, I lost at least £300 by that speculation. This was a bad state of things, and my wife would not hear of me going in the *Phantom* myself after her late distress and sickness so far from home. I therefore sent the chief officer in command once more, forwarding a power of attorney to Colvin and Co. to sell the vessel at Calcutta, but limiting them to a certain sum.

She was loaded for Mauritius and, after a thorough refit, she sailed for that island some time in May 1843, and from thence proceeded to Calcutta.[12] But the pilot who was put on board at the Sand Heads managed to run the brig on a sand, although the captain and the man at the masthead told him it was the sand he was steering for, and not a tide ripple as he persisted in calling it. The consequence was she lay there till the flood tide set in with a considerable swell, breaking her main keel before being hove off, which caused her to leak so much that they were obliged to run her on shore on Saugor Island to save her from sinking. There she lay till she was patched up, and then towed up the river by two steamers, to be placed in dock at Calcutta.[13] The expense, with repairs, came to £1,100! She was then put up for sale by auction, and bought in by my agents as she did not fetch my limit by £200. The excuse for this was that they could not risk my suing them for that sum of deficiency, giving no heed to the value of the vessel having been reduced at least that much by the damage sustained by wreck. The consequences of this conduct were ruinous to me and, as it turned out, a loss to their own selfish house of £1,700. Meantime, the pilot had been tried by his superiors, and dismissed the service, a very short time afterwards drowning himself in the river.

When I first learned these facts I thought of going to Calcutta myself and working the debt off, but the brig might have been sold since the date of the letter. Instead, I sent a general power of attorney and, if not sold, to take a bottomry bond on the vessel and send her on to China for sale.[14] Contrary to this they sent her to the Cape and Mauritius, by which voyage she sunk £600. She was then laid up to rot in the Hooghly, and after two years of humbug and selfish disobedience of my orders Messrs Colvin, Ainslie, Cowie and Co. sold the brig for £1,400, although they had previously refused £3,100.[15]

This climax was, of course, total ruin to me, more especially as they claimed £1,700 from me for losses, expenses, commissions and interest of money. I had to go through the Insolvent Court at Launceston[16] and, my whole property being in the brig, my agents got not a farthing more than they had already pocketed. I was adrift in the world with my Company pension only to keep my wife and family on. A few months before this unfortunate event took place I stumbled on my old enemy Captain Tommy, in from China and Melbourne, at the door of one of the hotels in Launceston. Immediately on my coming within speech of him, he sung out much to my surprise: 'Hullo'h Miller, who the devil would have thought of seeing you here!' I answered him by saying that I might with all propriety say, who would have thought of seeing him there. Then he asked me what I was doing, and when I told him of my distresses with the brig he said that if she was here he would buy her at once, but he did not see how he could help me otherwise.

I thanked him, and asked him to come out and see my wife who, I told him, knew him well by name, and would be very glad to see him within our little cottage. He said: 'Well, I will. I am living with Borrodaile[17] out your way, and I will come'. I knew that he would do what he said, and about eleven o'clock of the following day he came and spent an hour with us most pleasantly. When touching on our former battles, he said:

'Ah, you threw me off when I was most willing to be your friend.'

'You were too hasty in putting me under arrest, Sir,' I answered.

'Ah well, we are not likely to agree about these matters now,' he replied.

We dropped the subject after I had told him I was satisfied, from what I knew of him, that he would have acted exactly as I did, if he had been similarly situated, to which he quietly replied: 'Perhaps I would.' I was much pleased to find him so reasonable and friendly, and I could not help treating him with the same respect as if he had been my commander still.

Another occurrence took place during the absence of the brig which, being the affair of a very intimate friend of mine there, I must give it a place amongst these memoranda. It will prove the truth of the old saying of 'the course of true love never ran smooth', but the moral of the story I shall leave to the keen perception of my readers, only premising that every word of the narrative is true to the letter. A young man, a native of Scotland, on receiving an official appointment to Tasmania, thought, before leaving, that it might be well to secure a wife to come out to him when he should rise to that rank which would enable him to keep one. Accordingly, he got himself engaged to a very nice girl, to whom he had been known from his very young days at school, as well as ever afterwards. It was an agreed thing that in due time they should be married either by his coming home or her going out for that purpose.

Time rolled on and he was very successful in being able to make money with the little savings which he could lay aside from his pay, under the teaching of a canny Scot who had made £30,000 in Tasmania by lending to the needy, and other methods. When five years had elapsed, and a few hundreds had been made and carefully placed in the bank, letters passed more frequently than before between this loving pair on the subject of how the marriage was to be effected. At the end of the five years it was decided that the bride should come out to the bridegroom, as he found it impossible to get sufficient leave to go home. As a brother of hers was not in very good health, he was to chaperon his sister on the passage out on board of a certain ship in which the captain and his wife were well known to her 'intended'.

It unfortunately happened, however, that while these preliminaries were being carried out at home and on the passage, that Romeo (as I shall call him) had fallen in with a very handsome and fair young widow at Launceston with three children and £500 a year while unmarried, or if married with consent of her trustees. So powerful was this attraction that the recollection of poor Juliet (as I shall call her) was only that of vexation, and a sincere hope that she might never come out. When it was known that she had actually sailed, Romeo, being then over head and ears in love with the widow, was 'struck all of a heap', and quite beside himself as to how he was to act. Instead of tearing himself away from the widow, he was at her house daily for hours, plunging deeper and deeper into the abyss of love during the whole four months of the voyage. At last the ship arrived and the telegraph told of her coming up the river, his intended being near enough for Romeo to go down the river so far in a boat to meet her.

This was a dreadful day and, as he had previously told me, his friend, all his feelings on the subject, I could not but fear for the result. He had decided, much against my wish, to take Juliet to the widow's house till at least he should see how things were likely to be: this was making bad worse! Perhaps he hoped that Juliet might see 'how the wind sat there' and kick up a row, have a split, and be done with it. Down the river he went to meet her and, on coming alongside, I was told his face was like a sheet, he not knowing whether he stood or sat on his head or his heels. Of course, he made but a sorry appearance before his bride and her brother, but up they came in the boat and to the widow's house. She received them both kindly and tenderly, as it was really her nature to do, the brother soon after the introduction taking himself to the lodgings prepared for him.

From Romeo I learned all that was going on from time to time, as well as his inmost thoughts, from which I could plainly see that the right thing for him to do would be to make a clean breast of it to Juliet, and ask her to let him off the bargain, for both their sakes. This I advised should be done. Meantime, the widow was very kind to Juliet, who very soon saw the real state of the case, no doubt hoping against hope. Thus, nearly three weeks passed away without a word about taking a house or marrying passing Romeo's lips, who was now half dead with perplexity. In fact, he saw no necessity for any other house than the widow's, where he fully intended 'to hang his hat up' as soon as circumstances would permit. Seeing that some step must be taken, and that Juliet ought to be removed from where she then was living, I told Romeo so, recommending a 'council of war' being held between myself and the brother (to whom I had not then been introduced) in order to learn his mind on the subject, and to offer an asylum for Juliet in my cottage till matters of some decisions should be come to. All was agreed to and, on meeting the brother, whose vexation may easily be supposed, he at once agreed to his sister going to my house, being much relieved by the offered change which took place that same afternoon, my wife of course having been privy to the arrangement. Romeo was now left to the undisturbed revelling in the love of the widow, and only came out occasionally to see Juliet at our cottage. A couple of weeks, however, put an end in a great measure to this state of uncertainty.

The public of Launceston began to cry out against the widow for her share in the proceedings to such an extent as reached her ears. She, having a character at stake, thought it might be as well to save the same by a temporary sojourn at George Town for her health (which, by the way, was not very good), and trust to what might turn up. She agreed at the same time with Romeo to keep him duly apprised of her proceedings and feelings through a brother official there, who should individually report progress from time to time, and thereby save the scandal which might attach to either of them corresponding directly, under existing circumstances. This secret treaty doubtless placed the brother official in a very peculiar position, he being a very agreeable and good looking bachelor. To say the truth, he would have been something more than mortal if he had carried out that treaty strictly according to the wishes of his friend. He must have foreseen that the widow must soon have perceived her error with Romeo, and that her duty would be decidedly to let him complete his bargain with Juliet and, more particularly, when she found such another swain ready to jump into her arms when she might think proper to encourage the thing. I don't mean to say that this was the actual reasoning of either of those parties, but the result makes me think it at least very probable.

I must return to Juliet and her worthy brother, with whom my wife and I held frequent councils without any effect for two or three weeks after the widow's retreat, by which time we all saw that marriage was out of the question. All that remained to be done was to break off the match entirely, by getting Romeo to pay £400 to cover passage money out and home, and expenses. He agreed to this, after some bargaining, and accepted bills to that amount payable at different dates, and thus we supposed the end to have come. In this, however, we were mistaken because, a short time afterwards, the grand climax in the widow's affairs was arrived at, and wisely too: an engagement to marry the brother official of Romeo instead of Romeo himself, creating great surprise to everyone save myself, for the reasons before specified. Romeo was no sooner made acquainted with this, to him, awful blow than he came out to our cottage with new terms of proposal, which he never doubted would be accepted. Alas, for poor Juliet, none of us would listen to them for a moment, and to strengthen our argument the homeward passage money for herself and brother had then been paid at Hobart Town.

Romeo offered to marry Juliet and pay her passage money to her brother and do almost anything now, but we would not have it at any price, after such conduct. Although Juliet would, I have no doubt, have accepted this offer, late as it was, yet she was easily persuaded to give Romeo the 'coup de grace' for ever, and wend her way home again with a vexed heart indeed, yet not a broken one. She lived to be married to a clergyman in Scotland, and be the happy mother of six fine children, e're she died about three or four years ago rejoicing in God her Saviour. The marriage of the widow took place shortly after Juliet's departure: six months afterwards she was laid in her grave, a victim of consumption, one more lesson of the short-sightedness and vanity of this world of woe.

Not long after this love and marriage affair we had an invasion of bushrangers around Launceston: one of their attacks was worthy of note. Two men, armed with guns and pistols, went to the house of a Mr Oakden[18] on the side of Windmill Hill about midnight and, having got admittance by the usual method of knocking, they told Mr Oakden that he must come with them to Dr Browne's house who they knew had £100 in his study. They would not let him dress, taking him in his shirt to the doctor's little wicket gate which they found locked, but at once wrenching it open by putting the muzzle of one of their guns in between it and the post, which bent it a little. They had previously told him what to say to the doctor when the door should be opened, but the doctor looked out of an upper window, and on asking what they wanted, Mr Oakden said that Mrs Oakden was very ill, and she wanted him to come to her immediately. With this, he came down and opened the door, the bushrangers telling him to deliver up the £100 which was in his study. He denied having any money in the house, so the two men ransacked the library first and then other rooms.

During the disturbance the prisoner servant who slept above the outer kitchen, hearing what was going on, ran into the police office three-quarters of a mile off, getting the Chief Constable and another to come with him to the house. On arrival they burst open the front door and rushed in upon the two men, who met them by firing the bent gun (not then known to be so) right along the passage, at the farther end of which they were, but without effect, the slugs passing close to one side of them. The rush not being checked the two men were attacked by hand by the two constables, and captured in a very few minutes. Such wonderful preservation from so extraordinary a cause showed the hand of the Almighty most distinctly in this desperate affair. The result was the hanging of the two bushrangers.[19]

CHAPTER 20

They expected the bows to come out of her every moment!

1846

When I saw that the fate of the *Phantom* was sealed, and I had got my discharge from the Commissioner of the Insolvent Court, I tried to get Government employment or the command of a ship, but for a long time in vain. At length my friend Mr Raven,[1] having bought the wreck of a ship called the *Elizabeth and Jane* and put her into the floating dock for repairs, gave me the command at once.[2] For about three months I was busy looking after carpenters, taking in cargo and preparing for sea.

Our destination was London, where the ship was to be sold. My pay and allowance were very fair, and I was granted one of the after cabins and the one before it for the accommodation of my wife and family. By this time we had four sons, the youngest being only three months old,[3] besides our servant girl who was more of a nursery governess than a mere servant, and a great comfort to all. For six weeks before sailing we all lived on board, giving us plenty of time to sell off furniture and let the cottage, which had been bought in at the bankrupt sale, and given to my wife by a friend. We had also a Mr and Mrs Webster and their nine children, a young gentleman and a young girl of 16 who, with the wife of our mess servant, made 21 in the cabin altogether.[4]

The ship was only 360 tons burden, but her cabin accommodation was very large for a vessel of that size. We sailed on the 22nd April 1846 and got to sea on the 24th, taking the western route by Cape Lewin and the Cape of Good Hope. After clearing Bass Strait about 150 miles a westerly gale set in, and we found the ship made a good deal of water. I ran for Port Adelaide, or as near to it as the gale would allow, under a very small island near the southern entrance to Backstairs Passage, where I found a ship called the *Branken Moor* at anchor.[5] Here we had to remain for a couple of days till the gale moderated, and then made for Adelaide, getting in the same day.[6] The port was certainly much enhanced since

'The Miller Family', by John Adamson. Undated calotype photograph of Miller's four eldest sons from an album by their uncle. (The Trustees of the National Museums of Scotland.)

I had been there in 1838, but there was still a good deal of room left for improvement, in the shape of wharfage, etc.

We had some friends living here a little way in the country, but in business in the town, who kindly took my wife and family to their house till the ship's caulking should be completed. Most fortunately we succeeded in finding the leak, just a little above the water on the starboard bow. With one thing and another we were detained here a fortnight, but one benefit came out of it besides stopping the leak: the steward, a useless rascal, ran away, and I succeeded in getting a first rate man of colour who had been in an American liner and tried his hand at farming, with no effect at Adelaide. He turned out a real treasure to me and all my passengers.

While lying here we were visited on board a few hours before sailing by Mr Solly, a young gentleman who had been a midshipman with me in the *Abercrombie Robinson* in 1835 and 1836. He presented my wife with a very handsome gold broach, enclosing a malachite, both being the produce of South Australia. He is now Assistant Secretary to the Government at Hobart Town.[7] This was a mark of attention I little expected at such a place, but it appeared that it was done in gratitude for some trifling kindness I had shown him when sick, in days when he was young and at sea.

After leaving Adelaide, about the middle of May, we experienced a variety of weather, including half a dozen gales till, rounding Cape Lewin, we got into the south-easterly trade and bowled along in great comfort, saving and excepting occasional bursts of temper from Mrs Webster, our passenger, who was unfortunately very easily offended. She had, in the first gale of wind off Kangaroo Island, allowed one of her children to tumble out of its bed, cutting her head, for which she abused the ship and me most liberally. Another time she refused to mess at the table, and remained in the same mind to the end of the voyage, because I would not dismiss from the cabin duties the mess servant whom she had been calling a 'convict wretch'. It is not often that one meets with such ladies in the pent up space of a 400 ton ship but I never gave in to her whims, being not at all sorry that she messed in her own cabin during more than three-quarters of the voyage, as it prevented her making many disturbances no doubt.

When off the Cape of Good Hope on L'Agulhas Bank we had two days' calm weather during which we caught great quantities of fine fish, it being the first time I had ever seen the like in that part of the world. It was great fun to our 14 children, as well as everyone on board, and the fish, with a little salt, lasted for nearly a week. When we did get a breeze I was so anxious to get round Cape Point that I carried rather more canvas than usual and, in the dusk of the evening, two of the crew came aft to me and said that in the forecastle below, the ship was plunging and rushing through the water in such a manner that they expected the bows to come out of her every moment! This was certainly not a very agreeable prospect, but I attributed their fears chiefly to the fact of the ship having been so lately a wreck that they thought she would not stand much driving, and I did not shorten sail. Matters were soon all right in their eyes by our getting into somewhat smoother water.

On nearing St Helena, and not seeing it at sunset, I hove to till daylight when within about ten or twelve miles. In the morning I found we were right enough as to distance from the island, but the current must have set us a little to leeward so that we could not fetch in to windward. We therefore passed close round the west side of it, to let the passengers and my family see what they could of this extraordinary island, and stood on for Ascension, rather than lose time beating up against both wind and current, not having a Captain Lestrange on board, as in the *Portland*. We got to Ascension in four days more where we found the *Acteon*, a 28-gun frigate, and the *Sylph*, a 12-gun brig, hove down.[8] I lost no time in calling on Captain Mansel[9] of the former, who agreed to give me a couple of tons of coals, and some 'coast water', which I could only use for the stock, but it answered my purpose for want of better.

I took my family on shore to look at the place and have a run the next day. The island is evidently a volcanic eruption and there is only one green spot on it, about half way up 'Green Mountain' where the government garden is. There is now a good jetty, as at St Helena, a hospital and sundry houses of the officials, but the place is only kept as a store house and recruiting spot for the African squadron, and their invalid crews. The *Tortoise* store ship[10] was also lying here, and a transport with troops, the lieutenant in charge of which I may hereafter mention in these pages when serving in a very different capacity.[11]

On the second day after arrival we got under way for England, and ran out under easy sail till the anchor was stowed, shortly after which dinner was announced. We had only been seated a few minutes when our servant came down from the deck with the baby in convulsions. I was the only doctor and I knew that it would take us two hours at least to beat back from where we were, by which time the crisis would be over for good or evil, so we did the best we could with the medical book. But Mrs Webster came to our aid the moment she heard of the state of things, without invite, and tended the child in the kindest manner for more than three hours with hot water and so on, till at last he recovered, and I lanced his gums, which completed the cure so well that he never took another fit. I mention this affair to show that withal Mrs Webster's ill feeling, it was dropped at once when she thought she could be of use to a human being in distress. Yet when all was right she took to her cabin again at meal times as before, and continued to do so to the end.

From the western islands to the Channel we had gales almost continuously, and ran up as far as Beachy Head before sighting the land. This was an anxious time for this lady, who never doubted that we should run on shore, if we could neither see land nor lights. Often she was heard 'singing out' to her husband, a good natured man: 'Get up, you donkey, and tell me if they see the lights yet.' Had she known that my chronometer had run down when very near the Line, and how much the correct or incorrect making of the Channel and lights depended upon that fact, she might have been somewhat anxious on the subject. When this awkward piece of forgetfulness took place, caused by some squall calling me on deck, I immediately set the chronometer going again and took numerous sets of lunar observations every day while the sun and moon were 'in distance', and the mean of the whole gave me the correct time at Greenwich on a particular day. By this I set the chronometer and, in 14 days more, I did the same over again, thereby getting the rate of the chronometer for that number of days, and for one day by dividing by 14, of course. I went by this till I got to London, when I found on giving it to Mr Murray in Cornhill,[12] that the error was only ten seconds, a most extraordinary bit of good luck as it was hardly possible for it to have gone so steadily and with so small a rate as three-tenths of a second per day after having run down.

We were just about six miles off Beachy when we saw the Head, but had been steering for a line of about that distance off and going by our soundings. I knew the EIC ship *Thomas Coutts*, Captain A. Christie,[13] to run up Channel in thick weather right up to the Downs before seeing any land when he hove to, to let a higgler go on board. He asked him what he would take the ship into the Downs for, thinking he was only off the South Foreland, and the man said £20. The Captain turned him over the side, shortened sail and stood in a little further before anchoring. When the weather cleared up he found himself within a very little of the proper anchorage.

CHAPTER 21

I was so sickened with ship owners

1846–1848

In London, where we arrived early in October,[1] my wife and family only remained two weeks, before going off to the north, leaving me to sell the ship and settle matters with the agent Mr Brooks.[2] Accomplishing this very soon afterwards, and that most favourably for the owner, I followed them to Fifeshire and Edinburgh for a few months of leisure and quiet before returning to look out for another command, which I trusted might turn up. I did not then, however, see my way at all clearly towards that desirable result. I had no money to take a farm, and employment on shore for a nautical man is not easily obtained, as I afterwards experienced. I did what I could by correspondence while enjoying my otium, and kept up my pecker with hope till the month of February 1847 when the state of the funds showed the necessity for exertion in another spell at sea in some capacity. Therefore, I went to the great city, and cruised about the Jerusalem Coffee House for a fortnight without effect, but there is an end of all things, and so it turned out with my idleness.

Through an introduction from my brother Andrew to Mr Phillipps of the firm of Phillipps and Tiplady[3] I got the command of their ship *Boyne* of 670 tons,[4] bound to Baltimore for grain and flour. She was chartered and a teak ship, just returned from India,[5] having only to take in ballast and sail in six days, without any refitting of rigging or anything else! This was short warning, but a great deal may be done in six days, and the evening of the last one found me at Gravesend, ready for a start next day, with a ship's company of three officers and 23 men, making 27 in all, being three less than she had ever sailed with before.[6] Shipowners, however, suppose that fewer men are required on a short voyage than a long one, notwithstanding our having to cross the Atlantic in the month of

March; by the same logical reasoning a ship's rigging cannot require looking at after a four months passage from India.

Be that as it may, we got down Channel about the middle of that same month,[7] and well on for the Azores before we were attacked by the westerly gales. For three weeks it seemed as if the fiat had gone forth that: 'Thus far shalt thou go, but no farther'. We were hove to under a close-reefed main topsail and stay sails off these islands during nearly the whole of that time, when at last I bore up, and ran through them to the southward and westward, after which we got on pretty well, making the passage in six weeks from the Downs. In crossing the Gulf Stream, a day before making Cape Henry, I found the difference between the heat of the sea and the air to be so much as 20 degrees.

At the mouth of the Chesapeake we got a pilot who amused me very much on the run to Baltimore with his tales of different kinds, one of which was that a lawyer had lately come from New York to take the part of a certain captain against his crew in a trial which was soon to take place, for which kind of duties he had made himself rather famous in his own city. A select band of sailors watched his arrival and, getting hold of him, stripped him to 'the buff', tarring and feathering him well from head to feet. This was thought a capital joke, and the perpetrators left to enjoy the fun without any punishment whatever, which is too often the case even in such cities as Baltimore.

When the *Boyne* was fast to one of the quays,[8] many people came on board to look at her, being a teak built ship, not a very common thing to be seen there. One day, the numbers becoming a little troublesome, and one man having gone on the poop to hold conversation for some time with a few of the crew who were repairing a sail there, I told him to go on shore as he was obstructing the work. He moved off very slowly and sulkily, and at last went over the gangway on to the quay. Having occasion to go on shore about half an hour afterwards, I found the fellow a little way from the ship, when he said to me: 'You think yourself a very great man, don't ye. Go and tell your queen, when you get home, if she has no better fellows than you in England they are all a set of damned blackguards!' To this very eloquent harangue, of course, I said nothing, and thought myself rather fortunate afterwards in having been allowed to leave the place without incurring a similar fate to the New York lawyer.

My agent was a Quaker who I found a most correct and conscientious man, but who thought it right, during the whole of my six weeks' stay, not only to withhold his own hospitality from me, but never to accept mine when offered to him, for what reason I know not. I dined at a large hotel at Baltimore once or twice, and found a very large number of people at the table, where the viands were excellent, but no wine or spirits were drunk and, so far as I recollect, no beer either. Water only was the beverage, and of that very little, I alone being left to drink a pint of sherry, which I could well have dispensed with, but for the idea of incurring the expected scowl of the landlord and waiters as in England. I asked a young man who sat next to me to take a glass of wine during dinner, but he declined, although he had been in the 'old country' and on the Continent. The rapidity with which the dinner was got through quite astonished me, although I had been somewhat prepared for it by report. The drinking part was, after 15 minutes of gobbling up the victuals, carried on in conjunction with smoking and chewing tobacco in the bar, to which I did not resort, having got my neighbour to withdraw his refusal of wine after the cloth had been removed.

On another day I took the railway to Washington, 20 miles from Baltimore, and saw the Capitol with its Houses of Congress, of such a size on the top of a hill as evidently proves the truth of what has been often said: that it is to be the capital of the world. The vanity of the Yankees, I know, is great enough for this, and even more. If they would read and take a lesson from history, they will find that they will have quite enough to do when they govern their present possessions without losing some part of them, and without getting any other part of the world whatever. Indeed, it is more than probable that even these will be split up into half a dozen republics e're many years shall have passed.

The White House is a shabby place for the President of 'so great a country' to inhabit, and there is nothing in Washington to make it worthy of being the capital of this *large* country, *great* is not the name for it, as they have yet to make it so in the true sense of the word. I dined at one of the best hotels there, but as it was not 'the season' there were only about 20 people, including six ladies. The same rapidity of eating was practised as I had seen at Baltimore, and no drinking at the table. What struck me as to the newness of the country were the stumps of trees appearing for miles in the corn fields between the two cities, just the same as in Tasmania or Australia. I was told there were the same for a long distance between Baltimore and Philadelphia, which I had not time to visit. The women of the former place are without exception the most beautiful in face which I had ever seen in the world, and I frequently walked the chief streets there looking upon them with wonder and admiration. The features were quite like the chiselled Grecian, and the colour well diffused, it being quite rare to see a plain looking woman.

At the close of six weeks all the cargo was on board, and the *Boyne* ready for sea, but 12 men having run[9] I was obliged to take such as I could get in their stead, of whom three were 'black fellows'. By this time the ship had been moved 20 miles down the Bay to complete the loading, but the new men, half Yankees and half English, declared that they wouldn't allow a black man to live in the same forecastle with them, threatening to leave the ship at once, if they were not sent on shore. It came to this: that I must either lose nine men or three, so of the two evils I chose the least, sending the blacks back to Baltimore. But next day, these nine rascals, having been disappointed in getting clear of the ship by too good a lookout having been kept to allow a boat to come alongside during the previous night, refused to get the anchor up. I told them that I could do without their services till I should get down to the cutter at the mouth of the Bay, when I should hand them over to the commander for a good flogging. Still they would not work, so by perseverance we got the anchor up without them, and stood down the Bay of Chesapeake. Towards evening, when we were drawing near to the cutter, the cowardly rascals came aft and said they would go to work. I let 'bygones be bygones' and, after getting rid of the pilot, made all sail past Cape Henry, and out to sea. If it had not been to save a night at anchor I certainly should have got these nine rascals a severe flogging on board the cutter, my own power to do so being nil, both legally and physically.

This is only one of the hundreds of similar cases daily occurring in the merchant service. Nothing requires a more thorough overhauling than the total want of discipline in that service, if it can by any means be called such, with every existing paragraph in the Merchant Shipping Act in favour of the sailors, and hardly one for the captain and officers. Their lives are not only rendered miserable by the insolent and lazy conduct of these men, but those of passengers also. The safety of the ship and cargo are constantly imperilled by the want of power in the captain to enforce obedience to orders. Can there be anything more absurd or degrading to a commander than the law telling him that a man may refuse to do his work at any time and sit below in idleness, if he shall choose to lose two days pay for every one of disobedience, after he has signed articles of agreement 'to obey the captain and officers by night and by day and upon all occasions'? The wise concocters of the Act I can excuse for this and other sections from their ignorance of the subject. Not so those who are connected with the said service who have allowed such a total want of discipline to go on for many years, without a single petition or proper remonstrance against it, notwithstanding all captains and officers have been constantly crying out about it amongst themselves.

I shall mention one instance of a whole crew refusing to work at about the time of which I am now writing. It was that of a new ship called the *Sir Edward Parry*, bound to Baltimore, commanded by a young man who had never been in that responsible situation before, and who was unfortunate enough to lose all his three topmasts in one of those gales by which I had been also delayed so long.[10] The crew, excepting three boys, three mates and one steward, refused even to cut the wreck adrift, stowing themselves away below in the forecastle in perfect idleness. The whole of the work of the ship was carried on and jury topmasts rigged by the captain and the remaining seven, occupying more than three weeks e're they reached the Chesapeake. All that could be done to these rascals was to allow them only bread and water during that time. On arrival at Baltimore the Consul very properly put them all in jail, expecting them to be punished, but they were all taken out by writ of habeas corpus, the judge telling the Consul that American jails were not built for English sailors, no doubt after finding that the men could only be punished by two days' stoppage of pay for every one of refusing to do duty, according their own code of laws. They were all sent adrift to add to the number of American lawless seamen who are ruled by that of the club and the 'knuckle duster'. I shall only add that in my opinion philanthropy is highly praiseworthy, only when carried out in such a manner as shall not risk the lives or property of anyone, and it is misplaced entirely in the whole of the Merchant Shipping Act of the present day.

On getting fairly to sea in the *Boyne* I found the mutinous characters had changed their tactics, and I had no trouble with them during the short passage of three weeks to

England. On arrival at London I was well received by Mr Phillips, the owner (his partner having died during my absence), who told me that I should have to give up the *Boyne* to a senior commander of his, as he had told me would be required before sailing. He had purchased another smaller ship for me called the *Pathfinder*, bound to Hong Kong in three weeks![11] This I thought rather sharp practice, but there was no saying nay, so I made the best of it and got my wife up from Scotland to lend a hand with the refitting of clothes, etc.

This ship, I soon discovered, had been to China the former year, and had torn herself almost to pieces in beating up the China Sea against the monsoon, but gave little heed to the report, taking that of the Lloyd's surveyors for gospel. She was about 340 tons old measure burden and built at Sunderland, which did not improve her in my eyes. The cargo was taken in, most of which was coals (200 tons), and we sailed at the specified time in August 1847[12] and my wife returned to Scotland, the owner having told me that he would honour my drafts in her favour to a certain amount.

Nothing particular occurred till getting near the Cape when the ship, by tumbling about in a gale of wind, made a great deal more water than usual, even to six inches an hour. In rolling, her lower deck planks used to open at each side as much as one and a half inches, thereby showing great weakness, causing me to take the opinion of the carpenter and two officers as to the necessity of going into the Cape to strengthen the ship with some additional knees. On this being agreed upon, I steered for Table Bay, and there remained ten days, getting in 14 iron knees and caulking.[13] The coals had been giving signs of heating for some time previously, so I was glad to overhaul them and to find that they were alright. Another ship was lying there at the same time which had been in a state of combustion for a week before arrival from the heating of her coals and, with great difficulty and perseverance, they kept it under by pouring down water and digging down to the hot place.

I was very glad to find my brother Ebenezer here as parson of the Free Scotch Church, and enjoyed my stay with his family very much.[14] I had to get rid of the second officer for neglect of duty, and got another in the person of a Mr Baker who had formerly commanded the late Company ship *Thames*[15] for a time in China as a transport, after the death of the captain. He had been living with his married sister near Algoa Bay and wished to get back to employment in China: he suited me well and was an excellent officer. After leaving Table Bay[16] the ship was certainly stronger and did not make quite so much water as before. Being too late for the monsoon up the China Sea I took the Timor Passage, sailing through the Banda Sea to the northward of New Guinea, before passing the Pelau Islands to the westward, and then through the middle of the Bashee Islands into the China Sea and to Hong Kong, where we arrived late in December 1847.[17] By this time I had had repeated reason to find fault with the chief officer for sleeping on his watch, and took the first opportunity of discharging him and employing another, as Mr Baker expected to be better provided for.

The agents of the owner were in Canton so I was passed on to their agents at Hong Kong. In two weeks the cargo was discharged and the ship's hold cleared for survey, having consulted the carpenter and a couple of the senior men of the crew about the general grumbling of the whole, concerning the leaky state of the ship. I received for answer that they would not go to sea again in the ship without such survey having been carried out. The surveyors were: Captain I. Rickett, Lt Perry, RN, harbour master, Mr J. Lamont,[18] shipbuilder, and the carpenter of HM Ship *Melampus*.[19] They certified that the *Pathfinder* was rotten in the breast hooks and various other parts, both forward and aft. Numerous knees were broken, which to repair would cost so much money that they recommended the ship being sold for the benefit of all concerned. A copy of the certificate was sent home by me to Mr Phillips and the ship moored out of the way till an answer could be received. Meantime, I retained only the cook and three boys to clear hawse when necessary, working myself at all times to save expense during the whole 11 months which elapsed before the ship was finally out of my hands. The owner's answer was that he was quite satisfied with what I had done and he was to send me out a power of attorney to sell the ship by the next mail.

I must not omit to state that a few days after arrival at Hong Kong I was visited on board by my old captain, Tommy, then living there, to whom I mentioned all my distresses. He gave and promised me his advice at all times so as to satisfy Mr Phillips, the owner, and also a letter to him stating that all that had been done was by his approval and in conjunction with him, for which Mr Phillips begged I would give him his best thanks. Notwithstanding all this, Mr Phillips, in his next letter, told me that he was not satisfied on the matter. He had consequently sent a power to Messrs Dent and Co.[20] to sell the ship and not to me, and had ordered another survey to be held by his own surveyor, Captain De St C., in the first place. His certificate, I may add, was almost word for word the same as that of the former. The ship was then sold by auction to Messrs Jardine, Matheson and Co. and Messrs Dent behaved to me in their usual gentlemanly style, settling all my accounts and allowing me passage money by the mail steamer for England.

In September 1848 I left Hong Kong by the mail steamer via Singapore, Galle, Suez, Alexandria and Malta for Southampton, arriving about the third week of October 1848. I hastened up to London and called on Mr Phillips, whom I did not hesitate to reprove for his conduct towards me, and especially for refusing payment of a draft of mine in favour of my wife at the same time he sent the power to Dent and Co. He said he had seen his error and was very sorry for it, so I forgave him, and asked no questions as to informers or 'kind friends' who had misled him. We parted quite good friends though I was so sickened with ship owners that I determined in my mind I should never have any dealings either with him or them if I could help it in the future. I went home to Fifeshire after attending the marriage of my only remaining sister in Edinburgh,[21] where I met my wife.

While quietly resting on my oars, I heard that civilian officers were being admitted into the Coast Guard and, thinking that it might suit me to try that service for a time, if not for a full do, and look after the education and bringing up of my family, now five in number, I applied through some MPs, succeeding in getting an appointment from the Admiralty to a station on the east coast of England. The service was then under the Customs, but all appointments, both of Inspecting Commanders and officers, as well as the Controller and Deputy-Controller General belonged to the Admiralty.

I wrote to Mr Phillips in London for a certificate to send in along with others and was not a little surprised at his refusal, until he should have some matters concerning the *Pathfinder* further cleared up from China! The 'kind friend' I supposed had not told all his falsehoods when I saw him last, but I left the matter till I should go to London for further investigation, having in the meantime succeeded without this 'great little man's' certificate. I contented myself when I got to London, about a week later, with administering a public rebuke to Mr Phillips' partner S. in the Jerusalem Coffee House, having then heard that the chief officer whom I had dismissed had been my 'kind friend' all the time. Mr Phillips had been fool enough to be led by the nose by his lies, so far as to discredit the honest, straightforward statements of the brother of his very old and Christian chum.

Twelve years after this I met one of the *Pathfinder's* crew in London who was then a fireman in 'St Mary Axe'. I was not a little astonished when he said to me that he hoped I had got well out of the trouble with Mr Phillips who had kept him and a whole lot of the crew in pay when they got home, to appear against me in the court, but after a fortnight's being in pay, they were told they should not be wanted. What he intended to charge me with I never heard and never cared; mens conscia recti timet nihil [a mind conscious of rectitude fears nothing]. The man spent some money like a fool, but had sense enough to stop in time. I have letters from Dent and Co. and Mr Phillips' own surveyor at Hong Kong, which prove everything having been done by me entirely for the benefit of Mr Phillips from first to last, and that my conduct was highly satisfactory to them in every way. I have been somewhat minute in my memoranda concerning the *Pathfinder*, in the hope of its yet being possible that they may come to the ears if not the eyes of Mr Phillips e're he and I shall quit this world of woe, and that he may learn how foully he has wronged one whose only fault was serving him too well.

CHAPTER 22

This kind of discipline requires no comment

1849–1853

In January 1849 the Coast Guard Service was under the Customs and had been for many years, although intermeddled with by the Admiralty in more than one way, whether for good or otherwise. At the time I entered on 2nd February 1849, there were 56 Inspecting Commanders, six Inspecting Lieutenants, 255 Lieutenants of Stations, 18 Masters, three Marine Officers, five Second Masters and 26 Civilian or Naval Chief Officers of Stations. The last increased to 62 in 1854, being the largest number of that class at any time in the service. In addition to all the above there were, in 1849, about 25 or 30 of the old original Civilian Chief Officers, who had been gradually pensioned off from the time the Admiralty had first their finger in this pie. The station I was appointed to was a country one, being 12 miles from the nearest post town, and 20 from our headquarters where the Inspecting Commander lived and the drill battery or gun platform was placed. The nearest village with a church was two miles distant, so we were not likely to be troubled with much visiting, even had my duties allowed it.[1]

I had been informed by a clerk at the Coast Guard office that the sale of my predecessor's furniture would take place on a certain day.[2] I therefore took care to go on that day to relieve him and buy what I wished. On my arrival at the station I was met by my predecessor who immediately introduced me to the Inspecting Commander of the District[3] who happened to be there. He received me very kindly and talked about the important station I had got, hoping I would soon get acquainted with the duties. He then left me and I was introduced to two officers of the service amongst the people who were mustering for the sale. One belonged to a station 12 miles off and the other, a lieutenant who had been superseded by the Inspecting Commander's request and sent to another station a few months before. These two told me that I had got under the command of a

Newton-on-sea coastguard station, Miller's first posting. (Michael Nix, 2004.)

man who was a bear and everything that was bad, and I would not remain a fortnight with him. I thought that this description was anything but pleasant, and I decided at once to let my wife and family remain where they were for three months at least, till I should see how I got on with this 'bete noir'. I thought at the same time that I had been able to manage quite as big 'bow-wows' as he could be, and I hoped to do the same with him.

That day I dined with the vicar[4] along with my predecessor and his wife, took tea at the doctor's house, and then drove with my brother chip[5] and his wife 12 miles to his station where I remained till the morning, and got a lesson touching the duties, journal, etc. On my return to the village of Embleton I again dined with the vicar, and met my Inspecting Commander at his table, who did not appear to me to be a man to be afraid of. I was kindly invited to remain at the vicarage till I could get my house put to rights at the station, which I accepted for two days only. I then roughed it in my new home with all the energy of a determination to do my duty rigidly, as I had always been accustomed.

Captain Boys visited every fortnight and I very soon found that he was the lieutenant who was naval agent on board of the transport which we met at Ascension in 1846. He had got his promotion to Commander through the application of the officers of the regiment on board, on account of his exertions in a hurricane which they had experienced near the Mauritius. My duties were arduous at night, having to visit the men on their 'guards' twice during the dark hours, but in the day time I had little more to do than write the journal and occasional musket drill and sword exercise, besides visiting the detachment twice in the month six miles off.

Three months soon passed away very agreeably although solitarily, and having every reason to be satisfied with Captain Boys, notwithstanding his having got eight officers removed from his District in two years, I asked him to allow the cutter on the station to go to Fife for my wife and family and their furniture. He granted me this at once, the lieutenant in command having previously offered his services to me.[6] It was then the month of May and the lieutenant thought he might have a chance of falling in with a small smuggling cutter which had been reported as likely to come on our part of the coast. Away went the cutter and, after getting my family and their traps on board, she was going along under all plain sail when they saw something rather suspicious a long way ahead, to the southward of St Abb's Head. The lieutenant had taken the vessel at one time previously, but, from some flaw, was obliged to let her go again. So he knew the craft by the cut of her canvas and, thinking he was all right, made sail in chase.

Now was the anxious time and 'each heart was bounding then'! The two brass 6-pounders were loaded and run out, the breeze freshened, and they overhauled the chase rapidly. Bang went a shot across his bow, but no slackening was shown. Bang, bang went the shot, till at last the little smuggler, seeing that all was up, hove to and let the cutter come alongside. Down went the boat into the water with an armed crew and in a few minutes the lieutenant found himself 'master of the occasion', with a prize worth £900 under his lee. The crew were soon put on board the cutter and a few men with the chief mate placed in the smuggler, when both vessels stood to the northward for Leith, instead of bringing my living and heavy baggage to my station. On arrival there next morning the lieutenant advised my wife and bairns to take the railway from Edinburgh. He would bring on the traps as soon as he could after getting the smuggler condemned, which might be a week afterwards.[7] This was done and, the following morning, when I was busy with the glass looking out to sea and thinking the cutter was making a very long passage, the whole troop, two servants included, marched into my house without my knowledge. Then it was that I got the above account of the smuggler, which proved to be the last of any tolerable size, that was taken all round the coast during the whole of my servitude in the Coast Guard of sixteen and a half years.[8] It was fully a week e're the cutter appeared off my station, rather to the inconvenience of the household, but we were all glad that the lieutenant and his crew had secured so good a prize. His term of service was soon after completed and he was appointed to the headquarter station on shore, where his wife and family were.[9]

The houses for the men at my station were not all required, the complement having been reduced. I was therefore enabled to knock a door through from my kitchen into the next one and occupy it, which gave me four good additional bedrooms. But I was not allowed to do this without payment of additional rent, amounting to £4 10s. per annum, which I thought very contemptible, the rent of my own house being £9. But there were and are many anomalies in the Coast Guard service. The men were all charged £6 rent for their houses, their pay being 3*s.* per day, with nothing found them. This was pinching work to those with families, but there was the chance of prize money, which was only of rare occurrence. One of the men who had eight children I took pity on two different times, and asked him to work in my garden for which I paid him 5*s.* each day, though it was contrary to the regulations for an officer to employ a man for himself at all.

Now this man was very impertinent to me one night about a fortnight afterwards when I visited him on his guard, and I reported him to the Inspecting Commander, who forwarded the case to the Controller General.[10] This man's answer to the charge was then called for, which was not a denial, but an attack upon me for having employed him to work for me, contrary to the regulations. To this the Controller General was fool enough to listen at once, and wrote to know why I had done so. Of course, I told him as above stated, his answer being that he was sorry I had broken such and such a section of such an article of the instructions, as it prevented him punishing that man as he would otherwise have done. He was removed to another station at his own expense, about 400 miles off.

Nothing could be more puerile than this treatment of me, or show less knowledge of discipline. In my opinion the man ought to have been punished immediately for insolence to his superior officer irrespective of anyone's act and, if I acted wrongly, I also should have been punished afterwards. I condemn a superior for allowing a retaliatory charge at all from any man against his officer, more especially if that charge has not been sent in within one day after the offence had been committed. Had I been Controller General I should, under the circumstances of my offence, passed over it with a slight remark, and punished the man for ingratitude, besides that for the insolence. However, there is nothing which causes a greater variety of opinion than discipline, and this I have seen verified in numerous instances during my lifetime.

Commander Boys was one of those who would check all irregularities by severity, and a fine of a guinea was a very common punishment for even what might be called a trivial offence, such as omitting to hoist the ensign before he arrived at the station, thereby showing a bad lookout! On one of these occasions it fell to the lot of a Romanist chief boatman to be so fined.[11] He went to his priest and got him to use his influence with the Romanist chief clerk at the Coast Guard office, who managed to get an order sent from headquarters to the Inspecting Commander, to the effect that such was to be cancelled immediately! Commander Boys told me the fact himself and wondered at the counter-manding of his order, having no idea how it had been effected: he had left the district e're it came to my knowledge. This kind of discipline requires no comment.

Months, and even three years, passed away in the regular routine of Coast Guard duties without ever an unpleasant word passing between Commander Boys and myself. In short, I had uniformly received the greatest kindness from him, as also my wife and family, when his term of service came to an end in January 1852. He was succeeded by

The coastguard station at the Spanish Battery, Tynemouth Castle.
Although drawn in 1886, the station had changed little since Miller's day.
(Newcastle Libraries and Information Service.)

Commander Forsyth who was an easy going, kind hearted sort of man.[12] My boys were by this time getting beyond the teaching of a village school master, and I was anxious to get a removal to a town station where really good education could be got, no better shore appointment than the Coast Guard having cast up or appearing likely to do so. The good doctor, the vicar and their families, and one farmer and his wife, were all whom we could call visiting friends near our 'out of the way' station, so we did not feel at all tied to the place. By application through a very kind and powerful neighbour who was at all times anxious to serve me as a friend, I very soon got the wished for removal to one of the great ports on the east coast, to which we went in July 1852.[13]

At this my new station we very soon found plenty of society, and I plenty of work, having three detachments and almost constant wrecks occurring, especially in the winter time. The Inspecting Commander, Norcock, was a pleasant, but rather peculiar man, and his ideas of discipline were too much of the 'popularity hunting' kind for me, or for the benefit of the service.[14] It was perhaps fortunate for us both that he was removed in eight months to another district.

The custom of the service is for the Inspecting Commander to muster the crew at the main station once in each month, and then ask each man if he has any complaints to make of his officer or anyone or anything else. On one of these occasions a man said that I had sent him every night for a week to an extreme guard, which he looked upon as a grievance. The Inspecting Commander not only listened to this absurd complaint, but before asking me a question about it said that such was not to be done again. I then told him that it was entirely a false charge and, according to the instructions, I considered that I had a right to send a man to any guard I chose every night, turning up the journal to prove that the man had not been more than once to the extreme guard for 14 days back. I said: 'This man, Sir, has been proved to have brought a false charge against me, his officer, and deserves punishment, which I call upon you to inflict'. He refused to do so which the man took advantage of, asking the Inspecting Commander if his character was affected by anything which I had said. 'Oh no,' said the Inspecting Commander, 'your character stands exactly the same as it did before Miller came to the Station.' Of course, I then gave him a bit of my mind very plainly, for which I apologised next day, but he told me there was no need for any apology as I had not said anything that required one!

This Commander RN, incredible as it may seem, had been first lieutenant of a line-of-battle ship.[15] The only way I can account for his last speech is that he had come to see his error, and was afraid that I should send in a written charge against the man, who must then have been tried by a Court of Inquiry, when his own abominable conduct would certainly have been reproved in no very gentle terms. On the removal of this popularity hunting Commander Norcock, we were much favoured by his successor being a just and truly kind hearted man. Indeed, I may say that his only fault (if such it could be called) was that he sometimes had almost too much of the latter. He was an elderly officer, though young of his rank as Commander, and had seen a good deal of active service.[16] He soon became my friend and that of my family also, not only during eight years in which I served under him, but to the day of his death in 1867.

In his district of 60 miles of coast, with some thousands of vessels constantly knocking about in all weathers, he had a large field for the exercise of every kindly feeling, especially concerning wrecks, which were far more numerous within that range than on any other part of the coast of Great Britain of equal extent. He was always on the alert to the saving of life both by the lifeboats and mortar and rocket apparatus. The latter belonged exclusively to the Coast Guard under his command, and he was increasing in his endeavours towards its improvement and the efficiency of the officers and men in using it. The former he had much in his power to make effective also, and he did his best in conjunction with Captain Ward, RN, the able Superintendent of Lifeboats for the Royal National Institution,[17] at all times. Such was the man I had then as my superior officer.

I think it was in 1853 that the Admiralty formed the Corps of Royal Naval Coast Volunteers for the purpose of manning the Navy in a war emergency, from fishermen, boatmen, bargemen, etc., and all Coast Guard officers were ordered to assist the captains who were appointed for this duty.[18] Those who should be well reported of in this respect were promised by memo 'the good will of their Lordships'. To raise this force was no easy matter, as was soon found out by the captains, although one of the understandings was that the men would never be required to go beyond 300 miles from Great Britain. The wives had a great deal to say to it and they did not believe the Admiralty, who they suspected would send the men to a three or four years' station abroad at any time after entry. By perseverance, however, and a little palaver, I contrived to get about 70 men to enter. Captain Broadhead[19] was so much pleased with this number that he very kindly offered to report me favourably to the Admiralty, and ask for an appointment to be given to my eldest son if I wished it. I was too glad to accede to this offer, which was very soon carried out to my satisfaction, being one of several favours afterwards received by me from Captain Broadhead while he commanded that corps, as well as at a later date.

I believe about 4,000 men were induced to join the Coast Volunteers. They were regularly drilled and instructed in the great gun, musket and sword exercise on board the district ship or gun boats and, at a later date, on board the reserve ships. I fear they have fallen off in numbers very much lately and, if ever called out for active service, will muster very thinly indeed. In the meantime, it adds not a little to the duties of the Coast Guard officer to look after these men. This was, however, only one of many additions to their Coast Guard labours which came pretty thickly after this date both from the Admiralty and Board of Trade Marine Department, without one penny of extra pay either to officer or man. Indeed, there were several reductions in the allowance for salvage, saving lives, etc., that concerning the latter was and is most contemptible. It used to be a general thing for an officer to charge the owner of a ship whose crew he had saved by the rocket apparatus at the rate of £1 per head, which was divided amongst the crew and himself as prize money. This was disallowed, 2s. per man being granted for the whole crew of one ship if saved and 1s. if the apparatus was taken to the waterside without being used, and nothing whatever to the officer.

Now, it so happened that these changes and increase of duties in the Coast Guard took place a very few weeks after certain officials at the Board of Trade Marine Department found their duties had increased considerably, and they applied for more pay, asking £200 a year in addition, which was granted! Surely, a little of the same spirit of liberality might have pervaded their minds in the case of the Coast Guard allowances for increased duties, but self ruled everything, especially with one of these gentlemen, who ought to have been the last to cut down the paltry trifle. To show that £1 per head for saving life was not considered too much by shipowners of respectability, I may mention that on two different occasions when that sum had been refused, I summoned the captain of the ship before the police magistrates, both being shipowners,[20] and the £1 was ordered to be paid at once, with the remark to the captain who had refused payment: 'You ought to think yourself well off to have your life saved for so small a sum.'

CHAPTER 23

The reign of humbug and red tape

1854–1860

In February 1854, owing to the war with Russia, I received an order from the Inspecting Commander to take charge of 22 Coast Guard men from our District[1] to the flagship at Sheerness,[2] for distribution to other ships about to sail for the Baltic under Sir Charles Napier.[3] This was a little change from the general routine of my Coast Guard duties and, after a rather remarkable show of feeling on the part of wives and friends at the railway station, we started by the 5 p.m. train. We got along very well till we were about to leave York, when it turned out that all my men had got into second class carriages along with other passengers. When told to go into another by themselves only, they refused and I was called to use my authority in the matter. They persisted in saying they had a right to a second class carriage and, as they were in one, they would stay there. I then told the police to take them out by force immediately, and put them into another carriage and lock the doors, which was done in a few seconds, much to the astonishment of the 'Jacks', and off the train started.

My neighbour in the carriage wherein I was seated then began to talk to me about the Coast Guard, seeing me in uniform and having been called out to settle the dispute. After asking a number of questions about various things, especially the nature of our arms, and finding that only flint carbines were allowed to the service, he said it was shameful. When in his place in the 'Upper House' some evening, he would ask the Master of the Ordnance (not then done away with) how it came that such an absurdity as flint lock carbines were still served out in any of HM services. I was thunderstruck at the idea of having said so much to a lord, telling him that I was not aware I had been talking all that time to a member of the Upper House, as also at supper in the refreshment room. 'Oh yes, I am so,' he said, and handed me his card, on which was printed the name of the Earl of

Yarborough.[4] When I stood up to read it by the light of the lamp, he added: 'Perhaps you may recollect my father's name, he was a great yachting man.' I answered that I did, and had seen his beautiful yacht at Cowes more than once.

His lordship kept up the conversation most pleasantly till we arrived at Retford Station, where his carriage was waiting. He then asked me if I had any conveyance for the men on arrival in London at King's Cross, and on being told I had not ordered any, he at once went to the telegraph office, ordering an omnibus to be in readiness for us at 4 a.m. He came back to the carriage to tell me so before saying goodnight, which he did with great heartiness, telling me to be sure to write to him with any grievances I might have, and he would do his best to remedy them. Thus ended a most agreeable conversation of two and half hours with a nobleman, who I afterwards learned, was much beloved by all who ever had anything to do with him, and who died about six or seven years afterwards, deeply regretted by everyone.

Sure enough we found the 'bus waiting for us at King's Cross which just held our number and baggage. We drove to the London Bridge station where we had to remain till 9 a.m. for the Rochester train. During this time one of the men got out of the way, detaining me at Sheerness all night, he not arriving in time for me to take them all on board till the next morning. I was, however, fortunate in having so little trouble with them and, having delivered over my 22 to the commander of the *Waterloo*[5] and got his receipt to that effect, I retraced my steps to London. I remained for a night at Berners Street with my brother Andrew, and then returned to my station.[6]

The demand for men in the Navy caused a still further increase to my duties, by being obliged to open a *rendezvous* for seamen in one of the low streets of the town, get bills pasted up and keep the ensign flying at this abominable public house for about 18 months. During this time I entered upwards of 80 men for the Navy, hunting them out of this house and that, paying their lodging bills and other debts, keeping a book and accounts, and sending them off to the District ship or to the Inspecting Commander by a Coast Guard man, whenever there were three or four to go. All this additional duty was for the large sum of nil, while the men who assisted me got 10s. per man: one of them actually pocketed £16 in all for what is called 'bringing money'! This was the liberality of the Coast Guard Controller General who seemed to consider 8s. per day as a sufficient payment for all kinds of duties by night and by day.

The wrecks on the coast within range of my station were very numerous, and we never knew the hour we might be safe from being called to assist with the rocket apparatus. Some bungling fool who called himself a 'captain' and a sailor would get his ship on shore, even in a fresh breeze (and no gale), from gross ignorance of his duty. On one occasion of a strong easterly gale setting in on the morning after a large fleet had sailed, the sea appeared to be covered with vessels running for the port. Across the Bar they came 'helter skelter', fouling each other and driving on shore from want of sufficient canvas, 25 in one tide! There were two lifeboats inside the Bar which never attempted to cross it to save the

'Wrecks on the coast - Tynemouth', from the *Illustrated London News*, 14 January 1854.
(The Trustees of the National Library of Scotland.)

crew of an unfortunate schooner[7] beyond the reach of the rocket apparatus. I think we saved half a dozen crews on that day and £6,000 of silver from one of the ships, by sending one man on board by the hawser which had been used by the crew to be hauled on shore by us. I was afraid of the ship breaking up on the next flood tide, and lost no time in getting this silver on shore: fortunately, I was right as she did break up as I expected.[8]

The second day of this gale brought seven more ships on shore making 32 in all, nine-tenths of which (and of almost all the wrecks which I saw take place at that port) were caused by the want of canvas in crossing the Bar and the sea, in consequence, broaching the ship to. The small crew of the schooner mentioned above were all drowned. Two of them who had lashed themselves to the masthead were, for about 20 minutes, seen being banged into the sea every roll of the vessel and lifted up again as she righted by the force of the sea, in the most melancholy manner. The lashing at last having slipped down to their feet, the corpses were swung about like a whiff at each rising of the mast, till the rigging was carried away, and the whole lay surging in the sea. I sent a man by the apparatus into a brig that was nearer the shore, and he threw a rope with a piece of wood fast to it to two other men who were lashed low down in the schooner's rigging, but the poor fellows were too much benumbed to do anything or to lay hold of it: they were drowned when the masts went over the side.[9] I do not hesitate to say that either of the lifeboats might have saved these men, and they were repeatedly told to try, but they were afraid.

Touching the £6,000 worth of silver saved, the ship was from South America and the consignees in Glasgow and I had to retain the whole in the Hatch House for 14 days, under a sentry by day and night. It was then sent to the Bank of England and I claimed £150 salvage, but the Glasgow men would pay nothing as they considered that we 'only did our duty in saving it, this was before the Board of Trade had cut off all salvage from the Coast Guard. The decision of the Glasgow churls I was not at all inclined to put up with and I sued them at the Admiralty Court in London. Months passed away in doubt and botheration with lawyers, but at last a decision was given in my favour of £30 to the Coast Guard and £50 to the man I sent on board to sling the silver, who was a stranger, having kept my own men to guard and carry it to the Watch House. Expenses, however, of £90 on my side were paid by the opposite party, £15 extra falling to us. My share came to exactly £4 6s. for all my trouble and risk, to say nothing of anxiety about results. So much for the uncertainty of the law! The judge explained that the Coast Guard were not bound to save silver without salvage, any more than anyone else. It would be well for the Board of Trade Marine Department to bear this in mind, as also a trifle more liberality to the officers and men of the Coast Guard if they expect them to do their duty properly.

Somewhere about the end of five years' service at this important station, I found my expenses so great with the numerous duties I had to perform, especially in house rent, that I applied for a change to the southward, unless an allowance for rent should be granted, taking the assistance of a friend at court at the same time. For once, I received a 'lift' of £20 a year, rather than let me go to another station. This paid the half of my rent, and I was able to live on for a few years more during which, in 1857, the Coast Guard service was turned over to the Admiralty from the Customs entirely. District ships were commissioned to belong to the service, to the number of 11, under a Commodore, and many changes took place accordingly, but none for the benefit of the civilian officers or those who had not belonged the Navy.[10]

From the first, the Commodore seemed determined to get rid of them as fast as possible, as also the civilian men, by any means. He knew that these officers did their duty right well and, having signed an agreement on entry, that they were 'to serve as long as they should be able to do their duties efficiently', he could not with any reason ask for their discharge. He fell upon a plan to drive them out of the service by disgust and, I am sorry to say, he succeeded in too many instances, as their numbers in a year or two most distinctly pointed out. His plan was that of promoting Chief Boatmen to the rank of what he called Second Class Chief Officer on the pay of £100 a year, besides lodgings and a 1s. 4d. a day for provisions, with the rank and uniform of Second Masters, RN, and superior in rank to the First Class Chief Officers, or 'Naval Chief Officers' as in the Navy List. Here was the cut direct, but he persisted in this measure, and has passed it down to his successors to this day, although at the loss of all Lieutenants of Stations, save 15, and all other officers who cared for their respectability or were at all able to quit the service.

The reign of humbug and red tape official routine was soon thoroughly established, along with, in 1859, that most expensive piece of folly, the formation of the 'Royal Naval Reserve' corps.[11] I shall here take the liberty of making a few remarks, notwithstanding the high encomiums issued forth in the papers lately, as having come from Mr Childers, the First Lord of the Admiralty,[12] after his cruise in the Coast Guard fleet. I claim this right, from having been 30 years in the merchant service, 18 of which was in command, and also from having been connected with the Reserve in procuring and examining men for that Corps during the years 1859 and 1860, at one of the largest seaports on the east coast of England. During this time I examined and passed as ABs nearly 100 men into the Reserve. Had I not been told that I was 'to be easy' with them, as the authorities were anxious to get the list filled up, I would not have passed half a dozen of that number.

The men of the merchant service nowadays are not qualified for a man-of-war as there are few indeed who are ABs and still fewer who will submit quietly to the necessary discipline and cleanliness, having been accustomed to do as they like in almost every respect. Drill, of course, they can learn and, for the pleasure of variety, learn well, treated as they always are with every kindness in the drill ships, but when it comes to anything save gun, musket and cutlass, I feel sure that there will be nothing but growling at what they would call unnecessary work. Should such a case happen in any ship they might belong to as once took place in July at Portsmouth in the *Trafalgar*,[13] of topgallants and royal masts and yards being sent up and down 19 times, with no cessation whatever, because they were not smart enough, I will venture to say that the captain's life would not be worth five minutes purchase after the first half dozen times!

For years past there have been no apprentices in the merchant service, and men of any kind have been taken to be hauling and pulling machines only. They have nothing to do with rigging the ship, stowing cargo or getting out cargo, these are all separate branches of their trade. When a mast is carried away the grand difficulty is to find two or three sailors in a ship's company who know anything about getting up another. This being quite general in merchant ships, how can these Reserve men be all 'prime seamen', as is so often stated by the papers and Registrar General. Most of the coasting seamen are married, and my experience with these viragos has told me that, when the Reserve may be called out for active service, not one married man in 100 will be allowed to join the Navy! This is rendered quite simple to effect, by the man and his wife going to another port, changing his name and then joining a merchant ship as a plain seaman without RNR being added to it. There are no 'register tickets' now obliged to be shown at all times and, without them, any man can get clear of the Navy if he wishes it, as I have shown.

I have pointed this out to more than one captain of a Coast Guard ship and have always found them agree with me: why it is not done I do not know. Until some such measure is started and carried out, not one-fourth of the men of the Reserve will be forthcoming when wanted. Their object in entering is solely to get the £6 a year and £12 pension: they can keep their own counsel for future purposes. To give these men £12 a year pension after eight or ten years' service is a monstrous and unjustifiable expense, for so very great an uncertainty as getting them to serve.

The Reserve should be formed of an increased Coast Guard or of ten-years' men from the Navy with sixpence a day pension. Thousands would be glad of it and the Navy also sure of their men who would be the right sort and not such as would be a continual torment to their officers. No one will ever convince me that there are more than 100 'prime' seamen in all the 16,000 the Registrar so frequently boasts of. For a thousand reasons, the sooner the present Reserve shall be knocked in the head the better. My worthy Inspecting Commander was most zealous in his endeavours to get up this RN Reserve and succeeded by various manoeuvres in obtaining about 400 men in all during the first year, including those from my own port, notwithstanding great opposition from the wives, the force gradually increasing by sheer perseverance of the Coast Guard officers. The number has at no time exceeded 16,000 (and is now down to 13,000), little more than a half of that allowed by the Act, and which the Admiralty expected would have been filled up in a month from their terms being so uncommonly liberal. But little did they know of merchant seamen then.

CHAPTER 24

To be retired without pension

1860–1865

Although the men composing the Coast Guard were and I believe are still, very well conducted generally, and a great proportion have been petty officers in the Navy, yet there were not wanting those of another stamp. I may state that I do not know a service in which the vigilance of the officers is more required, or perhaps less exerted. Commander Boys used to say frequently that he never liked to see a continuation of 'no defaulters' lists', as it made him think that the officers were so peccant themselves in dereliction of their duties, as to terrify them from reporting a man who might be caught tripping, from a fear of retaliation. Be this as it may generally, I boldly say that I never passed over more than a first offence and, in the case of drunkenness, not even that. We were especially told by general memo from the Controller General that, regarding such, we were not to be allowed any discretion whatever. I used to read to the crew occasionally by way of refreshing their memories on the subject, that they might not blame me for doing my duty whenever necessity should call for it.

There was one man of my crew who had been very troublesome to the officer of another station, and been removed to mine by application of the Inspecting Officer to the Commodore, as he thought I would look better after him than he could do. This was a compliment I could willingly have dispensed with, but 'mum was the word'. For some months this man contrived to escape my notice as to drunkenness, but this did not last long and I had to report him twice within a year at most, when of course, he was punished by fine. The third report was sure always to bring the defaulter to trial by court-martial if he had belonged to the Navy, or by Court of Inquiry if a civilian.

The third came with this man in the following manner. It was blowing from the east and the coast was guarding itself, as the saying is, and only one man on the look out for wrecks near the Watch House. A few minutes past midnight I went down to see that all was right and, before reaching the Watch House, by about 200 yards, I met the man, William Moore, coming out from under a wooden shed. When seeing that he was drunk, I told him so, but he denied it in a very disrespectful manner, saying he was waiting for his relief. I told him to come with me to the Watch House. We had scarcely turned to go up a little rising part of the path when he began to abuse me with his tongue, suddenly turning round before me and striking me with his fist on the forehead, which I returned by two smart blows of a cane, which I held in my hand, under the left ear. He then closed and grappled with me, trying to strike me again for a minute or two, when I saw that I could not long hold out against him, a six feet tall drunken man. Throwing him off me, as far as I could, I ran up the hill towards the Watch House, but, being tripped by a stone, I fell, my hat and stick taking leave of me at the same moment. Moore overtook me immediately and, seizing my stick from the ground, he struck me repeatedly on my bare head with it before I could get up, then stopped. I said to him that he surely did not consider what he was doing in attacking me so, and asked for my stick, which he gave me. He looked about to find my hat, then I left him and got to the men's houses, calling out the Chief Boatman and another man immediately, ordering them at the same time to make a prisoner of Moore and take him to the police office. On the way I told him it was lucky for him that I had not got my heavy stick with me, to which he replied that it was lucky for me that he had not his pistols on him.

We soon left him at the police office where I learned that they were keeping a bright look out after this very man who, along with a certain woman, had been for some months suspected of murdering a waiter of a hotel by throwing him over the cliff. One of the police saw the same woman with him near the shed that very night just before I met him. I knew he was a man of a most ungovernable temper and, for a long time previous to this occurrence, I had always got my pistols ready when meeting him on his guard at night. Indeed, I suspected him so much of an intent to throw me into the river when he was pulling me across in the punt one night, that I kept a pistol in hand all the time saying nothing, being determined to have shot him if he had risen from the thwart. His having seen this probably prevented the act. I wrote next morning a full statement of this case to the captain of the district ship, as also to a master RN, who had been left in charge of the Division by the Inspecting Commander who had gone on leave.

This officer had then only lately entered the Coast Guard service and was much my junior, but his belonging to the Navy made him my superior. With much pomposity and ignorance, he came the following day to investigate, and report on my charges against Moore. The District Captain ordered him to be sent to the ship where he was kept in irons till the Court of Inquiry should meet which, of course, I expected was only preliminary to a court martial. In this I was mistaken, as the former only took place, attended by three Commanders as members and the Paymaster as secretary. All that I have related above was retold and a great deal more by a policeman from the town where the waiter of the hotel was murdered, as also by the Chief Boatman and the man who took him to the police office. Although proved to be guilty of attacking and striking his officer, yet, after several days' consideration by the Commodore, he was only sentenced 'to be dismissed the service with disgrace'. He was thereby thrown loose upon me to wreak his vengeance at any convenient season.

Two cases of men striking their officers had occurred on board men-of-war only a short time before, and in both the criminals were sentenced to four dozen lashes, two years in jail and to be dismissed the service. I can see no reason why some such punishment should not have been inflicted upon Moore by order of a court-martial also. I was told afterwards by the Paymaster that they, the authorities, had committed a mistake. If so, it might have been remedied, but perhaps it may have been thought that a man striking a civilian officer was not guilty of such criminality as one who actually belonged to the Navy! If such was the reasoning of the Commodore and others, I do not hesitate to say that they were totally unworthy of holding their high positions. Whatever may have caused them to treat me in the manner they did showed at least a great want of knowledge of discipline, and total disregard for the benefit of the Coast Guard service.

For nearly a year after this happy decision, I was obliged to go armed both by day and night, the man Moore living in his old haunts, and only occasionally going to sea in a coaster for a week or two. I therefore was surprised one day to learn from the Chief Boatman that Moore wanted to speak with me, to apologise for his bad conduct. I met him where I knew he was waiting for me and, after very strong expressions of regrets and stating that he was aware that I only did my duty in reporting him, he held out his hand which I shook, wishing him well while in this world of iniquity, and to profit by what had passed.

In October 1860 an Order in Council was issued for all Lieutenants, RN, of 60 years old to be pensioned from the service and promoted to the rank of Retired Commander. This made a number of vacancies for Inspecting Officers of Coast Guard, and I thought now or never was my time for promotion. At the same period I was quite aware of the extra difficulty to be surmounted by being a civilian officer only and that my chance of success would be small indeed with only official recommendations. I was also determined against any Irish appointment. I set myself to work to obtain the interest of my former kind and powerful neighbour, applying through him privately, and my superiors officially, for one or other of two Divisions in England, which in a short time was successful.

On the 7 November 1860 I presented myself to my astonished and respected predecessor about 200 miles south of where I had been for eight and a half years, holding out my appointment to him.[1] Without it, he declared, he would not have listened to me: with it, he was kind and obliging. He was 70 years of age and had been 40 years at and about that part of the coast as Lieutenant of Stations, in command of cutters and of the Division to which I had been appointed. He looked like a man of only 60 and died aged 81 years. I soon learned from this worthy old commander all that was necessary concerning the Division, and he drove me round the whole of it next day, the distance being 25 miles in length, a long day's journey.

After this I had to look for a house in the town, which was exactly at one end of the Division, as also lodgings for a temporary residence till my family could leave their old quarters. Both having been found, I took time to look about the Division, getting acquainted with the men at the different stations and detachments. The walking was considerable, but I could not afford to start a trap just at first, having a little leeway to make up, but my allowances were increased by nearly £80 a year, which made us very comfortable. My family came to me on the 2nd December 1860, bag and baggage, by railway and all expenses paid, on promotion to Inspecting Officer. Our house was in the High Street, and of a good size and convenience, but we did not like a town, so we kept a good look out for one in the country somewhere nearer the sea, which in two months did really cast up.

I may as well mention here that, after I had left my former station, my late Inspecting Commander on his first visit to my wife (who had not then removed) told her that he had some money lying idle in the bank. If she required any to clear scores there was £100 at her service in a minute, and not to scruple to take it, as he would be delighted to assist us if we required it. This was an offer which proved his true friendship and kind Irish heart most markedly, but we did not require it and, of course, it was declined. It was only of a piece with his unflinching friendship for the whole of the seven and three-quarter years I was under his command. I had by this time two sons in the Navy as Master's Assistants, another in the Peninsular and Oriental Company service. The Inspecting Commander was always looking out how he could assist them and push them on in the service, doing much one way and another by letters and other plans, after I left him. To Captain Broadhead also I have been much indebted for assistance in getting my sons on, and yet I never had to ask anything, it was always offered by these two most generous and friendly officers.

In February 1861 we shifted our quarters to within one and a half miles of the sea, and four from the town, placing me much more conveniently for my duties. The house was large and roomy with garden, gig house and stable, and two or three nice families within a moderate distance which, when my duties permitted, made the time pass very agreeably till early in 1864.[2] At that period it entered into the heads of the Admiralty to give an order that civilian officers of Coast Guard were to be retired without pension at the age of 60, the same as naval officers, so far as age and quitting the service went![3] Such an order as this I knew well could only emanate from the man who had already most grossly insulted the civilian officers. He was then a member of the Board at Whitehall and in full charge of the Coast Guard,[4] though headed by another commodore who, fortunately, was a clever, gentlemanly man and always inclined to listen to just and honourable complaints.

To him I went in London to point out that I and all civilian officers had signed an agreement on entry stating that we were not to be entitled to a pension on retiring, but we never doubted that we should serve as long as health and strength were given us to do the duties efficiently. If such was not stated in the written agreement, it was for him to show. I was 60 years of age, but I was as well able to serve as ever I had been. The officer I relieved was then 70, and many others had been even older than that. I trusted that he would use his influence with the Admiralty, either to retain us while able to serve, or to give us a respectable pension, whereby we might be prevented from starving. To this speech he replied that he would be very glad to do all he could for us, but he did not think that we would succeed in getting a pension. I saw it would be of no use arguing the question more at that time, but through the application of the District Captain I succeeded in obtaining another year of service to 1st August 1865.

In the meanwhile a petition was got up, and Commodore Ryder[4] promised to recommend it. We had also found out that part of our written agreement, which all had separately signed, stated distinctly the fact of our being 'entitled to serve as long as we should be able to do our duties efficiently'. We thought this to be a great point in our favour, but when the petition was sent to the Board of Admiralty by the Commodore who strongly recommended that a pension should be granted, it was returned with a decided negative, at which the Commodore expressed by general memo his 'extreme regret'.

Indeed, he must have taken this refusal as anything but complimentary to himself, as in three weeks' time he issued another general memo expressing his great satisfaction at being able to inform us that he had succeeded in obtaining from the Admiralty their recommendation to the Treasury for a suitable pension to the civilian officers of the Coast Guard, or words to this effect. But what is the pension granted? It is of the Civil Service only which, for a few years and a small salary, gives a mere trifle. I know two officers who had served 16 and 16½ years whose pensions were £34 and £36 or thereabouts. I wonder if any Admiralty clerk has been pensioned on such sums, for having 'read the papers and played dominoes' for that length of time! I wonder also how any Government Board could treat hard working officers with such contempt, but it was not the decision of the Board. It was the decision of one man who persuaded one or perhaps two others to pinch for the few remaining days of their lives a small number of gentlemen who had rigidly done their duty. They had worked for a very paltry pittance under the impression of being allowed to serve their country so long as they were able, according to their written agreement, but who, like too many more, have been deceived by the selfishness of mankind.

It is not yet too late to remedy this great evil, and I trust that some of the remaining civilian officers may, through their friends in Parliament, bring the matter before the notice of the present efficient heads of the Admiralty, in such a manner as would gratify all concerned, both retrospectively and prospectively. Since 1st August 1865 I have ceased to serve under the Admiralty, or anyone else, and do the best I can with my small means to keep my family in that respectable sphere to which we have always been accustomed, being quite as able for all Coast Guard duties as on this day nearly nine years ago when forced to relinquish HM service.[6]

London, 1st March 1874 [altered from 1869].
    John Miller,
    Mount View Road,
    Crouch Hill,
    Hornsey North.

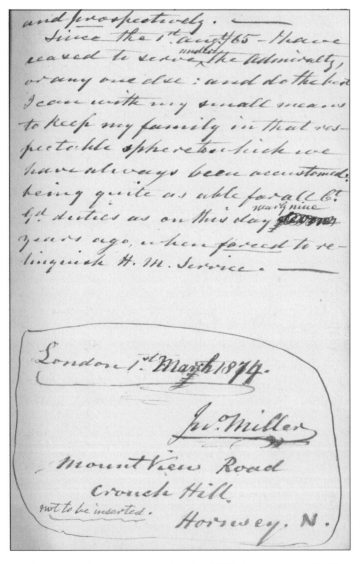

Last page of the manuscript, bearing Miller's signature and address.

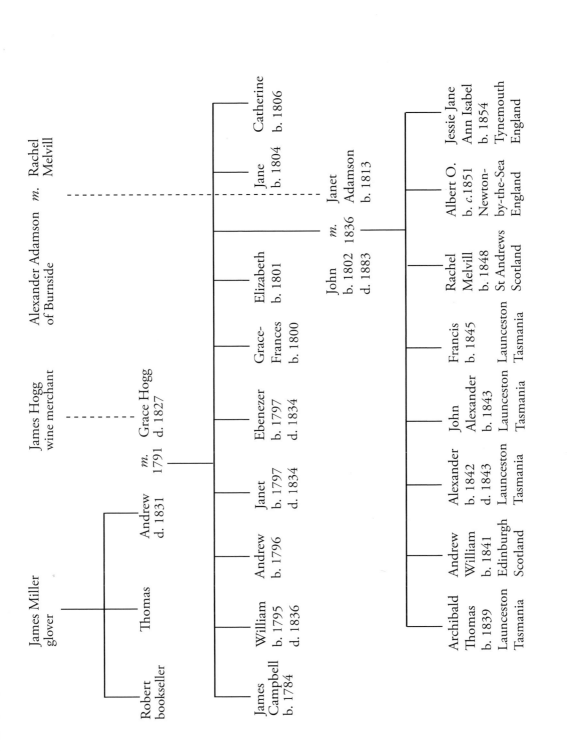

James Miller
glover

Robert
bookseller

Thomas

Andrew
d. 1831

James Hogg
wine merchant

m.
1791

Grace Hogg
d. 1827

Alexander Adamson
of Burnside

m.

Rachel
Melvill

James
Campbell
b. 1784

William
b. 1795
d. 1836

Andrew
b. 1796

Janet
b. 1797
d. 1834

Ebenezer
b. 1797
d. 1834

Grace-
Frances
b. 1800

Elizabeth
b. 1801

Jane
b. 1804

Catherine
b. 1806

John
b. 1802
d. 1883

m. 1836

Janet
Adamson
b. 1813

Archibald
Thomas
b. 1839
Launceston
Tasmania

Andrew
William
b. 1841
Edinburgh
Scotland

Alexander
b. 1842
d. 1843
Launceston
Tasmania

John
Alexander
b. 1843
Launceston
Tasmania

Francis
b. 1845
Launceston
Tasmania

Rachel
Melvill
b. 1848
St Andrews
Scotland

Albert O.
b. c.1851
Newton-
by-the-Sea
England

Jessie Jane
Ann Isabel
b. 1854
Tynemouth
England

APPENDIX

An Adventure in China

(Reprinted from *Leisure Hour, X*, 1861, pp. 69–71)

In August, 1822, when opium smuggling into China by English ships was in its infancy, three of these vessels were at anchor in the pretty little land-locked bay called Cumsen-moon, about 12 miles to the north-east of Macao. The inhabitants about that part of the country had, up to this time, scarcely ever been visited by foreigners; and, although it turned out that they were filled with the usual Chinese ill feeling towards them, yet the report from the ship which had been longest there was so favourable, as to cause all arms to be dispensed with by the crews on going on shore at any time, until the following occurrence took place.

Soon after breakfast one fine clear day, Mr. A-, a young officer belonging to the *Swinger*, was sent on shore to fill water in the launch, with a crew of eight Lascars and one Englishman. It so happened that he met another officer from the *Nymph* on shore, who was on the same duty as himself. The two youngsters proceeded to take a walk into the country, for the purpose of amusement and information. In doing so, however, they had to leave the boats and ships entirely out of sight, turning sharp round a bluff point very near to the watering place; which will be proved in the sequel to have been a gross want of prudence, giving the hidden enemy all the advantage which they seem to have been stealthily watching for.

The walk was pursued for about a mile inland, towards a hill, and then, on returning by the same path, about 500 yards from the boat, but hidden by the bluff, they were met by 30 or 40 Chinamen, some with hoes, and some with heavy sticks, used for carrying weighty things across their shoulders. The Chinamen, after passing, and having a great deal to say amongst themselves, came after the officers, pulled them by the sleeve once or twice to stop them, and stood in the way also to prevent progress. Mr. A.-, seeing that they were bent on a disturbance, thought, under the circumstances, that discretion would be the best mode of tactics. He stopped and turned round, but in a moment was knocked down by a blow from some of the crowd of Chinamen. This was followed up by tying the unfortunate officer's hands and feet, stealing his neckerchief (nearly strangling him in the act), and one shoe from his foot, and then letting him lie on the ground.

Mr. B-, seeing this state of things, and possessing good long legs, considered that now was the time to use them, by running through the mob to the boats for assistance, which he fortunately effected. The two crews of Lascars and the one English sailor now took oars and stretchers from the boats and bravely fought the Chinamen for a short time till they were driven back to their boats by overpowering numbers, and shoved off, without further loss, to their respective ships, to tell the tale of Mr. A- being in the hands of the enemy.

The captain of the *Swinger* (an old lieutenant, RN) immediately boarded the *Nymph* and the *Sea Gull*, and advised a razzia of the country until Mr. A- should be found and brought back, dead or alive, which was forthwith put into execution, by mustering on shore in due time all the officers, petty officers, Lascars, and sepoys who could be spared from the three ships, well armed with muskets, fowling-pieces, swords, pistols, etc., of which opium ships in those days had no niggardly supply.

But we must now return to Mr. A-. The moment the Chinamen saw the boats shove off from the shore, the order was given to put Mr. A- on his legs, by untying them; and he, having picked up his hat, but still minus the shoe and neckerchief, stood for a moment, until the words 'Fye, fye', were given by one of four villanous-looking fellows who were now left in sole charge of the prisoner. Not knowing the meaning of this, however, at the time, – viz. 'run, run' – he still stood and was forthwith saluted by a stroke from a bamboo across the back of the legs near the heels, and dragged forward at the same instant by two of the four men, the other two following in the rear with bamboos, in case any slackening of the pace should appear.

In this manner, at a hard trot, did these wretches drive Mr. A- through paddy fields, and all sorts of ground, till they reached the top of a hill, about 200 feet high, although he was in great pain from the blow which he had received, and hardly able to move at all. Before ascending the hill on the other side, Mr. A- turned round to look at the ships in the distance, with feelings of a somewhat melancholy nature, as may be supposed, when the same man who had struck him said, in half Portuguese, half Chinese, 'Do you want to look? Look! It is your last look!' These words Mr. A- happened to understand, from having heard occasionally a little of this jargon at Macao, and they certainly did not tend to soothe his mind in its then anxious state. Still he had a kind of hope that dollars might gain his release, although up to this time appearances were far from favouring such an idea. Having descended the hill towards the beach, on the opposite side from the ships, and after a two miles run with the heat at 100 degrees at least, they halted under some trees close to a small stream of water, of which Mr. A- asked to be allowed to drink, which was granted. He then, seeing that his wrists were already considerably swollen from the tightness of the rope by which they were bound, asked to have it slackened. This was also not only granted, but he was then tied by only one hand; and in a few moments the run was again commenced for a further distance of about two miles, nearly the whole of which was through heavy sand, till at last a village was entered, and Mr. A- was safely housed in a large ground-floor room on one side of a square court, where were two long tables, and benches on either side of them.

Tired and fagged with a four mile march at the double, and dragged along by the rope like a bullock to be slaughtered, he sat down at one of the tables with feelings more easily imagined than described. These were certainly not much relieved when, in a few minutes, the demon of the bamboo brought some huge knives from a corner of the room, and put them to his neck with a grin of delight, saying that the mandarin would soon be there to pass sentence of death on him, when he should cut off his head in the manner then shown.

Meanwhile, hundreds of people came to see the Fankwei – men, women, and children – who had never beheld one in their lives before; some wondered at his dress, others at his hair, and nearly all jeered and laughed at his position; even the women, whose compassion Mr. A- had tried to gain, abused him and talked of the mandarin, making signs also of cutting off a head.

The crowd being by this time very great, and adding much to the almost insufferable heat, Mr. A- begged to be relieved from such unwelcome visitors if possible, which request was immediately acceded to, by his being placed in a small room on the other side of the court, where was the usual Chinese bed, viz. a mat and glazed pillow on a board, and a stool and table with a teapot and a cup on it. The door of this place was only a mat hung from the top, which was occasionally lifted up, to allow the favoured few to have a peep at the Fankwei, or foreign devil.

Mr. A- here threw himself down on the mat bed, to await, as he hoped, the coming of the captain to his rescue, which he knew from experience he would do immediately on learning the circumstances of the case from the boat's crew (for he did not then know of the escape of Mr. B-), and he prayed sincerely that this might happen before the arrival of the said mandarin. The natives offered him tea, which he gladly accepted, after he had first seen them drink out of the same pot; and in a short time, amongst the 'favoured few' who were allowed to peep into this raree-show, appeared a man who accosted Mr. A- with the well-known sounds of 'Hey, yah, how you do? I have seen you before; I thinkee at Macao!' Never was mongrel English more welcome! Mr. A- recollected having seen the man somewhere, and at once looked upon him as a friend, and asked if he thought there was any danger of his being killed, as had been threatened; to which the man said in a careless unsatisfactory sort of way, 'No, I no thinkee so!'

'Do they want dollars?' asked Mr. A-.

'Yes,' was the reply.

'How much?'

'Two thousand,' said the man.

'Maskee' [never mind], answered the prisoner. 'If you will give me a pen and ink, with a sheet of paper, and take a letter to the captain when written, he will give you the dollars.' To this an assent was at once given, and the necessary articles being produced, a letter was forthwith written by Mr. A-, descriptive of the state of the case and his whereabouts, as near as he could guess, not forgetting the bearing of the village from the ship by compass, and requesting that the number of dollars should be paid which were demanded, and no killing or wounding at the watering-place; as Mr. A- was then so completely in the Chinamen's hands, that he would then be sure to be beheaded. He also asked for a pair of shoes to be sent, to enable him to walk back to the ship.

When this letter was despatched, Mr A- lay down once more on the mat, and was now in a comparatively composed state of mind, being under the impression that he would be a prisoner for four or five days at least, as the captain would require to get the ship under way and proceed to Macao for such an amount as 2,000 dollars, if that sum should really be demanded by the messengers. Far different was the result, however.

On the man's arrival at the watering-place, he found a considerable number of well-armed men and officers all ready for an attack, and vowing vengeance against all Chinamen. The letter was delivered to the captain, and when read, the man was asked how many dollars were demanded, Mr. A- having in the letter stated no particular number, but merely 'to pay' the amount 'demanded'. His answer was 50, which the captain immediately went on board the ship and procured, taking the opportunity of getting a pair of shoes to send, and writing a letter to Mr. A- at the same time; all of which he delivered into the hands of the messenger, the dollars sealed up in a bag, addressed to Mr. A-.

As this man objected to any Englishman going to the village along with him, from fear of a fight, it was thought advisable to give in to him, and send a Chinese carpenter, who belonged to one of the ships, to assist in the negotiation, and show the road back to Mr. A-, no difficulty being apprehended, as the whole sum asked for had been given, and the captain having no knowledge of any greater having been spoken of. He told the man, however, that, having satisfied his demands, he would allow a reasonable time for the release of Mr. A-; but if this was not then accomplished, he would burn the village, and 'make a second Lintin business of it, and take him by force!', alluding to what had been done there a few months before by HM frigate *Topaze*, which caused a stoppage of trade for six weeks at Canton.

With this warning, the two Chinamen left the little 'army' at the watering-place, and in due time made their appearance at the village, and delivered the bag of dollars, letter, and shoes to Mr. A-, who, on recognising the carpenter, immediately gave him the dollars to hand over to the four 'braves', and expected to be allowed to decamp forthwith. But, 'man, man!' [stop!] was the order, and a long angry conversation took place in the large room amongst many Chinamen, who were not a little annoyed at the small sum received by their messenger; but they had not seen the 'guns and swords, and rungs and gads' which caused this craven to reduce his figures so instantaneously; and it took at least 20 minutes of verbal war for him to convince his friends that it was better to pocket 50 dollars with a whole skin, than lose their village and their lives by standing out for a larger sum. The carpenter, no doubt, had some weight in the argument, and at last Mr. A- was 'granted a pass' to the watering-place, in company with the carpenter. He tried hard to induce the four braves to accompany him back, by way of showing the road, having a distant glimmering of seeing them tied up at the gangway of his ship, and expiating their offences under the boatswain's tuition; but as the probability of such a climax had no doubt been hinted to their own minds, the invitation was politely refused, saving so far as to the skirts of the village.

With a light heart, Mr. A- now travelled along with the carpenter, and in the course of an hour had the gratification of being welcomed at the watering-place by three cheers from the armed party in waiting, and many a hearty shake of congratulation by the hand; feeling at the same time deeply thankful to the Almighty for his merciful escape, and particularly for having so willed it that he should have been without arms on the occasion of his capture; as they certainly would have been used, and, as a consequence, would almost as certainly have been the cause of his murder.

As it is customary in China for all mandarins to live upon those under them, by 'squeezing', or making them pay dollars, it was not much to be wondered at that some of them should try to make capital out of the above occurrence; and consequently, three or four days afterwards a man-of-war junk, sent by the admiral from Chuen-pee, came to anchor in the bay, and in a short time the mandarin went on board the *Swinger*, and made inquiries touching the description of the attacking parties, and particularly that of the four 'braves', which was easily given by Mr. A-, their features being indelibly imprinted on his mind, and he having in addition been able to get hold of their names from some of the natives at the watering-place.

The mandarin said he should go on shore and seize those men, and, if successful, bring them on board the *Swinger* the following day for Mr. A- to identify, when he should tie them up and flog them till Mr. A- was satisfied. But on that same evening an East India Company's ship arrived and anchored at Lintin, and the captain of the *Swinger*, having business to transact with it, it was necessary for him to get under way at daylight on the following morning, and sail for that island, distant about six or seven miles, which prevented Mr A- witnessing the flogging of the four 'braves'; for it was shortly afterwards known that the mandarin did seize them and not only flogged them well, but 'squeezed' them well also.

The ship which had arrived was that to which Mr. A- properly belonged (he having only been lent to do duty in the *Swinger* during her temporary absence at Penang); and as he then for ever quitted the opium service, he has had no subsequent opportunity of learning any further particulars concerning the men who committed this outrage, or even the name of the village to which he was dragged. The facts are, however, strictly true, and will tend to show how absolutely necessary it is for all boats' crews to use the greatest caution on landing on the coasts of China.

REFERENCES

CHAPTER 1

1　John Miller's father, Andrew, was Depute Clerk of the Bills, the Bill Chamber being part of the Court of Session (*Register of the Society of Writers to Her Majesty's Signet*, Edinburgh, 1983, p. 224). At the time of John's birth the family lived at 5 St James Street, South Side. In 1806–7 they were listed at 8 New Street, and in 1811–12 at the newly constructed 11 York Place (*Post Office Annual Directory*, Edinburgh). His mother Grace Hogg was the eldest daughter of James, wine merchant (Edinburgh Old Parochial Registers, 685[1]/52, p. 104).

2　The Royal High School at that time was located in the 1777 building at High School Yards, Infirmary Street. Mr Algionby Ross Carson, M.A., L.L.D., was born at Holywood, Dumfriesshire. He became a master at the RHS in 1806 and was Rector from 1820 until 1842. James Pillans, MA, was rector from January 1810 until 1820 when he became Professor of Humanity at Edinburgh University. His portrait was painted by Raeburn and engraved by Turner (see W. Steven, *History of the High School of Edinburgh*, Edinburgh, 1849).

3　George Dundas (1802–1869), son of James Dundas of Ochtertyre, W.S., was Sheriff of Selkirk 1844–68, Vice-Dean of Faculty 1855–68 and created Lord Manor 14 October 1868 (F.J. Grant, *The Faculty of Advocates in Scotland, 1532–1943*, Edinburgh, 1944, p. 62).

4　John Dundas, brother of George, was born 19 December 1803 and died 1873 (*Society of Writers*, p. 94).

5　Sir David Dundas (1803–77) was son of Sir Robert Dundas of Beechwood (Grant, *Faculty of Advocates*, p. 61).

6　Sir Francis Grant (1803–78) was born at Kilgraston, Perthshire. Best known as a portrait painter, he was ensured success in 1840 when his painting *Queen Victoria Riding at Windsor Castle with her Gentlemen* won royal approval (J. Halsby and P. Harris, *Dictionary of Scottish Painters, 1600-present*, Edinburgh, 2001, p. 87).

7　From the new edition, Glasgow, 1824, lines 508–9: Scott may perchance his name and influence lend, And paltry Pillans shall traduce his friend.

8　*Ramillies,* 74-gun ship, *Culloden/Thunderer* class, built by Randall at Rotherhithe and launched in 1785 (D. Lyon, *The Sailing Navy List: All the Ships of the Royal Navy Built, Purchased and Captured, 1688–1860*, London, 1993, p. 71).

9　Alexander Reid Junior, merchant, 25 Charlotte Street, Leith (*Post Office Annual Directory*, Edinburgh, 1819, p. 394).

10　No. 11 York Place.

11　James, John's eldest brother, born 1793, and Andrew, his third brother, born 1796. According to the *Post Office London Directory*, 1820, they were 'general agents and insurance brokers' at 12 Bishopsgate Street Without.

12　*Lord Castlereagh,* 812 ton, three-decked ship, built by Barnard of Deptford and launched 1802. Keel length 117 ft 10 in, breadth 36 ft and depth of hold 14 ft 9 in (A. Farrington, *Catalogue of East India Company Ships' Journals and Logs, 1600–1834*, London, 1999, p. 396).

13　For the size and composition of ships' companies see Sir H.E.A. Cotton, *The East Indiamen: the*

East India Company's Maritime Service, London, 1949, p. 24.

14 William Younghusband, born 1772 at Chatton in Northumberland. EIC Service 1786–1826; captain, *Alexander* 1809–10; *Union* 1812–13; *Lord Castlereagh* 1816–19; *Cornwall* 1825–26 (A. Farrington, *Biographical Index of East India Company Maritime Service Officers, 1600–1834*, London, 1999, p. 885).

15 John Rennie Manderson, born 1791, married Margaret Rennie at Prestonkirk, East Lothian, 1828. EIC Service 1807–1832; captain: *Bridgewater* 1824–29; *Charles Grant* 1831–32 (Farrington, *Biographical Index*, p. 515).

16 John Williams, born 1784 at St Marylebone, London; EIC Service 1798–1819 (*ibid.*, p. 854).

17 Patrick Lindesay, born 1796 at Newburn, Fife; EIC Service 1810–22, died 4 June 1822 (*ibid.*, p. 475). *Sir David Scott* , 1,342 ton ship, built by Bailey of Ipswich in 1821 (Farrington, *Catalogue*, pp. 604–5).

18 George Alfred Legget, born 1795, London; EIC Service 1810–19 (Farrington, *Biographical Index*, p. 468).

19 William Whitmarsh, EIC Service 1818–21 (*ibid.*, p. 847).

20 This was the only recorded voyage Richard Somerville made with the Company (*ibid.*, p. 736).

21 Mr Muir is probably Robert Muir who graduated from Edinburgh University in 1813 (*List of Graduates in Medicine in the University of Edinburgh, 1705–1866*, Edinburgh, 1867, p. 47).

22 Walter Lorimer, EIC Service 1803–24, died Whampoa 17 November 1824 (Farrington, *Biographical Index*, p. 485).

23 Ellis Bostock, EIC Service 1810–19 (*ibid.*, p. 84).

24 Richard Oakes Hardy is not recorded by Farrington for this voyage.

25 John Say Sparkes, born 1800, England; EIC Service 1815–29 (*ibid.*, p. 437).

26 Henry Bonham Shepherd, born 1800, Wales; EIC Service 1818–30 (*ibid.*, p. 711).

27 Charles D. has not been identified.

CHAPTER 2

1 The *Lord Castlereagh* departed the East India Dock in March for Gravesend, sailed from there on 14 April and arrived at the Downs on the 18th (A. Farrington, *Catalogue of East India Company Ships' Journals and Logs, 1600–1834*, London, 1999, pp. 396–7). See also the voyage journal (BL, India Office Records, India Office: Marine Records, L/MAR/B/188H), ledger (BL, L/MAR/B/188-O [1]) and pay book (BL, L/MAR/B/188-O [2]).

2 Idlers: those members of a ship's company liable to constant day duty and therefore not subjected to keep the watch at night, except when all hands were called on deck (W.H. Smyth, *The Sailor's Word-book: an Alphabetical Digest of Nautical Terms*, London, 1867, p. 399).

3 'On 3 Sept. at 6 a.m. Mr Bostock, purser, returned from Macao with a pilot', ship's journal (BL, L/MAR/B/188H).

4 Arrived Whampoa 5 September 1819 (Farrington, *Catalogue*, pp. 396–7).

5 Departed China 19 November 1819 (*ibid.*, p. 397).

6 *Lowther Castle*, ship, 1427 tons, built by Pitcher at Northfleet and launched in 1811. Sold in 1830 to Joseph Somes for £8,650 (*ibid.*, pp. 412–4).

7 Arrived St Helena 13 February 1820 (*ibid.*, p. 397).

8 Sir Hudson Lowe (1769–1844), Governor of St Helena, 1815–21, was intensely disliked by Napoleon. There was little face to face communication between the two men (*DNB*, XI, pp. 189–93). The *Lord Castlereagh* arrived at the island just over a year before Napoleon's death on 5 May 1821.

9 *Conqueror*, 74 guns, 1842 tons, built by Graham, Harwich, launched 1801 (D. Lyon, *The Sailing Navy List: All the Ships of the Royal Navy Built, Purchased and Captured 1688–1860*, London, 1993, p. 110).

10 *Tees*, 26 guns, 444 tons, built by Taylor, Bideford, 1817 (*ibid.*, p. 132).

11 *Menai*, 26 guns, 444 tons, built by Brindley, Frindsbury, 1814 (*ibid.*, p. 133).

12 *Redwing*, brig sloop, 18 guns, 382 tons, built by Warren, Brightlingsea, 1806 (*ibid.*, p. 141).

13 *Leveret*, brig sloop, 10 guns, 235 tons, built by Perry, Blackwall, 1808 (*ibid.*, p. 145).

14 *Rosario*, brig sloop, 10 guns, 235 tons, built by Bailey, Ipswich, 1808 (*ibid.*, p.144).

15 George Rennie, captain 7 June 1814, dismissed 14 July 1821, restored 1822. Died 11 February 1844 (D. Syrett, and R.L. DiNardo, eds, *Commissioned Sea Officers of the Royal Navy, 1660–1815*, Aldershot, 1994, p. 375).

16 Arrived Downs 9 April 1820 (Farrington, *Catalogue*, p. 397).

17 Act 6 Geo. IV, c. 108, s. XXXVII: by this legislation Customs officers were permitted to make a body search only after taking a suspect before a Justice of the Peace, or a Collector or Comptroller of Customs, or other superior officer.

CHAPTER 3

1 *Marquis Camden,* 1216 ton three-decked ship, built by Pitcher at Northfleet, launched in 1812. Length: 165 ft 8 in; keel: 133 ft 11 in; breadth: 42 ft 1 in; depth of hold 17 ft 1 in; height between decks: 6 ft 5 in and 6 ft 4 in (A. Farrington, *Catalogue of East India Company Ships' Journals and Logs, 1600–1834*, London, 1999, pp. 432–3). See also the voyage journal (BL, India Office Records, India Office: Marine Records, L/MAR/B/58D), ledger (BL, L/MAR/B/58N [1]) and pay book (BL, L/MAR/B/58N [2]).

2 *Repulse*, ship, 1334 tons, John Paterson commander, built by Wigram of Blackwall and launched in 1820 (*ibid.*, p. 555).

3 In fact, the *Lord Castlereagh* continued trading.

4 The British Library has a copy of Charles H. Adams, of Edmonton, *The Explanatory Letter-press to Accompany the Plate of the Solar System*, London, 1822.

5 Thomas Larkins, EIC Service 1808–32; captain of *Marquis Camden* for most of her voyages 1816–32 (A. Farrington, *Biographical Index of East India Company Maritime Service Officers, 1600–1834,* London, 1999, p. 460). Of the five principal owners of the vessel three were members of the Larkins family (Farrington, *Catalogue*, p. 432). See E.W. Bovill in *Mariner's Mirror*: 'Some Chronicles of the Larkins Family, The Convict Ship 1792', 40, 2, pp. 120–7; 'Some Chronicles of the Larkins Family, The Wreck of the *Halsewell*, 1786', 40, 4, pp. 251–7; 'Some Chronicles of the Larkins Family, The Loss of the *Warren Hastings*, 1806', 42, 3, pp. 188–200.

6 William Miller, born 23 January 1795, Edinburgh. Attended the Military Seminary at Addiscombe

in 1809, promoted to lieutenant 1811, captain 1818 and fought in the Mahratta War of 1817–19. From April 1820 he was Brigade-major of Artillery, the Director of the Depot of Instruction, 1822–31, and Officer-in-Command of the Northern Division from 1835. He died on 14 May 1836 at Mahableshwar having become Judge Advocate General that year (E. Dodwell and J.S. Miles, *Alphabetical List of the Officers of the Indian Army*, London, 1838; F.W.M., Spring, *The Bombay Artillery: List of Officers who have Served in the Regiment of Bombay Artillery*, London, 1902, p. 81).

7   Charles Butler, born 1786, Gamston, Notts; EIC Service 1801–21, died 30 March 1822 (Farrington, *Biographical Index*, p. 121).

8   John Fenn, born 1796, London; EIC Service 1812–32, serving on the *Marquis Camden* between 1816 and 1832. Killed 1 July 1832 by a shot fired from EIC Schooner *Royal Tiger* (*ibid.*, p. 265).

9   Gilson Reeves Fox, born 1797, Bow, Middlesex; served RN six years, EIC Service 1816–30; captain: *Marquis Camden* 1825–26; *Bengal Merchant* 1829–30 (*ibid.*, p. 280).

10   Thomas Andrew Hutchinson, born 1800, England, EIC Service 1815–24 (*ibid.*, p. 406).

11   Horatio M. Hogarth, EIC Service 1820–27 (*ibid.*, p. 384).

12   James Veitch, graduated Edinburgh University 1808 (*List of the Graduates in Medicine in the University of Edinburgh, 1705–1866*, Edinburgh, 1867, p. 40).

13   David Scott, *Marquis Camden* 1820–21; *Sir David Scott* 1825–26 and 1827–28 (Farrington, *Biographical Index*, p. 698).

14   Stoddart Drysdale; EIC Service 1816–21 (*ibid.*, p. 232).

15   Miller is mistaken. The *AJ*, XI, No. 62, p. 208, shows that Captain Falconer, Mr Beck, cadet, and Mr W. Hodges of the Bombay Marine were passengers on this voyage. Those mentioned in the text took passage subsequently (see Chapter 6).

16   Samuel John Crofts Falconer, born 14 December 1793, Bombay Artillery; Addiscombe 1809–11, lieutenant fire-worker 1811, lieutenant 1816, captain 1818, died 20 August 1835 at Ahmedabad (Spring, *Bombay Artillery*, p. 82).

17   Arrived off Portsmouth 23 January 1821 (Farrington, *Catalogue*, pp. 432–3).

18   The ship's log states: '18 May at 6 pm punished Thos Lynch with 7 doz lashes, Jno Dugen, Jno Sutherland and W. Knowlson 6 doz lashes for mutiny. Confined the prisoners in irons. Punished P. Earl with 1 doz lashes for not coming aft where the hands were called out' (BL, L/MAR/B/58D). There is an account of this flogging in a letter to *Shipping and Mercantile Gazette*, 4 June 1875, from A.B., dated Hornsey, 27 May 1875. John Miller was almost certainly the author; he was living in Hornsey at this date.

19   *Bombay Merchant*, ship, 433 tons, built Hull 1816, J. Clarkson master (*LR*, 1821).

20   Arrived 21 May 1821 (Farrington, *Catalogue*, p. 432; *LL*, 28 Sep. 1821).

21   William Miller married Catherine Sarah Russell, daughter of James Graves Russell of Clifton House, Gloucestershire, on 13 November 1822 (*AJ*, XV, No. 90, p. 636).

22   According to the ship's log Moseley is Thomas Molyneaux who died at Bombay 10 June 1821 (BL, L/MAR/B/58D).

23   For accounts of the cholera epidemic in Asia and the Middle East see frequent articles in the *Asiatic Journals* during the early 1820s. The official return for cholera deaths between 23–28 May 1821 was 235 (*AJ*, XII, 71, p. 513).

24   Departed 29 July 1821 (*ibid.*, XIII, 74, p. 193).

25   A very similar, and maybe the same, incident is recorded in the ship's log on 6–7 May (BL, L/MAR/B/58D).

REFERENCES

CHAPTER 4

1 Arrived 14 August 1821 (A. Farrington, *Catalogue of East India Company Ships 'Journals and Logs, 1600–1834,* London, 1999, pp. 432–3).

2 *Topaze*, 1060 tons, formerly French *l'Etoile*, built Nantes 1814, taken by *Hebrus* 1814 (D. Lyon, *The Sailing Navy List: All the Ships of the Royal Navy Built, Purchased and Captured, 1688–1860*, London, 1993, p. 273). Charles Richardson, knighted 1841 and Vice-Admiral of the White 1849 (W.R. O'Byrne, *Naval Biographical Dictionary*, London, 1849, pp. 974–5).

3 Henry Blackwood (1770–1832), Commander-in-Chief in the East Indies, 1819–22 (*DNB*, II, pp. 612–4).

4 East India House, Leadenhall Street, built by Richard Jupp between 1796–9, was the headquarters of the Company (A. Farrington, *Trading Places: the East India Company and Asia, 1600–1834*, London, 2002, p. 110).

5 Arrived Singapore on 6 September and sailed on the 8th; arrived Whampoa 4 October (Farrington, *Catalogue*, pp. 432–3).

6 For more details about the *Merope's* opium smuggling activities see: H.B. Morse, *Chronicles of the East India Company Trading to China, 1635–1834*, Oxford, 1926, IV, *passim*; and M. Greenberg, *British Trade and the Opening of China, 1800–1842*, New York and London, 1979, Ch. 5.

7 James Matheson, born Lairg, Sutherland, in 1786. An independent agent for Country traders, he went into partnership with the surgeon and shipowner William Jardine (1784–1843), the two men taking control of the well established firm of Cox and Beale in 1829. Three years later they established the firm of Jardine, Matheson and Company. Matheson died in 1898 (J. and J. Keay, eds, *Collins Encyclopaedia of Scotland*, London, 1994, p. 558; S. Leiper, *Precious Cargo: Scots and the China Trade,* Edinburgh, 1997, pp. 39–47). For the history of the Company see M. Keswick, ed., *The Thistle and the Jade*, London, 1982.

8 George Parkyns became lieutenant in 1811 and died 1844 (D. Syrett and R.L. DiNardo, eds, *Commissioned Sea Officers of the Royal Navy, 1660–1815*, Aldershot, 1994, p. 347).

9 Sir James Brabazon Urmston, 1785–1850, President of the Select Committee, Canton, knighted 1820 (Sir H.E.A. Cotton, *The East Indiamen: the East India Company's Maritime Service, London*, 1949, p. 175).

10 The Typan was the HEIC's chief supercargo and most senior civil servant in Canton.

11 *General Harris*, ship, 1200 tons, George Welstead, built by Brent at Rotherhithe and launched in 1812. (Farrington, *Catalogue*, pp. 265–6).

12 The official report on *Topaze* incident from the Committee at the Canton Factory, 27 February 1822, to the Governor General at Fort William is reproduced in H.B. Morse, *Chronicles of the East India Company*, IV, pp. 27–30, which also includes Peter Auber's account, pp. 31–41. See also G.S. Graham, *The China Station, War and Diplomacy, 1830–1860*, Oxford, 1978, pp. 15–16.

CHAPTER 5

1 Arrived 15 April 1822 (A. Farrington, *Catalogue of East India Company Ships 'Journals and Logs,1600–1834*, London, 1999, pp. 432–3).

2 *Samarang*, ship, 406 tons, Captain Gover, taken as a prize off Java in 1812 and a receiving vessel for opium 1822–24; *Eugenia*, 350-400 tons, of Calcutta from 1820; *Quiroga* or *Quirogo* : a

Spanish brig (A. Bulley, *The Bombay Country Ships, 1790–1833*, Richmond, 2000, p. 162; H.B. Morse, *Chronicles of the East India Company Trading to China, 1635–1834*, Oxford, IV, 1926, p. 61, 77; *LR,* 1822).

3   'An Adventure in China', *Leisure Hour,* X, 1861, pp. 69–71 (see Appendix).

4   Charles Butler died on 30 March 1822 (A. Farrington, *Biographical Index of East India Company Maritime Service Offices, 1600–1834,* London, 1999, p. 121).

5   *Sir David Scott,* ship, 1342 tons, built 1821 by Bailey of Ipswich (Farrington, *Catalogue,* pp. 604–5).

6   William Hunter, born 28 May 1784, Scotland, EIC Service 1800–22; captain *Coromandel* 1819–20, *Sir David Scott* 1821–22 (Farrington, *Biographical Index,* p. 404).

7   Nathaniel Grant, graduated Edinburgh University 1814, EIC Service 1815–24 (*ibid.,* p. 321; *List of Graduates in Medicine in the University of Edinburgh, 1705–1866,* Edinburgh, 1867, p. 48).

8   On 1 November 1822 at 9.30 pm a report reached the factories that a great fire was raging about a mile and a half to the north. The British factory fire engines were unable to obtain water and the wind drove the fire rapidly towards the factories. The Chinese authorities failed to create a fire break by demolishing houses. The losses to both foreign traders and Chinese were enormous: about 7,000 shops were destroyed and many warehouses (H.B. Morse,*Chronicles of the East India Company Trading to China, 1635–1834,* Oxford, 1926, IV, pp. 64–6).

9   Departed 27 November 1822; arrived Downs 17 April 1823 (Farrington, *Catalogue,* p. 433).

CHAPTER 6

1   Miller's future wife was Janet (Jessie) Adamson, born 16 February 1813, daughter of Alexander Adamson of Burnside, near St Andrews, and his wife Rachel Melvil (St Andrews Old Parochial Registers, Baptisms, 1813, 454/4). Two of her brothers, John and Robert, were distinguished pioneers in the art of photography (see D. Bruce, ed., *Sun Pictures: the Hill-Adamson Callotypes,* London, 1973; C. Ford and R. Strong, eds, *The Hill / Adamson Collection: An Early Victorian Album,* London, 1974).

2   William Morgan, born 29 February 1785, St Ives, Cornwall, EIC Service 1800–24, drowned Whampoa 18 November 1824 (A. Farrington, *Biographical Index of East India Company Maritime Service Officers, 1600–1834,* London, 1999, p. 559).

3   Jackson Sparrow, born 14 October 1798, Heddington, Middlesex, EIC Service 1819–27 (*ibid.,* p. 738).

4   Anthony Forbes, born 15 August 1803, Ireland, EIC Service 1819–24, 'run' 10 August 1824 (*ibid.,* p. 275).

5   Paul Storr; this is the only known voyage with the EIC (*ibid.,* p. 756).

6   Dr Frederick Fowler, EIC surgeon 1819–24 (*ibid.,* p. 280).

7   Thomas Collingwood, EIC Service 1819–32, purser on the *Marquis Camden* 1823–32 (*ibid.,* p. 164).

8   Sailed from Gravesend 1 March 1824 (*AJ,* XVII, No. 100, p. 475).

9   At Cowes 23 March 1824 (A. Farrington, *Catalogue of East India Company Ships' Journals and Logs,1600–1834,* London, 1999, pp. 432–3). On page 15 above Miller incorrectly lists these passengers: Major Deschamps, Captain Riddock and Mr Taylor (They are listed for this voyage in the *AJ,* XVII, No. 100, p. 475). Henry R. Deschamps of the Bombay Army, died at Hythe 1829 (E. Dodwell and J.S. Miles, *Alphabetical List of the Officers of the Indian Army,* London, 1838);

almost certainly Thomas Riddock of the Country service (see A. Bulley, *The Bombay Country Ships: 1790–1833*, Richmond, 2000, p. 202); and John Taylor, Assistant Surgeon, Bombay Artillery, 1811, died 6 December 1821, Sheraz, Persia (F.W.M. Spring, *The Bombay Artillery: List of Officers who have Served in the Regiment of Bombay Artillery*, London, 1902, p. 118).

10 Arrived Bombay 23 June 1824 (Farrington, *Catalogue*, pp. 432–3).

11 Mountstuart Elphinstone (1799–1859), Governor of Bombay 1819–27 (*DNB*, VI, pp. 744–6).

12 Montgomerie Hamilton, born *c*.1781, Scotland, EIC Service 1797–1832; captain *Bombay* 1811–14, *Dunira* 1817–1832 (Farrington, *Biographical Index* , p. 345); *Dunira*, ship, 1325 tons, built by Wigram of Blackwall, 1817 (Farrington, *Catalogue*, pp. 189–90).

13 *Cambridge*, ship, 770 tons, built Bengal 1810 (*LR*, 1825); departed 11 August, arrived Gravesend 11 December 1824. 'Mr Fowler of the *Marquees* [*sic*] *Camden*' is listed amongst the passengers (*AJ*, XIX, No. 109, p. 107).

14 Alexander Manson, born 26 February 1793, Bombay Artillery; Addiscombe 1809–10, lieutenant fire-worker and lieutenant 1810, captain lieutenant 1816, captain 1818, major 1829, lieutenant-colonel 1833, brevet-colonel 1844, colonel 1849, died 23 February 1852 at Bombay (Spring, *The Bombay Artillery*, p. 80).

15 Arrived 24 September 1824 (Farrington, *Catalogue*, pp. 432–3).

16 James Walker, captain of the *Macqueen* (Farrington, *Biographical Index,* p. 816).

17 *Macqueen*, ship, 1333 tons, built by Brindley at Rochester, 1821 (Farrington, *Catalogue*, pp. 421–2).

18 *Earl of Balcarras*, ship, 1417 tons, Captain Peter Cameron, Company ship built Bombay, launched 1811 (*ibid.*, pp. 202–4).

19 *Castle Huntley*, ship, 1311 tons, built Bengal 1812, Captain Henry Andrews Drummond (*ibid.,* pp. 109–10).

20 *Lady Melville*, ship, 1263 tons, built by Wells, Blackwall, 1813 (*ibid.,* pp. 372–3), Richard Clifford, born 14 April 1788, Monthrath, Queens County, Ireland, EIC captain 1821–9 (Farrington, *Biographical Index,* p. 156).

21 Arrived in the Downs 10 May 1825 (Farrington, *Catalogue*, pp. 432–3); arrived Gravesend 12 May (*AJ*, XIX, No. 114, p. 867).

22 The duties of the Committee of Shipping included receiving tenders, signing charter parties and purchasing exports (C. Northcote Parkinson, *Trade in the Eastern Seas, 1793–1813*, London, 1966, p. 25).

23 Jerusalem and East India Coffee House, Cowper's Court, Cornhill, is described in the *Universal British Directory* 1791 as being 'frequented by gentlemen who are, or have been, in the service of the honourable East-India company, and by managers owners of ships employed in their service; also, by under-writers, policy and insurance brokers, and others, connected with the East-India trade. And to this coffee-house, and Lloyd's, are transmitted the earliest accounts of the departure, arrivals, or loss, of ships in the company's service, and of all important events that happen'.

24 Andrew Kedslie, surgeon on the *Dunira*, 1817–24 (Farrington, *Biographical Index*, p. 435).

CHAPTER 7

1   *Asia*, ship, 958 tons, built by Barnard, Deptford, 1811, three decks, length 149 ft 3 in, keel length

120 ft, breadth 38 ft 9 in, depth of hold 15 ft 1 in, between decks 6 ft 3 in, 6 ft 5 in; voyage journal (BL, India Office Records, India Office: Marine Records, L/MAR/B/24BB), ledger (BL, L/MAR/B/24AAA [1]), pay book (BL, L/MAR/B/24AAA [B]) (A. Farrington, *Catalogue of East India Company Ships' Journals and Logs*, London, 1999, pp. 35–6).

2   Thomas Frederick Balderston, born 28 December 1788, England, EIC Service 1802–28; captain *Asia* 1817–28 (A. Farrington, *Biographical Index of East India Company Maritime Service Officers, 1600–1834*, London, 1999, p. 37).

3   The *Asia* departed Deal 14 June 1826 (*AJ*, XXII, No. 127, p. 125).

4   Henry M. Sterndale, born 8 March 1795, England, EIC Service 1810–26 (Farrington, *Biographical Index*, p. 746).

5   2nd officer: Lionel Ripley Pearce, baptised 20 Oct. 1799, St Buryans, Penzance, Cornwall, EIC Service 1813–26 (*ibid.*, p. 611); 4th officer: G.M Abbott, born 13 May 1807, St Dunstan's Kent; EIC Service 1825–33 (*ibid.*, p. 1); surgeon: Stanley Sterndale (*ibid.*, p. 746); purser: Robert Guild (*ibid.*, p. 330).

6   Almost certainly Paul Marriott Wynch of the Bengal Civil Service who returned to India from home leave on 20 October 1826. At home on absentee allowance from 1834 and pensioned in England from 1836 (E. Dodwell, and J.S. Miles, *Alphabetical List of the Honourable East India Company's Bengal Civil Servants*, London, 1839, pp. 580–1).

7   Irwin Maling, entered Indian army 1799, major 1825 (E. Dodwell, and J.S. Miles, *Alphabetical List of the Officers of the Indian Army*, London, 1838, pp. 180–1).

8   Paul M. Wynch married Sophia M. Maling 30 December 1826 (*East-India Register and Directory, 1827, 2nd ed.*, p. 517).

9   Almost certainly Edward Cornwallis Wilmot, qualified as an East India Company writer in 1825 and died 24 December 1826 at Calcutta aged 19 (Dodwell and Miles, *Bengal Civil Servants*, pp. 570–1; *AJ*, XXIII, No. 138, p. 857).

10 Arrived 20 October 1826 (Farrington, *Catalogue*, pp. 35–6).

11 Probably James Grierson, graduate of University of Edinburgh, 1810 (*List of Graduates in Medicine in the University of Edinburgh*, *1705–1866*, Edinburgh, 1867).

12 At this time the Bengal Pilot Service had one steam vessel, the *Enterprise*, Captain J.H. Johnston (*East-India Register, 1827, 1st ed.*, p. 143).

13 Thomas Clarke (*ibid.*). A branch pilot was the holder of a Trinity House diploma, known as a branch (W.H. Smyth, *The Sailor's Word-book: an Alphabetical Digest of Nautical Terms*, London, 1867, pp. 128–9).

14 A passenger list with 23 names was published in the *AJ*, XXIV, No. 140, p. 269.

15 Arrived London 28 July 1827 (*ibid.*).

16 *Scotsman*, 4 April 1827: 'At Edinburgh on the 27th ult. Mrs Grace Miller wife of Andrew Miller, Esquire, Writer to the Signet, Depute Clerk of the Bills'. Miller's eldest sister was Janet, born Edinburgh 1797.

CHAPTER 8

1   *Eagle*,196 ton smack, Peter Allan master, built by Davy of Topsham for the Edinburgh, Glasgow

and Leith Shipping Company in 1814 and owned by the London, Leith, Edinburgh and Glasgow Shipping Company in 1828 (NAS, CE 57/11/1, Leith Register of Shipping, 12/1827, *Post Office Annual Directory*, Edinburgh, 1828–29).

2 Robert Pitcher, born 25 March 1786, Deptford, EIC Service 1802–28 (A. Farrington, *Biographical Index of East India Company Maritime Service Officers, 1600–1834*, London, 1999, p. 627).

3 Robert Renwick, graduated University of Edinburgh 1812 (*List of Graduates in Medicine in the University of Edinburgh, 1705–1866*, Edinburgh, 1867, p. 246).

4 William John Irwin, born 1806, Swansea, EIC Service 1821–32 (Farrington, *Biographical Index,* p. 412).

5 3rd officer: John Copling, born 13 March 1803, London, EIC Service 1817–30 (Farrington, *Biographical Index*, p. 173); 4th officer: George Abbott, as for the previous voyage.

6 This was the Cameronian Regiment's first deployment in India. The *Asia*, one of four troopships, sailed 23 May 1828 and the men were landed at Madras on 9 September (T. Carter, ed., *Historical Record of the Twenty-sixth or Cameronian Regiment*, London, 1867, pp. 165–6).

7 Waldron Kelly joined the Cameronians in 1828 and was cashiered in November 1830 (*ibid.*, p. 251).

8 Miller could be referring to Ensign James Gordon Campbell who was cashiered in India 29 December 1828. (E. Dodwell and J.S. Miles, *Alphabetical List of the Officers of the Indian Army*, London, 1838, Bengal Presidency, pp. 76–77).

9 Stewart Paxton, appointed writer 1819, at home on absentee allowance 1826, returned to India 21 September 1828, died 20 October 1830 Cawnpore (E. Dodwell and J.S. Miles, *Alphabetical List of the Honourable East India Company's Bengal Civil Servants*, London, 1839, pp. 386–7). His name and that of his wife are in the passenger list (*AJ*, XXV, No. 150, p. 840).

10 Twist: a hearty appetite (*OED*).

11 Pintado: a species of petrel, *Daption capensis*, also called Cape Pigeon (*ibid.*).

12 Mrs Colonel Thompson and a Miss Thompson are recorded in the passenger list (*AJ*, XXV, No. 150, p. 840).

13 Arrived Diamond Harbour, 23 September 1828 (A. Farrington, *Catalogue of East India Company Ships' Journals and Logs, 1600–1834*, London, 1999, p. 36).

14 Andrew Ramsay, born 6 May 1776, married 1800 Rachel daughter of James Cook of Rampore, Benares, died 2 April 1848. His brother George, ninth Earl of Dalhousie, was Colonel of the Cameronians between 1813 and 1838 and Commander-in-Chief, India, 1829–39 (J. Balfour Paul, *The Scots Peerage*, Edinburgh, 1906, p. 105).

15 In Tobias Smollett's *Roderick Random* Lt Tom Bowling RN, Roderick's uncle, ties up and flogs the brutal schoolmaster as revenge for the teacher's mistreatment of his nephew and classmates (see the *Everyman* edition, London, 1927, Ch. 5).

16 Burns met William Nicol through the freemasons in Edinburgh in 1786. During his second stay in the city (1787–88) Burns lodged with William Cruickshank. The verse is:

> 'O Willie brew'd a peck o'maut,
> And Rob and Allan cam to see;
> Three blyther hearts, that lee lang night,
> Ye wad na found in Christendie.'

(J. Kinsley, ed., *The Poems and Songs of Robert Burns*, Oxford, 1968, I, pp. 476–7).

17 Arrived Blackwall 21 May 1829 (Farrington, *Catalogue*, p. 36).

CHAPTER 9

1   *Portland*, ship, 38535/94 tons, built by Hilhouse Sons and Company, Bristol, 1822. Dimensions:
    keel 107 ft 5 in; breadth: 28 ft 4 in; between decks: 6 ft 1 in (G. E. Farr, ed., *Records of Bristol
    Ships, 1800–1838 Vessels Over 150 tons,* Bristol, 1950, p. 93).

2   The Australian Company commenced operations on 31 October 1822 with the objective of '. . .
    conveying and carrying of goods and passengers between Leith and the ports of Australia,
    comprehending New South Wales, and adjacent territories . . . with leave for the vessels of the
    Company to call, for the purpose of trade, at such intermediate ports and places as shall for the
    time be lawful . . .' (NAS, CS 46/June 21/1857, Reclaiming Note for the Australian Company of
    Edinburgh . . . in the Action against them at the instance of William Weymss, Contract of Co-
    partnery, article 4). The first shipping concern to operate a regular service between the United
    Kingdom and Australia, the Company was dissolved in October 1830 following bankruptcy. When
    Miller took command the *Portland* was being redeployed from the Australian to the India trade
    prior to her being sold (see M. Nix, *Portland: 'The Scotch Frigate'*, http://www.maritime-
    scotland.org.uk/VESSELS/portland.htm, 2003).

3   Robert Brown, the manager and a former shipping agent for the West India merchant James
    Ewing of Strathleven, was brother-in-law to James Wyld, an original or founding director.

4   Cleared 1 May, sailed 12 May 1830 (*LCL*, 4, 14 May 1830).

5   Reported at Deal 20 May (*ibid.* 25 May 1830).

6   Charles Baird Handyside, graduated in 1827 from Edinburgh University (*List of Graduates in
    Medicine in the University of Edinburgh, 1705–1866*, Edinburgh, 1867, pp. 171, 194). Appointed
    Assistant Surgeon, Bengal Establishment, 12 May 1830 (E. Dodwell, and J.S. Miles,
    Alphabetical List of the Medical Officers of the Indian Army, London, 1839, pp. 30–1).

7   Probably William Fuller Cumming, appointed Assistant Surgeon, Bengal Establishment, 2 June
    1828 (*ibid.*, pp. 14–15).

8   Arrived Bengal 9 October 1830 (*LCL*, 25 Feb. 1831).

9   Robert Hand (*East-India Register and Directory, 1830, 1st ed.*, p. 146).

10 Henry McKenzie of Buchanan and Co., merchants (*East-India Register and Directory, 1830, 2nd
    ed.*, p. 169).

11 There is a detailed description of St Andrew's Day celebrations in Calcutta in: 'A Griffin',*Sketches
    of Calcutta, or Notes of a Late Sojourn in the 'City of Palaces'*, Glasgow, 1843, pp. 166–9.

12 John Peter Grant of Rothiemurchus, 1774–1848, Chief Justice of Calcutta, died on passage
    home, buried Dean Cemetery, Edinburgh (*DNB*, VIII, p. 398).

13 The Buckinghamshire Regiment.

14 Assistant Surgeon R. McIsaac, appointed to the Presidency General Hospital, 17 November
    1830 (*AJ*, NS V, No. 2, p. 87). Died 25 December 1830, Madras (E. Dodwell, and J.S. Miles,
    Alphabetical List of the Medical Officers of the Indian Army, London, 1839, pp. 42–3).

15 Tumblehome: the extent to which the sides of a vessel slope inwards, diminishing its width at
    deck level.

16 *Alligator*, Atholl class, 499 tons, built Cochin, launched 1821 (D. Lyon, *The Sailing Navy List: All the
    Ships of the Royal Navy Built, Purchased and Captured, 1688–1860*, London, 1993, pp. 133–4).

17 Alexander Duff, 1806–1878, missionary in India, arrived Calcutta 1830 and established a school
    later known as Duff College (N.M. de S. Cameron, ed., *Dictionary of Scottish Church History*

REFERENCES

and Theology, Edinburgh, 1993, pp. 259–60).

18 All-a-taunt-o: a vessel having all her light and long spars aloft (W.H. Smyth, *The Sailor's Word-book: an Alphabetical Digest of Nautical Terms*, London, 1867, p. 675).

19 Miller mistakenly wrote the 12th Regiment.

20 Sailed 15 December 1830 (*AJ*, NS V, No. 2, pp. 88).

21 Reported St Helena 28 February 1831 (*LCL*, 3 May 1831).

22 *Reliance*, ship, 1416 tons, built by Wigram of Blackwall, launched 1827 (A. Farrington, *Catalogue of East India Company Ships', Journals and Logs, 1600–1834*, London, 1999, p. 555).

23 The surgeon of the *Reliance* was James Grant (*East-India Register and Directory, 1830, 1st ed.*, p. lxxiii).

24 Plantation House, the residence of Brigadier-General Charles Dallas, Governor St Helena 1828–36 (P. Gosse, *St Helena 1502–1938*, Oswestry, 1990, pp. 300, 423).

25 Arrived Deal 4 May 1831 (*AJ*, NS V, No. 2, p. 116).

26 Death notice in *The Scotsman*, 9 February 1831: 'At his house, 45 East Claremont Street, on 27 ult. Andrew Miller, Esq. W.S. Depute Clerk of the Bills.' The uncle was possibly Robert Miller, bookseller at 92 Princes Street, Edinburgh, who died 19 March 1831 (*Edinburgh Evening Courant*, 24 March 1831).

27 The *Portland's* purchaser, Captain William Ascough, made two voyages to Sydney: the first, with 178 males and 29 soldiers, departed Portsmouth on 27 Nov. 1832; the second, with just under 200 male convicts and a guard from the 21st Fusiliers, departed from Cork on 21 February 1833 (Nix, *Portland*; C. Bateson, *The Convict Ships, 1787–1868*, Glasgow, 1969 ed., pp. 59, 350–1, 388).

CHAPTER 10

1 *Countess Dunmore*, brig (first voyage), barque (second voyage), 230 tons, built Dunmore, Stirling, 1826. First registered Alloa 24 / 15 March 1826 and registered in London 6 / 4 Jan. 1833, John Miller master. Dimensions: keel length 90.4 ft; breadth 24.3 ft; 6.1 ft between decks. James Scott's address was Saint Helen's Place, Bishopgate's Street, City of London (NA, BT 107, London Register of Shipping).

2 Departed from Deal 13 January 1832 (*AJ*, NS VII, No. 26, p. 119).

3 Arrived Mauritius 28 April 1832 (*LL*, 10 Aug. 1832).

4 Colonel G.J. Hall, of the 99th Lanarkshire Regiment, and Captain John Weir of the 29th, Worcestershire Regiment (*Army List*, Dec. 1831).

5 *Talbot*, 500 tons, 6th rate, 28-gun sloop, built Pembroke Dock 1824 (D. Lyon, *The Sailing Navy List: All the Ships of the Royal Navy Built, Purchased and Captured , 1688–1860*, London, 1993, p. 133).

6 *Paul et Virginie*, a very popular romantic novel by the Abbè Bernardin de Saint-Pierre, published in 1788 and based on the wreck of the *St Geran* in 1745. For a description of the tombs see F.P. Flemyng, *Mauritius, or the Isle of France*, London, 1862, p. 134.

7 Monsieur Fillifay made his dawn observations from the signal station on Long Mountain. He looked up towards the clear sky, seeing inverted images of vessels (*ibid.*, p. 117–9).

8 William Norton Taylor, born 24 October 1798, Flushing near Falmouth. Commander 1841 and

Coastguard service 1841–48 (W.R. O'Byrne, *Naval Biographical Dictionary*, London, 1849, pp. 1163–4). On this particular feat see W.N. Taylor, 'Account of the Ascent of Peter Botte Mountain (Mauritius) on 7th September 1832', in *London Geographical Journal*, III, p. 99.

9 Departed Mauritius 31 May 1832 (*AJ*, NS IX, No. 35, p. 150).

10 Arrived Gravesend 4 October 1832 (*ibid.*).

CHAPTER 11

1 'Ship and Insurance Brokers and Wine and Spirit Merchants', of 33 Mark Lane, London (*Post Office London Directory*, 1836).

2 Sailed from Deal for Van Diemen's Land 19 May 1833 (*AJ*, NS XI, No. 43, p. 201).

3 The passengers were: 'Miss Tayspill, Miss Clarke, Messrs Forster, Laderwig, Rudkin, and Master Thomas Dowling, Mrs Plummer, Mr and Mrs Bullock, William Emery & 2 children (O'Neils)' (*Launceston Advertiser*, 31 Oct. 1833).

4 On 6 November 1833 Miss Eliza Tayspill married Henry Dowling, the editor and publisher of the *Launceston Advertiser* (*ABD*, I, pp. 316–7).

5 HMS *Spartiate*, the former French prize *La Spartiate*, captured at the Battle of Aboukir Bay, 1798 (D. Lyon, *The Sailing Navy List: All the Ships of the Royal Navy Built, Purchased and Captured, 1688–1860*, London, 1993, p. 237).

6 Michael Seymour, born 1768, joined the Royal Navy in 1780. In 1832 he became Commander-in-Chief South America. He sailed February 1833 for Rio where he died of a fever in the following year (*DNB*, XVII, pp. 1262–4).

7 Pedro II became Emperor in 1831 aged five. Crowned 1841 and personally ruled from 1847 until 1889 (G. Pendle, *A History of Latin America*, Harmondsworth, 1969, pp. 150–6).

8 *Samarang*, Atholl class, 500 tons, built Cochin, launched 1822 (Lyon, *Sailing Navy List*, pp.133–4).

9 Charles Henry Paget (1806–45) joined the Royal Navy in 1819 and commanded *Samarang* in South America between 1831 and 1835 (W.R. O'Byrne, *Naval Biographical Dictionary*, London, 1849, pp. 849–50).

10 John Grant joined the Royal Navy 1806, first lieutenant of *Spartiate* from 18 Oct. 1832 (*ibid*, pp. 422–3).

11 Hobart Tait, born 23 January 1793, joined Royal Navy 1806, commander of *Spartiate* from 1832 and acting senior officer in South America on Admiral Seymour's death (*ibid.*, p. 1155).

12 The old lighthouse on Low Head was commenced in 1832 and completed 10 December 1833 (*The Cyclopedia of Tasmania*, Hobart, [1899?], p. 22).

13 James Reid of Richmond Hill, near Sidmouth (J.G. Branagan, *The Historic Tamar Valley: its People, Places and Shipping, 1798–1990*, Launceston, 1991, p. 70).

14 Pearson Foote was commissioned in the Royal Navy on 22 December 1827 (O'Byrne, *Naval Biographical Dictionary*, p. 368).

CHAPTER 12

1   Patricious William Welsh of Dublin arrived Launceston in 1829. Employed as chief constable, poundkeeper and inspector of distilleries before establishing himself as a 'shipping and commission salesman' at King's Wharf. In 1832 he married Margaret, eldest daughter of George Allan of Allan Vale (Launceston Library, Tasmania, Whitfield index). For background information useful in understanding Miller's experiences in Tasmania see B. Dyster, 'The Port of Launceston before 1851', *Great Circle*, 3, 2, Oct 1981, pp. 103–24.

2   The cargo included an 'elegant four-wheeled carriage', a 'strong-built gig' and two whale boats with 'oars and sails', as well as soap, boots and shoes, clothes, etc. (*Launceston Advertiser*, 7 Nov. 1833).

3   Samuel Dugdale, baptised Dissenters' Congregation, Exeter, Devon, 21 January 1787. EIC Service 1808–13 (A. Farrington, *Biographical Index of East India Company Maritime Service Officers, 1600–1834*, London, 1999, p. 233).

4   Andrew Barclay, bap. 28 June 1759, Kembock, Fife. EIC Service 1784–1810. Arrived Van Diemen's Land 1816. Became a supplier of meat to the Commissariat and by 1828 considered largest owner of good land on the island. Died 1839 (*ibid.*, p. 41; *ADB*, I, pp. 56–7).

5   A convict still under sentence assigned as a servant to a private household.

6   William Page Ashburner, mayor of Bombay 1824 (*AJ*, XVIII, No. 103, p. 83), appointed justice of the peace in Van Diemen's Land 1828 (*HTG*, 19 July 1828).

7   The four bushrangers were W. Ward, S. Newman, John Buchan and Thomas Dawson. They robbed Dr Browne at about 9 pm on 20 December 1833 after tapping on the door which was opened by Dr Browne's younger brother. Because Mrs Browne was unwell after the birth of a daughter two days before, the bushrangers were asked to go about their business quietly. They did so, at times on tip-toe! Dr Browne promised to assist them if they gave themselves up, and it appears they wrote at least one letter offering to do this, but were unable to deliver it to him (W.B. Dean, *Notorious Bushrangers of Tasmania*, Launceston, 1891, pp. 85–90).

8   The four bushrangers were captured at the Wool Pack near Auburn on 29 June 1834 by a constable called Dixon and a small party of volunteers after a tip-off, and taken to the police magistrate at Campbell Town. They were hanged at Launceston in March 1835, although Buchan 'received a respite' due to a mistake in the name on the warrant (*ibid.*).

9   The *Portland*, Captain Coghill, was lost 17 miles to the eastward of George Town Heads. A baby and the ship's carpenter died. The wreck was advertised to be sold by auction on the 16 October and those articles saved 'more or less damaged' on the 19th (*Launceston Advertiser*, 3, 10, 17 Oct. 1833).

10 Charles Inches graduated from the University of Edinburgh 1829 (*List of Graduates in Medicine in the University of Edinburgh, 1705–1866*, Edinburgh, 1867, p. 203).

11 James Ward (*The Cyclopedia of Tasmania*, Hobart, 1899?, p. 23).

12 Reported 11 July 1834 off Eastbourne (*AJ*, NS XIV, No. 56, p. 308).

CHAPTER 13

1   The death of Miller's eldest sister Janet was announced in *The Scotsman*, 15 October 1834. His youngest sister was Catharine.
2   Miller was ranked second mate and his pension commenced 22 April 1834. The sum is confirmed in Parliamentary Papers, 1835 (23) XXXIX, 73, Proceedings of the Court of Proprietors Concerning Compensations, Superannuations, Allowances, etc.: List 1–5.
3   Robert Scott, born 22 June 1801, Ecclesgrieg, Kincardine. EIC Service 1815–32; captain, *Vansittart* 1828–32 (A. Farrington, *Biographical Index of East India Company Maritime Service Officers, 1600–1834*, London, 1999, p. 701).
4   The *Abercrombie Robinson*, ship, 1331 tons, built by Wigram, Blackwall, launched 1825. Three decks; length 165 ft 10 in, keel 133 ft 4 in, breadth 43 ft 33/4 in, hold 17 ft 2 in, between decks 6 ft 8 in and 6 ft 4 in (A. Farrington, *Catalogue of East India Company Ships' Journals and Logs, 1600–1834,* London, 1999, p. 1). Registered London 925 / 16 Nov. 1825; 386 / 23 Dec. 1834; 425/1840 (NA, BT 107, London Register of Shipping).
5   Reported sailed from Portsmouth 15 March 1835 (*AJ*, NS XVI, No. 64, p. 302).
6   Thomas Pattle, Lieutenant Colonel, 1st King's Dragoon Guards, 1859–68. In 1835 he was a lieutenant in the 16th Lancers (J. O'Donnell, *1st King's Dragoon Guards, 1685–1912*, London, 1913, p. 24; *AJ*, NS XVI, No. 63, p. 215). Sir William Grey, 1818–1878, Lieutenant Governor of Bengal, 1867–71 (*DNB*, VIII, pp. 659–61).
7   Arrived Hooghly 21 July 1835 (*AJ*, NS IXX, No. 73, p. 38).
8   Departed Saugor 20 September 1835 and arrived Singapore six days later (*ibid.*, No. 75, pp. 205, 210).
9   *George the Fourth*, ship, 1329 tons, a former EIC vessel built by Pitcher, launched 1825. Owned by J. Nicholson and Co., trading to Madras, Bengal and China (Farrington, *Catalogue*, p. 272; *AJ*, NS XV, No. 60, p. 243). George Waugh, born 1789, Rotherhithe, London, EIC Service 1804–30; captain *Protector* 1827–30 (Farrington, *Biographical Index* , p. 831).
10 Arrived 8 December 1835 (*AJ*, NS IXX, No. 76, p. 305).
11 Departed China 30 January (*ibid.*, NS XX, No. 79, p. 203).
12 Reported Deal 6 June 1836 (*ibid.*).
13 The following announcement appeared in *The Scotsman* on 25 August 1836: 'At Burnside, near St Andrews, on the 22nd inst. by the Rev. Dr Buist, Mr John Miller of the Hon. East India Company's late Sea Service, to Jessie, second daughter of Alexander Adamson, esq., of Burnside'.

CHAPTER 14

1   Thomas Andrew Hutchinson, fourth mate on *Marquis Camden*, 1820–21 (A. Farrington, *Biographical Index of East India Company Maritime Service Officers, 1600–1834*, London, 1999, p. 406).
2   *Black Joke*, brig, 219 tons old measure, length 88 ft 6 in, breadth 24 ft 6 in, depth of hold 7 ft 9 in; with figurehead. Formerly the *Esperança*, she was condemned as a slaver on 2 November and registered 9 / 28 November 1836 at Sierra Leone in the name of John Hamilton, merchant. She

was registered *de novo* 295 / 9 August 1837 at London by Miller and at Launceston 4 / 22 April 1838. Her tonnage was given as 113.6 tons, new measure. The bill of sale dated 24 June 1837 from John Hamilton, Sierra Leone merchant, to John Miller gives Miller's address as Goodge Street, Tottenham Court Road, Middlesex (R. Parsons, *Ships of Australia and New Zealand before 1850*, Magill, 1983, I, p. 23; NA, BT 107, London Register of Shipping).

3   Probably Edward Luckie of Luckie Brothers, 14 Birchin Lane, London, shipping agents (*Post Office London Directory*, 1839). *LL* 20 September 1837 states that they were the agents for the *Black Joke*.

4   Reported sailed from Deal 22 September 1837 (*AJ*, NS XXIV, No. 94, p. 122).

5   *Adelaide*, ship, 640 tons, built Calcutta 1832 and owned by Baring Bros., London (*LR*, 1836). Departed Bengal 2 September 1837, bound for England and reported off Hastings 19 Feb. 1838 (*AJ*, NS XXV, No. 99, p. 197).

6   Robert D. Guthrie, EIC Service, first mate on the *Ganges* 1828–29 (Farrington, *Biographical Index*, p. 332).

7   Arrived 7 December 1837 (*AJ*, NS XXV, No. 99, p. 190).

8   For a description of Port Elizabeth and the difficulties of landing there see E.E. Napier, *Excursions in Southern Africa, Including a History of the Cape Colony*, London, 1849, pp. 283–4, 300–8.

9   A similar excursion from Port Elizabeth to Uitenhage is described in Napier's *Excursions*, pp. 290–2.

10 A submerged reef with about six feet of water on it surrounded by heavy breakers near Robben or Penguin Island.

11 The *Abercrombie Robinson* was carrying contingents of the 27th and 91st regiments and Cape Mounted Rifles, with women and children, when she was wrecked on 28 August 1842, 33° 54.90 S and 18° 27.94 E. There was no loss of life. The ship's bell is in the Dutch Reformed Church, Caledon (M. Turner, *Shipwrecks and Salvage in South Africa, 1505 to the Present*, Cape Town, 1988, p. 147). For a little light relief see William McGonagall's poem 'The Wreck of the *Abercrombie Robinson*'.

12 The convict ship *Waterloo*, Ager master, had sailed from Sheerness on 1 June 1842: 143 prisoners, 14 crew, 15 soldiers of the 99th Regiment and 18 women and children died (C. Bateson, *The Convict Ships, 1787–1868*, Glasgow, 1969 ed., pp. 283–90).

CHAPTER 15

1   Edward M. Orr, Bengal Army. He and his wife left Calcutta on 15 November 1837 for London via the Cape on board the *Perfect* and arrived Portsmouth 10 April 1838 (*AJ*, NS XXVI, No. 101, p. 56).

2   There is some uncertainty about the departure date from Table Bay: the *Sydney Gazette* (18 March 1838) gives 26 December 1837, the *AJ* (NS XVI, No. 101, p. 53) 25 January 1838; and I.H. Nicholson, *Shipping Arrivals and Departures: Sydney 1826–40*, Canberra, 1984, p. 186) 22 January 1838. The *Sydney Gazette* of 20 March 1838 gives the *Black Joke's* arrival as 17 March 1838.

3   Miller arrived on St Patrick's Day when a big regatta was organised. The jubilee celebrations were held earlier, on 26 January, now Australia Day.

4   Cook wrote in his journal: '... at Noon we were by observation in the Latitude of 38° 50' about 2 or

3 miles from the land and abreast of a Bay or Harbour wherein the apperd to be safe anchorage which I call'd Port Jackson. It lies 3 leag^S to the northward of Botany Bay' (J.C. Beaglehole, ed., *Journals of Captain Cook*, London 1999, p. 130). The harbour was named after Sir George Jackson, Secretary to the Admiralty.

5   The *Sydney Gazette* of 22 March 1838 reported: 'For Hobart Town to sail in fourteen days the first class brig *Black Joke*, 200 tons, John Miller, commander, will commence loading in 4 days and sail positively on 1st April. The sailing of this vessel and her excellent accommodations, render her a most eligible opportunity. For freight and passage apply to Lamb & Parbury, Darling Harbour, 19th March 1838'. From 24 March the advertisement was changed to read Launceston instead of Hobart Town.

6   Sailed 8 April 1838 (Nicholson, *Shipping Arrivals and Departures: Sydney*, p. 186).

7   HMS *Conway*, Tyne class, 6th rate, 28 guns, 633 tons, built Chatham Dockyard, launched 1832 (D. Lyon, *The Sailing Navy List: All the Ships of the Royal Navy Built, Purchased and Captured, 1688–1860*, London, 1993, pp. 134–5).

8   Charles Ramsay Drinkwater Bethune, born 27 December 1802. Joined Royal Navy 1815; 9 September 1836 appointed to *Conway* as Senior Officer New South Wales, then Bengal. Fought in China during Opium War 1840–42 (W.R. O'Byrne, *Naval Biographical Dictionary*, London, 1849, p. 77).

9   J. Waterland became a pilot in 1835 and was one of five pilots when the Pilotage Department was established as part of the new Launceston Marine Board in 1858 (R.A. Ferrall, *The Story of the Port of Launceston*, Launceston, 1983, pp. 16–17).

10 Arrived 16 April 1838 (*Cornwall Chronicle*, 21 April 1838).

11 Departed 28 April 1838 (I.H. Nicholson, *Shipping Arrivals and Departures: Tasmania, 2, 1834–1842*, Canberra, 1985, p. 109).

12 Miller is referring to the *Lady Emma*, ex HMS *Philomel*, built Portsmouth Dockyard and launched 1823, sold by Royal Navy and registered London 210 / 1833. Registered Launceston 1 / April 1838, owners J. and J. Raven (R. Parsons, *Ships of Australia and New Zealand before 1850*, Magill, 1983, II, p. 2). Her master from London to Adelaide was John Witherden Hurst (R.T. Sexton, *Shipping Arrivals and Departures, South Australia, 1627–1850: a Guide for Genealogists and Maritime Historians*, Ridgehaven, South Australia, 1990, p. 33).

13 Arrived 17 May 1838 (*ibid.*, p. 36).

14 The new colony was proclaimed 28 December 1836.

15 Sir John Hindmarsh (1785–1860), Royal Navy 1793–1832. Appointed first governor of the new colony of South Australia 1835 (*ADB*, I, pp. 538–41).

16 Thomas Lipson, Royal Navy 1793–1819, retired with rank of Commander. Arrived South Australia with family in 1836. First harbour master of Adelaide (O'Byrne, *Biographical Dictionary*, pp. 660–1; D. Day, *Smugglers and Sailors: the Customs History of Australia 1788–1901*, Canberra, 1993 rep., pp. 364–5).

17 Cleared at Adelaide for Launceston 24 May 1838 (Sexton, *Shipping Arrivals and Departures, South Australia,*. p. 36).

18 Arrived 1 June 1838 (Nicholson,*Shipping Arrivals and Departures: Tasmania, 2*, p. 112).

19 The chief officer was called Freeman (*Launceston Advertiser*, July-August 1838).

20 Departed for Sydney 12 July 1838 and returned to Launceston 15 Aug. Prior to this Freeman

had made a voyage to Port Phillip (Nicholson, *Shipping Arrivals and Departures: Tasmania*, 2, pp. 112–3, 116).

21 Haddon Cottage, Patterson's Plains Road, now Elphin Road.

22 The Dry family lived at Elphin. Richard Dry Snr (1771–1843), born near Wexford, was transported as a convict in 1800 after involvement in the Irish Rebellion of 1798. Pardoned, he eventually became a leading agriculturalist in Van Diemen's Land. Richard Dry Jnr, born 1815 at Elphin, became the eighth premier of Tasmania and was knighted in 1859 (*ADB*, I, pp. 328–9; *The Cyclopaedia of Tasmania*, Hobart, 1899?, I, p. 57).

23 Arrived Launceston from Sydney 15 August 1838 under the command of Freeman who was replaced there by James Harding. The vessel departed for Sydney about 26 August (Nicholson, *Shipping Arrivals and Departure: Tasmania*, 2, p. 116).

24 Michael Bates had a chemist shop in Brisbane Street in 1835 (*Launceston Advertiser*, 28 May 1835).

25 The Hentys became a prominent family in Van Diemen's Land. Edward and Francis Henty arrived in the early 1830s and engaged in whaling until 1834 when they moved to Victoria, establishing successful sheep stations. William Henty, a solicitor, settled in Launceston in 1837 and Charles S. Henty became manager of the town's Cornwall Bank in 1833 (M. Bassett, *The Hentys: an Australian Colonial Tapestry*, Melbourne, 1962, *passim*; *Cyclopaedia of Tasmania*, p. 14).

26 *Henry*, William Walmsley master, barque, 419 tons, reported arrived Sydney from London 24 January 1840 and departed for Valparaiso, 17 March (Nicholson, *Shipping Arrivals and Departures: Sydney*, 2, p. 233).

27 The Collier story is referred to in Bassett, *The Hentys*, pp. 444–7.

CHAPTER 16

1 Archibald Thomas' birth was announced in the *Cornwall Chronicle*, 30 March 1839. He served in the Royal Navy and the merchant service, rising to command with the Liverpool firm of Messrs Lamport. From 1881 until 1903 he was the captain of the trading ship HMS *Conway* (J. Masefield, *The Conway*, London, 1953, 'The cadet ship *Conway*', Shipping, VI, No. 36, pp. 1834–43).

2 The cottage was advertised in the *Cornwall Chronicle*, 4 May 1839, and described as having: 'Six rooms, with a kitchen, pantry, etc., also 3½ acres of land attached'.

3 Departed 25 June 1839 (I.H. Nicholson, *Shipping Arrivals and Departures: Tasmania*, 2, *1834–1842*, Canberra, 1985, p. 138).

4 George Ashburner, ranked ensign in the 8th Native infantry, 24 July 1839 (*AJ*, NS, XXXI, No. 121, p. 82).

5 The Right Reverend Thomas Carr, 1788–1859, Bishop of Bombay 1837–51 (C.E. Buckland, *Dictionary of Indian Biography*, London, 1906, p. 74).

6 Departed Sydney for China 7 July 1839 (I.H. Nicholson, *Shipping Arrivals and Departures: Sydney 1826–40*, Canberra, 1984, II, p. 218).

7 G.G. Chisholm's *Longman's Gazetteer of the World* (London, 1895) describes the Torres Strait as 'one mass of shoals, reefs and islands, the principal of which are Prince of Wales and Clarence Islands'.

8 Between Whitsunday Island and the coast of Queensland.

9 *Royal Saxon*, ship, 510 tons, Captain Towns, reported London loading for New South Wales, Oct. 1838. The vessel was jointly owned with Robert Brooks. Robert Towns established wide commercial connections including Jardine, Matheson and Co. and John Burd, a rice exporter on Lombok and Bali (see F. Broeze, *Mr Brooks and the Australian Trade: Imperial Business in the Nineteenth Century*, Carlton, Victoria, 1993, *passim*). Arrived Sydney 31 March 1839; departed for Manilla and India 6 June (*AJ*, NS, XXVII, No. 106, 126; Nicholson, *Shipping Arrivals and Departures, Sydney*, 2, p. 212).

10 Arrived 22 August 1839 and departed for Macao 27 August (*Sydney Gazette*, 10 January 1840).

11 Hypothecation: a loan against security – on the cargo in this case.

12 Following the break up of the East India Company's China monopoly in 1833 a relatively stable commercial system built up over a long period was overthrown, increasing tensions. In particular, opium smuggling, used by the British to finance their legal trade, strained relations. In 1837 the Chinese authorities tried to stamp it out, leading to a series of incidents culminating in August 1839 in the evacuation of the British community to Hong Kong. Hostilities, known as the first Opium War, broke out in the following year (see G.S. Graham, *The China Station: War and Diplomacy, 1830–1860*, Oxford, 1978).

13 Arrived Hong Kong from Singapore and Launceston 20 September 1839 (*LL*, 1 Feb. 1840).

14 Charles Elliot, born 1801. Joined RN 1815, at battle Algiers 1816, captain 18 August Accompanied Lord Napier to China, 1834, HM. Plenipotentiary in China, 1838, during the Opium Wars (W.R. O'Byrne, *Naval Biographical Dictionary,* London, 1849, p. 332; Graham, *China Station,* p. 73).

15 Interestingly, the two vessels were similarly confused by A.B. Lubbock in *The Opium Clippers*, Glasgow, 1933, pp. 169–71. The schooner incident occurred on 17 August 1839 (see *AJ*, NS XXXI, No. 122, p. 143).

16 *Scaleby Castle,* former EIC ship, 1242 tons, built Bombay, launched 1798, sold to Henry Templer 6 August 1834 (A. Farrington, *Catalogue of East India Company Ships' Journals and Logs, 1600–1834*, London, 1999, pp. 593–4).

17 *Volage*, 6th rate, 521 tons, built Portsmouth Dockyard, launched 1825. *Hyacinth*, Favourite class, sloop, 429 tons, built Plymouth Dockyard, launched 1829 (D. Lyon, *The Sailing Navy List: All the Ships of the Royal Navy Built, Purchased and Captured,1688–1860*, London, 1993, pp. 134, 138).

18 Dadabhoy Rustomjee, prominent amongst the Parsee merchants in Canton, son of Rustomjee Cowasjee of Calcutta, owner of the largest fleet of ships trading out of India (Lubbock, *Opium Clippers*, pp. 292–3).

19 *General Wood*, arrived Macao from Bombay with a cargo of cotton, 9 July 1839 (for an account of the activities of this vessel see A.R. Williamson, *Eastern Traders*, np, 1975, pp. 155–71).

20 John Rickett, born 1801, EIC Service 1813–27 (A. Farrington, *Biographical Index of East India Company Maritime Service Officers, 1600–1834*, London, 1999, p. 665).

21 *Hercules*, purchased by Jardine and Matheson, December 1832, to replace the *Samarang*, their opium receiving vessel at Lintin from 1827 (Williamson, *Eastern Traders*, p. 175).

22 *Charles Forbes*, an opium receiving vessel (Lubbock, *Opium Clippers*, p. 103).

REFERENCES

CHAPTER 17

1   *Fort William*, ship, 1137 tons, built Calcutta, launched 1806 (A. Farrington, *Catalogue of East India Company Ships' Journals and Logs, 1600–1834*, London, 1999, pp. 252–3).

2   Departed China for Bombay 7 December 1839 (*LL*, 14 March 1840).

3   Arrived Bombay 24 January 1840 (*AJ*, NS XXXI, No. 214, p. 397).

4   *Berenice*, paddle-sloop, 630 tons, built by John Wood, engined by Robert Napier, Glasgow, 1836. She operated a regular mail packet service between Bombay and Suez (J.J. Colledge, *Ships of the Royal Navy*, London, rev. 2003. p. 52; W.J. Roff, 'Early Steamships in Eastern Waters', R. Gardiner, ed., *The Advent of Steam: The Merchant Steamship before 1900*, London, 1993, pp. 36–7, 40–1).

5   Departed 31 January 1840 (*AJ*, NS XXXI, No. 124, p. 434).

6   Major and Lady Elizabeth Wathen were listed as passengers (*ibid.*, p. 434).

7   *Marquis Camden* arrived Bombay 29 May 1819 (Farrington, *Catalogue*, p. 432). The second officer was Timothy Curtis, Lieutenant Royal Navy 1815 (*AJ*, VII, No. 37, p. 118; D. Syrett and R.L. DiNardo, eds, *Commissioned Sea Officers of the Royal Navy*, 1660–1815, Aldershot, 1994, p. 110).

8   Tonjon: a kind of sedan chair slung on a pole and carried by four bearers (*OED*).

9   Almost certainly Captain Hume, 10th Bombay Native Infantry, who married Annette, eldest daughter of J.S. Moore, Esquire, of Belvidere, on 14 February 1839, in Hobart, Tasmania (*AJ*, NS XXIX, No. 115, p. 202).

10 See *ibid.*, NS XXXI, No. 124, pp. 349–50, for a contemporary description of the stations and the scale of charges.

11 Horace Vernet, 1789–1863, professor at the École des Beaux Arts, Paris, who had a special interest in Africa and the Near East (J. Turner, ed., *The Dictionary of Art, London*, 1996, 32, pp. 335–7).

CHAPTER 18

1   Andrew William, baptised Portobello 11 March 1841 (Duddingston Old Parochial Registers, 684 / 7).

2   *Phantom*, registered Leith 35 / 23 September 1841. Built in 1841 by the shipbuilder John Miller of Brucehaven; 141 3455/3500 ton brig; length 85.4 ft, breadth 22.5 ft, depth of hold 11 ft; standing bowsprit; square stern; woman figurehead (NA, BT 107/441, Leith Register of Shipping Transcripts, 35 / 1841).

3   The *Phantom* was cleared 18 October and sailed for Port Phillip and Launceston on 19 October (*LCL*, 22 Oct. 1841).

4   Joseph Somes (1787–1845), prominent London shipowner. Many of his vessels were chartered by the Government and, at the time of his death, he was Governor of the New Zealand Company and Member of Parliament for Dartmouth, Devon (P. Burns, *Fatal Success: a History of the New Zealand Company*, Auckland, 1989, pp. 147, 262).

5   Sir James Meek, 1778–1856, Comptroller of the Victualling and Transport Service, 1830–50, knighted 1851 (*DNB*, XIII, pp. 209–10).

6   James Thomas Gambier, one of the first class clerks in the Storekeepers Department of the

Admiralty, and William Rumble, Inspector of Machinery Afloat, were found guilty in 1869 of offering to obtain Admiralty contracts for the timber merchant Nicholas Mahon Maxwell for a bribe of £30 (*The Times*, 18, 26 Feb., 5, 12 March, 6, 10 April 1869).

7   The *Phantom* was one of the earliest wire rigged vessels to operate in Australian waters, if not the first.

8   G.C. Fox and Co., Consular and Shipping Agents, founded in 1759 and in Arwenack Street, Falmouth, (D. Mudd, *The Falmouth Packets*, Bodmin, 1978, caption to Plate 19).

9   A James Teague is listed master in the *Navy List* of 1851; seniority 4 September 1829.

10 Probably John Tilly commander of the leased Admiralty packet vessel *Camden* at Falmouth during the 1820s. Listed as a master, seniority 3 September 1805 (*Navy List*, 1825, 1829). His son Tobias Harry is listed in the 1841 Census for Penryn as a solicitor living at Tremough, now part of the campus of the Combined Universities in Cornwall.

11 Departed Falmouth 5 November 1841 (M.A. Syme, *Shipping Arrivals and Departures, Victorian Ports, 1798–1845*, Melbourne, 1984, I, p. 74).

12 Arrived Table Bay 29 December 1841 (*Shipping and Mercantile Gazette*, 9 March 1842).

13 Arrived 13 or 14 February 1842 (Syme, *Shipping Arrivals and Departures*, p. 74).

14 Probably the *Manlius*, 703 ton ship, built Quebec 1839, Hodge master, registered Whitehaven (*LR*, 1841); arrived Port Phillip 14 February 1842 from 'Leith and Greenock' (Syme, *Shipping Arrivals and Departures*, p. 74), although the *LCL* does not show her sailing ladened from Leith. Advert in the *Times*, 14 September 1841: 'Port Phillip, New South Wales, from Greenock - the fine new coppered ship Manlius, Captain Hodge, 700 tons, has room for a few cabin passengers. Price 40 guineas cabin fare, sailing almost immediately from Greenock...'.

15 James Gordon, the Water Police Magistrate, appointed on the recommendation of Governor Gipps. The two men had arrived on the *Upton Castle* in February 1838 (A.G.L. Shaw, ed., *The Gipps-La Trobe Correspondence, 1839–1846*, Carlton, 1989, pp. 70–6).

16 Charles Joseph La Trobe, 1801–1875, appointed Superintendent of Port Phillip District, January 1831. Arrived 30 September. Retired and returned to England 1854 (*ADB*, II, pp. 89–93). The *Port Phillip Herald* of 11 March 1842 published a letter addressed to La Trobe from Captain Miller, dated 22 February 1842. It gives a detailed account of what took place when the *Phantom* arrived at Melbourne and requested an investigation. Miller stated that Melbourne's port practices were not consistent with Hobart, Sydney and Launceston and states he had appealed to the Quarter Sessions.

17 Sir George Gipps, 1791–1847, appointed Governor of New South Wales, 5 October 1837, retired 1846 (*ADB*, I, pp. 446–53).

18 Miller's appeal was reported in the *Port Phillip Herald* on 5 and 19 April 1842.

19 Gordon was dismissed following a private letter from La Trobe to Gipps expressing a concern about Gordon's behaviour regarded as verging on insanity (Shaw, *Correspondence*, pp. 129–30).

20 Arrived 4 March 1842 (*Cornwall Chronicle*, 5 March 1842).

21 Sailed 17 March 1842 (*Shipping and Mercantile Gazette*, 23 July 1842). James Langston, listed as master in the *Cornwall Chronicle* on 12 March, but the ship register records Thomas Sangster as master on 16 March (NA, BT 107/ 441, Leith Register of Shipping, Transcripts, 35 / 1841); the *Gazette* of 23 July 1842 supports this.

22 The spelling of the name of this vessel varies in different sources. Miller uses 'Nourmahull', but

the *LR* version is used here. The 197 ton *Noormuhul* was built in London in 1823 and registered there. Captain Stephenson sailed from Launceston for Sydney and London (*LR*, 1841). The vessel probably foundered on passage, but it was later rumoured that the crew had mutinied. In 1849 there was an unconfirmed report that a convict at Port Arthur was recognised as having been her carpenter (I.H. Nicholson, *Shipping Arrivals and Departures: Tasmania, 2, 1834–1842*, Canberra, 1985, p. 212).

23 Michael Connolly, established in 1831 or 1832 the Launceston branch of Hewitt, Gore and Co., a Hobart agency. In 1838 the branch became Connolly and Co. (B. Dyster, 'The Port of Launceston before 1851', *The Great Circle*, 3, 2, Oct. 1981, p. 111).

CHAPTER 19

1 Alexander, born 4 June 1842 (Register of Births, District of Launceston, Tasmania, 1842, No. 994).
2 Arrived 16 June 1842 (*Cornwall Chronicle*, 18 June 1842).
3 Miller resumed command on 6 July 1842 (NA, BT 107/441, Leith Ship Register Transcripts, 35 / 1841) and sailed on 15 July for Singapore (*Cornwall Chronicle*, 16 July 1842).
4 Arrived Singapore 26 August 1842 and sailed for Penang on the 30th (*LL*, 12 Dec. 1842).
5 *Vanguard*: presumably the snow of 247 tons, built Sunderland in 1840, and owned by Clark and Co., London (*LR*, 1843).
6 Arrived 18 September 1842 at Calcutta (*AJ*, NS XXXIX, No. 156, p. 427).
7 Listed in the *East-India Register and Directory*, 1843, first edition, p. 151 as: Colvin, Ainslie, Cowie & Co.; partners J. Colvin, D. Ainslie, H. Cowie and D. Cowie.
8 Departed Calcutta 14 December 1842 (*AJ*, NS IL, No. 158, p. 145).
9 Robert Jaques, born 1806, London, midshipman *Marquis Camden*, 1823–24; master *Mary Ann*, 500 tons, which left Madras 3 February 1842, for the Cape and London (*ibid.*, NS IL,No. 60, p. 419; A., Farrington, *Biographical Index of East India Company Maritime Service Officers*, 1600–1834, London, 1999, p. 420). The *Phantom* sailed from Madras 30 December 1842 (*AJ*, NS IL, No. 159, p. 318).
10 Arrived Launceston 16 February 1843 with a cargo of sugar, rice and coffee and two passengers and four 'natives' (*Cornwall Chronicle*, 18 February 1843; G. Broxham, *Shipping Arrivals and Departures Tasmania, Volume III, 1843–50*, Canberra, 1998, p. 239).
11 Alexander died 28 January 1843 (Register of Deaths in the District of Launceston, 1843, entry 801).
12 Thomas Sangster became master on 23 March 1843 (NA, BT 107/441, Leith Ship Register Transcripts, 35 / 1841) and sailed for Mauritius 23 March (*Shipping and Mercantile Gazette*, 23 July 1843). Arrived 7 May (*LL*, 3 Aug. 1843).
13 *LL* of 23 October 1843 states: ' Arrived 15 July *Phantom*, Sangster, Launceston, Etc., with considerable damage, having been aground in the River'.
14 'Bottomry is in the nature of a mortgage of a ship when the owner or master borrows money to enable him to carry on the voyage and pledges the keel or bottom of the ship, as a security for the repayments' (J. Blunt, *The Shipmaster's Assistant and Commercial Digest*, New York, 1837 [facsimile reprint, London, 1974], p. 193).
15 *Phantom*, registered Calcutta 33 / 17 December 1844. Returned to Australia, registered *de novo*

Sydney, 7 / 1847, Thomas Woolley owner. Traded between Sydney and South Australia. Lost Newcastle, NSW, July 1860 (R.T. Sexton, *Shipping Arrivals and Departures, South Australia, 1627–1850: a Guide for Genealogists and Maritime Historians*, Ridgehaven, South Australia, 1990, pp. 191–2).

16 Insolvency notices were published in the *Cornwall Chronicle*, 12, 19 November 1845.

17 William Borrodaile succeeded Michael Connolly as John Gore's Launceston agent (F. Broeze, *Mr Brooks and the Australian Trade: Imperial Business in the Nineteenth Century*, Carlton, Victoria, 1993, p. 161)

18 Philip Oakden (1784?–1851), entrepreneur and founding director of the Union Bank of Australia. Married Georgiana Cowie, daughter of a London alderman, in 1839 (*ADB*, II, p. 290). See *The Examiner* of Launceston, 18 August 1962, for a full-page biographical article, and S.J. Butlin, *Australia and New Zealand Bank*, London, 1961, pp. 18–19.

19 The *Launceston Examiner* reported this robbery on 7 March 1846. Three 'armed ruffians', it states, 'presented themselves at the residence of Philip Oakden Esq. in High street, and having first secured a manservant they took from Mr Oakden, a gold watch, and about three pounds six shillings and six pence in money . . . One man was left in charge, whilst the other two pressed Mr Oakden and insisted upon his accompanying to the residence the Rev. Dr Browne . . . They then went to work and took from Dr Browne a gold watch, about one pound thirteen in cash, and likewise possessed themselves of a loaded double-barrelled gun, a quantity of wearing apparel, etc. A servant of the doctor's [Mr Midgely] luckily heard the confusion in the house . . . and ran with all possible speed to the residence of the chief constable . . .' The two bushrangers, Henry Smart and Henry Food, were apprehended by a party of constables led by Midgely. The article confirms a shot was fired which missed because the barrel had been bent in forcing open a gate leading to the house. The remaining thief ran away on hearing the gunshot.

CHAPTER 20

1 James Raven, Launceston entrepreneur and shipowner (see B. Dyster, 'The Port of Launceston before 1851', *The Great Circle*, 3, 2, Oct. 1981, pp. 112–4).

2 *Elizabeth and Jane*, barque, 366 tons, built Monkswearmouth, Sunderland, 1828. Dimensions: 102 ft 7 ins, breadth 27 ft 7 ins, between decks 5 ft 11 ins. Stranded Circular Head, Van Diemen's Land, 10 August 1844. Salvaged by Captain John Hart and registered by James Raven at Launceston 2 / 1846. Transferred to Sunderland 15 / 1847 (R. Parsons, *Ships of Australia and New Zealand before 1850*, Magill, 1983, I, p. 59).

3 Francis Miller was born Launceston 23 September 1845 (Register of Births for the District of Launceston, No. 1115).

4 The passengers were: Mr and Mrs Webster and nine children, Miss Bray, Mr Jones, Mr and Mrs Smeaton and three children, Miss Black, Hannah Boylan (*Launceston Advertiser*, 23 April 1846).

5 *Branken Moor*, barque, 371 tons, built Whitby 1827, arrived at Port Adelaide from Launceston with troops of the 11th Regiment (R.T. Sexton, *Shipping Arrivals and Departures, South Australia, 1627–1850: a Guide for Genealogists and Maritime Historians,* Ridgehaven, South Australia, 1990, p. 113).

6   The *Elizabeth and Jane* arrived 3 or 4 May and departed about 26 or 27 May (*ibid.*, p. 115).

7   Benjamin Travers Solly, born Kent *c.*1820. On leaving school joined the EIC Service as a midshipman. Unable to pursue this career due to ill-health he emigrated to South Australia in 1840. A sheep farmer before joining a mining company, he became, in 1855, the Private Secretary to the Governor of Tasmania, Sir Henry E. Fox Young. Assistant Colonial Secretary 1857–94; died 1902 (*Tasmanian Mail*, 23 Aug. 1902).

8   *Acteon*, 6th rate, 26 guns, 620 tons, built Portsmouth Dockyard, 1831, completed as 18-gun survey ship (D. Lyon, *The Sailing Navy List: All the Ships of the Royal Navy Built, Purchased and Captured, 1688–1860*, London, 1993, p. 135). The *Sylph* has not been identified.

9   George Mansel, RN 1808, commander of *Acteon* 14 December 1844 (W.R. O'Byrne, *Naval Biographical Dictionary*, London, 1849, p. 719).

10 *Tortoise*, 962 tons, formerly *Sir Edward Hughes*, East Indiaman, built Bombay 1787, purchased 1806–7 as a store ship and renamed in 1809; hulked 1824 and sent to Ascension Island as receiving ship in 1844 (Lyon, *Sailing Navy*, p. 274).

11 The lieutenant was William Boys.

12 James Murray, chronometer, clock and watchmaker, 30 Cornhill (*Post Office London Directory*, 1846).

13 *Thomas Coutts,* ship, 1344 tons, built by Barnards of Deptford, launched 1817 (A. Farrington, *Catalogue of East India Company Ships' Journals and Logs, 1600–1834*, London, 1999, pp. 649–50). Alexander Chrystie, born 1787, Newburn, Fife, commander *Thomas Coutts* 1821–32 (A. Farrington, *Biographical Index of East India Company Maritime Service Officers, 1600–1834,* London, 1999, p. 149).

CHAPTER 21

1   Passed Deal 3 October 1846 and reported arrived at London Dock with 16 crew. The cargo included 618 bales wool, 2,783 bags wheat, 11,165 treenails, 20 tons mimosa bark, 8 cases books 'to order' and 20 bales wool consigned to Favell and Co. (*London Bill of Entry,* 13 October 1846).

2   Robert Brooks, shipowner and merchant, St Peter's Chambers, Cornhill (*Post Office London Directory*, 1846). See F. Broeze, *Mr Brooks and the Australian Trade: Imperial Business in the Nineteenth Century*, Carlton, Victoria, 1993.

3   Phillipps and Tiplady, ship and insurance brokers, 3 George Yard, Lombard Street (*Post Office London Directory*, 1846).

4   *Boyne*, ship, 619 ton, built Calcutta 1817, registered London 430 / 25 November 1845. Miller appointed master 23 February 1847. The three owners of this vessel were: William Phillips, shipbroker, Royal Exchange Buildings, City; William Henry Tiplady of the same address; and George Robertson, ship's chandler and sail maker, St Ann's Place, Limehouse (NA, BT 98/1305, Admiralty and Board of Trade, Agreements and Crew Lists, Ser. 1; *LR*, 1847).

5   Arrived Gravesend from Madras 23 January 1847 (*The Times*, 25 Jan. 1847).

6   Cleared London 27 February 1847 (*Shipping and Mercantile Gazette*, 1 Mar. 1847).

7   Sailed from Deal 1 March 1847 (*LL*, 2 March 1847).

8 Arrived 22 April 1847 (*ibid.*, 15 May 1847).

9 *The Times* of 10 November 1847 reported: 'John Wood, a seaman was charged . . . with having deserted the *Boyne* at Baltimore in May 1847 and committed for 30 days'.

10 *Sir Edward Parry* departed Portsmouth for Baltimore 11 February 1847. She arrived at Gravesend on 11 July, the same date as the *Boyne* (*ibid.*, 15 Feb., 12 July 1847).

11 *Pathfinder*, barque, 362.8 tons, built 1841, Cocks Green, County Durham, by Josiah Hall, registered London 275 / 26 July 1847. Miller appointed master the same day (NA, BT 98/1326, Admiralty and Board of Trade, Agreements and Crew Lists, Ser. I; *LR*, 1847).

12 Sailed from Deal 6 August 1847 and Portsmouth on the 10th (*LL*, 7, 12 Aug. 1847)

13 Arrived Table Bay 26 October 1847 from London to China (*The Times*, 21 Dec. 1847).

14 Ebenezer Miller, 1799–1857, studied theology at Edinburgh and Glasgow Universities, ordained 1827. Minister to the English congregation, Rotterdam, 1839–46 when he became a member of the Free Church and appointed missionary to Cape Town. Transferred to Bengal in 1850 (W. Ewing, ed., *Annals of the Free Church of Scotland, 1843–1900*, Edinburgh, 1914, I, pp. 267–8).

15 *Thames*, ship, 1330 tons, built by Barnard at Deptford, launched 1819 (A. Farrington, *Catalogue of East India Company Ships' Journals and Logs, 1600–1834*, London, 1999, p. 645).

16 Sailed from Cape of Good Hope 9 November 1847 (*LL*, 20 Jan. 1848).

17 Arrived Hong Kong 28 January 1848 (*ibid.*, 25 March 1848).

18 John Lamont, an Aberdonian shipwright who maintained the vessels operated by Jardine, Matheson and Co. Later, he was the proprietor of the Lamont Dock, Aberdeen (M. Keswick, ed., *The Thistle and the Jade*, London, 1982, pp. 134, 196).

19 *Melampus*, 5th rate, 46 guns, 1052 55/94th tons, built Pembroke Dock 1820, Leader class, the largest class of sailing frigate built. Two vessels of this class, the *Trincomalee* and *Unicorn*, still survive (D. Lyon, *The Sailing Navy List: All the Ships of the Royal Navy Built, Purchased and Captured, 1688–1860*, London, 1993, pp. 119–20).

20 The main rival house of Jardine, Matheson and Co. in the opium trade (Keswick, *Thistle and the Jade*, pp. 21–2, 35–6).

21 Grace Frances Miller married James Mackay, Esquire, goldsmith, of 24 Forth Street, Edinburgh, 7 November 1848 (Edinburgh Old Parochial Registers, 685[1]/69).

CHAPTER 22

1 Newton near Embleton, Northumberland, in the Coast Guard's Berwick District. Miller is listed in the *Navy List* of April 1849 as Chief Officer.

2 Miller's predecessor was John Theodore Page who had requested a transfer to North Berwick, Scotland (NA, ADM 175/7, Coast Guard Establishment Books, p. 285).

3 Commander William Boys (*Navy List*, 1849).

4 G. Rooke, MA, appointed vicar of Embleton in 1830 (*The Clergy List for 1850*, London, 1850).

5 Probably an obsolete usage connected to the expression, 'chip off the old block'.

6 The cutter was the *Mermaid*, Lt George S. Brittain (*Navy List*, 1849).

7 The smuggling vessel was the *Helena Maria* (alias *La Comëte*), Persloie or Pozoly master, from Flushing for the Faroe Isles, with 20 large bales of tobacco. She fell in with *Mermaid* off Fast

Castle near St Abb's Head and was taken into Leith Roads on 27 April. On 3 May the vessel was taken into Leith harbour and the cargo discharged and stored in the Custom House. The master and crew were brought before magistrates on 7 May and fined £100 and threatened with imprisonment if unpaid. The vessel was confiscated. She had been captured twice before by the *Mermaid* and chased once (*LCL*, 1,4,11 May 1849).

8 Miller's dates of service were 2 February 1849 to 1 August 1865.
9 Brittain is listed living in Ravensdowne, Berwick-upon-Tweed in 1855 (W. Whellan and Co., *History, Topography and Directory of Northumberland*, London, 1855, p. 968).
10 Captain Houston Stewart, 1791–1875, Controller General of the Coast Guard 1846–50. Knighted 1855 and Admiral of the Fleet 1872 (*DNB*, XVIII, pp. 1180–1).
11 Either John Ralph, Chief Boatman, January 1848 to February 1850, or Jeremiah Connor, Chief Boatman, February 1850 to April 1852 (NA, ADM 175/7, p. 284).
12 Charles B. Forsyth, Commander 26 January 1849; appointed 15 January 1852 (*Navy List*, 1850, 1852).
13 Tynemouth, in the Coast Guard's Sunderland District. Miller was listed there in the *Navy List* October 1852. In 1855 his address was 9 Tynemouth Place (Whellan, *Directory of Northumberland*, p. 492). Two years later he was listed at the same address. The watch house was located at the Spanish Battery (*Ward's North of England Directory*, Newcastle-upon-Tyne, 1857–58, pp. 31, 47).
14 George Lowcay Norcock, appointed 4 May 1852 to the Sunderland District; transferred to Fowey, Cornwall, July 1853 (*Navy List*, 1852, 1853).
15 In 1849 first lieutenant *Caledonia*, 120 guns (*ibid.*, 1849).
16 Commander Thomas Heard, appointed 9 April 1853, Sunderland District (*ibid.*, 1853).
17 John Ross Ward, born 3 August 1813, was appointed Inspector of Lifeboats, 1852, and subsequently Admiral 1885. Died 23 June 1890 (A.J. Dawson, *Britain's Life-Boats: the Story of a Century of Heroic Service*, London, 1923, pp. 63, 86, and information supplied by RNLI, Poole).
18 The Coast Volunteers were first mentioned in *Navy List* in January 1854. Its Captain Superintendent was Robert Smart who was appointed on 29 November 1853. The corps was founded by Act 16 and 17 Victoria *c*.73, passed 15 August 1853 and abolished 20 years later. The men signed on for five years and had to undergo four weeks training annually (F.C. Bowen, *History of the Royal Naval Reserve*, London, 1926, p. 4).
19 Henry Broadhead, captain in the Coast Volunteers (*Navy List*, 1854). He was responsible for the District from Berwick-upon-Tweed in Northumberland to Great Yarmouth in Norfolk (*The Times*, 17 March 1854).
20 Two local magistrates were recorded as shipowners in Whellan's *Directory of Northumberland*: Thomas Barker and John Dale (pp. 475, 478, 482).

CHAPTER 23

1 Seventeen of the Sunderland District Coast Guard are listed in the muster roll of HMS *Monarch*, 1854, and most transferred to HMS *Exmouth* in December (NA, ADM 38/4186, Ships' Musters, Ser III, HMS *Monarch*).

2   The flagship was HMS *Waterloo*, 120 guns (*Navy List*, 1854).

3   Sir Charles Napier, 1786–1860, Royal Navy 1799, Vice-Admiral 28 May 1853 and appointed to the command of the Baltic Fleet. MP for Southwark 1855 (*DNB*, XIV, pp. 38–45).

4   Charles Anderson Worsley, born 12 April 1809, Marylebone, London. Whig MP for Newtown, Isle of Wight, then Lincolnshire, and then North Lincolnshire from 1830 until 1846 when he succeeded to his title. Died 1862 (G.H. White, ed., *The Complete Peerage, or a History of the House of Lords and all its Members from the Earliest Times*, London, 1959, XII, 2, pp. 885–6).

5   Lord Frederick Kerr (*Navy List*, 1854).

6   Andrew is not listed in the Post Office Directory, however a James Miller was the Secretary of the Protestant Reform Society, 17 Berners Street (*Post Office London Directory*).

7   The schooner was the 62 ton *Eliza* of Kirkwall, Walter Scott master.

8   This gale occurred on 4–5 January 1854 and is described in detail in a series of reports sent to the *Times* from Tynemouth and published 5–9 January. The newspaper reported the vessel carrying the silver to be the *Sir Robert Peel* of Dundee from Valparaiso. She was a 252 ton barque, built in Dundee in 1848 and registered there (*LR*, 1853). The crew and nine pigs of silver were saved (*Shipping and Mercantile Gazette*, 5 Jan. 1854).

9   A detailed account of the loss of the *Eliza's* crew can be found in the *Times* 6 January 1854. The *Shipping Gazette*, 7 January 1854, reported: 'At one time some hopes were excited by a line having been thrown from the ship *Sir Robert Peel*. The line reached the *Eliza* but owing it is supposed to their exhausted state no advantage was taken of it'.

10   The transfer occurred in May 1857 and was authorised by The Coast Guard Service Act, 19–20 Vict. c. 83. The Controller General, Charles Eden, was given the rank of Commodore, giving him superiority over his deputy who was a captain. The district ships were: *Cornwallis*, built 1813, stationed on the Humber; *Southampton*, 1820, Harwich; *Melampus*, 1820, Southampton; *Meander*, 1840, Portland; *Eagle*, 1804, Falmouth; *Amphitrite*, 1816, Milford Haven; *Hawke*, 1820, Kingstown, Ireland; *Conway*, 1832, Queenstown, Ireland; *Hastings*, 1818, Liverpool; *Wellington*, 1816, Greenock; *Pembroke*, 1812, Leith.

11   Founded in 1859 under the Naval Reserve Act, 22 and 23 Victoria, c. 40. Initially a reserve of seamen only, the officer reserve was formed later. See F.C. Bowen, *History of the Royal Naval Reserve*, London, 1926, pp. 8–10. Included is a description of the first official inspection of an R.N.R. Division at Tyneside in July 1861.

12   F.C. Bowen states: 'When Mr Childers was First Lord of the Admiralty reform was the order of the day, and many of the measures he introduced were harsh and ill-judged' (*His Majesty's Coast Guard: The Story of this Important Naval Force from the Earliest Times to the Present Day*, London, 1928, p. 155).

13   *Trafalgar*, St George class, 120-gun first rate, 2693 tons, built Woolwich Dockyard, launched 1841 (D. Lyon, *The Sailing Navy List: All the Ships of the Royal Navy Built, Purchased and Captured, 1688–1860*, London, 1993, p. 105).

CHAPTER 24

1   Miller was appointed to the Wrangle Division, Lincolnshire, and succeeded Lieutenant Jonathan

REFERENCES

Butcher (*Navy List*, 1860).

2   Miller resided at Coppledyke Hall in the parish of Freiston (Morris and Co., *Commercial Directory and Gazetteer of Lincolnshire*, Nottingham, 1863, 1866).

3   The pensions issue and compulsory retirements are discussed briefly in F.C. Bowen, *His Majesty's Coastguard: The Story of this Important Naval Force from the Earliest Times to the Present Day*, London, 1928, pp. 153–4.

4   Miller was probably referring to Charles Eden who was, by that time, one of the Lords of the Admiralty (*The Times*, 7 Aug. 1861).

5   Alfred P. Ryder, Commodore of the Coast Guard 1863–66 (*Navy List*).

6   John Miller died at his home, 'Henley Lodge', 12 River Court Road, Hammersmith, Middlesex, on 2 February 1883 (Register of Deaths, St Peter Hammersmith, 1883, entry 253).

SOURCES AND BIBLIOGRAPHY

Archival

British Library
India Office Records: Marine Records, L/MAR.

General Register Office for Scotland
684/7, Duddingston Old Parochial Registers, Births 1819–54.
454/4, St Andrews Old Parochial Registers, Baptisms, 1813.
Edinburgh Old Parochial Registers.

National Archives
ADM 175/7, Coast Guard Establishment books.
ADM 38/4186, Ships' Musters Series III, HMS *Monarch*.
BT 107/441, Leith Register of Shipping, transcripts.
BT 98/1305, Admiralty and Board of Trade, Agreements and Crew Lists, Ser. I, London Ship Names BA-BO.
BT 98/1326, Admiralty and Board of Trade, Agreements and Crew Lists, Ser. I, London Ship Names PA-PO.
CUST 130/22, London Register of Shipping.

National Archives of Scotland
CE 57/11/1, Leith Register of Shipping.
CS 46/June 21/1857, Reclaiming Note for the Australian Company of Edinburgh . . . in the action against them at the instance of William Weymss, Contract of Co-partnery.

Other archival
Register of Births in the District of Launceston, Tasmania.
Register of Deaths in the District of Launceston, Tasmania.
Register of Deaths, St Peter Hammersmith, 1883.

Official Publications
Parliamentary Papers, 1835 (23) XXXIX, 73, *Proceedings of the Court of Proprietors Concerning Compensations, Superannuations, Allowances, etc.*

Primary Printed

Directories
East-India Register and Directory.
Morris and Co., Commercial Directory and Gazetteer of Lincolnshire, Nottingham.
Post Office Annual Directory, Edinburgh.
Post Office London Directory, London.
Universal British Directory, London.
Ward's North of England Directory, Newcastle-upon-Tyne.
Whellan and Co., *History, Topography and Directory of Northumberland*, London.

Newspapers and Periodicals

Asiatic Journal.

Cornwall Chronicle.

Edinburgh Evening Courant.

The Great Circle, Journal of the Australian Association of Maritime History.

Hobart Town Gazette.

Launceston Advertiser.

Launceston Examiner.

Leisure Hour.

Leith Commercial List of Imports and Exports.

Lloyd's List.

Lloyd's Register.

London Bills of Entry.

London Geographical Journal.

Navy List.

Port Phillip Herald.

Shipping and Mercantile Gazette.

Shipping Gazette.

Sydney Gazette.

Tasmanian Mail.

The Examiner.

The Scotsman.

The Times.

Secondary Printed

'A Griffin', *Sketches of Calcutta, or Notes of a Late Sojourn in the 'City of Palaces'*, Glasgow, 1843.

A List of the Officers of the Army and Royal Marines on Full, Retired, and Half-pay with an Index, London (Army List).

'An Adventure in China', *Leisure Hour*, X, 1861.

Australian Dictionary of Biography, Melbourne and London, 1966–91.

Bassett, M., *The Hentys: an Australian Colonial Tapestry*, Melbourne, 1962.

Bateson, C. *The Convict Ships, 1787–1868*, Glasgow, 1969 ed.

Beaglehole, J.C. , ed., *Journals of Captain Cook*, London, 1999.

Blunt, J., *The Shipmaster's Assistant and Commercial Digest*, New York, 1837, London, 1974 [facsimile reprint of 2nd ed.].

Bowen, F.C., *His Majesty's Coastguard: the Story of this Important Naval Force from the Earliest Times to the Present Day*, London, 1928.

Bowen, F.C., *History of the Royal Naval Reserve*, London, 1926 (reprinted from *Lloyd's List and Shipping Gazette*).

Branagan, J.G., *The Historic Tamar Valley: its People, Places and Shipping, 1798–1990*, Launceston, 1994.

Broeze, F., *Mr Brooks and the Australian Trade: Imperial Business in the Nineteenth Century*, Carlton, Victoria, 1993.

Broxham, G., *Shipping Arrivals and Departures Tasmania, Volume III, 1843–50*, Canberra, 1998.

Bruce, D., ed., *Sun Pictures: the Hill-Adamson Calotypes*, London, 1973.

Buckland, C.E., *Dictionary of Indian Biography*, London, 1906.

Bulley, A., *The Bombay Country Ships: 1790–1833*, Richmond, 2000.

Burns, P., *Fatal Success: a History of the New Zealand Company*, Auckland, 1989.

Butlin, S.J., *Australia and New Zealand Bank*, London, 1961.

Byron, G.G., *English Bards and Scotch Reviewers*, Glasgow, 1824.

Cameron, N.M. de S., ed., *Dictionary of Scottish Church History and Theology*, Edinburgh, 1993.

Carter, T. ed., *Historical Record of the Twenty-sixth or Cameronian Regiment*, London, 1867.

Chambers's Encylopaedia, London, 1967.

Chisholm, G.G., *Longman's Gazetteer of the World*, London, 1895.

Colledge, J.J., *Ships of the Royal Navy; the Complete Record of all Fighting Ships of the Royal Navy*, London, rev. 2003.

Cotton, Sir H.E.A., *The East Indiamen: the East India Company's Maritime Service*, London, 1949.

Dawson, A.J., *Britain's Life-Boats: the Story of a Century of Heroic Service*, London, 1923.

Day, D., *Smugglers and Sailors: the Customs History of Australia 1788–1901*, Canberra, 1993 rep.

Dean, W.B., *Notorious Bushrangers of Tasmania*, Launceston, 1891.

Dictionary of National Biography: from the Earliest Times to 1900, London, 1921–22.

Dodwell, E., and Miles, J.S., *Alphabetical List of the Honourable East India Company's Bengal Civil Servants*, London, 1839.

Dodwell, E., and Miles, J.S., *Alphabetical List of the Medical Officers of the Indian Army*, London, 1839.

Dodwell, E., and Miles, J.S., *Alphabetical List of the Officers of the Indian Army*, London, 1838.

Dyster, B., 'The Port of Launceston before 1851', *The Great Circle*, III, No. 2, Oct. 1981.

Ewing, W., ed., *Annals of the Free Church of Scotland, 1843–1900*, Edinburgh, 1914.

Farr, G. E., ed., *Records of Bristol Ships, 1800–1838: Vessels Over 150 tons*, Bristol, 1950.

Farrington, A., *Biographical Index of East India Company Maritime Service Officers, 1600–1834*, London, 1999.

Farrington, A., *Catalogue of East India Company Ships' Journals and Logs, 1600–1834*, London, 1999.

Farrington, A., *Trading Places: the East India Company and Asia, 1600–1834*, London, 2002.

Ferrall, R.A., *The Story of the Port of Launceston*, Launceston, 1983.

Flemyng, F.P., *Mauritius, or the Isle of France: being an Account of the Island, its History, Geography, Products and Inhabitants*, London, 1862.

Ford, C., and Strong, R., eds, *The Hill / Adamson Collection: an Early Victorian Album*, London, 1974.

Gardiner, R., ed., *The Advent of Steam: The Merchant Steamship before 1900*, London, 1993.

Gosse, P., *St Helena 1502–1938*, Oswestry, 1990.

Graham, G.S., *The China Station: War and Diplomacy, 1830–60*, Oxford, 1978.

Grant, F.J., *The Faculty of Advocates in Scotland, 1532–1943, with Genealogical Notes*, Edinburgh, 1944.

Halsby, J., and Harris, P., *Dictionary of Scottish Painters, 1600–present*, Edinburgh, 2001.

Keay, J., and J., eds, *Collins' Encyclopaedia of Scotland*, London, 1994.

Keswick, M., ed., *The Thistle and the Jade*, London, 1982.

Kinsley, J., ed., *The Poems and Songs of Robert Burns*, Oxford, 1968.

Leiper, S., *Precious Cargo: Scots and the China Trade*, Edinburgh, 1997.

List of Graduates in Medicine in the University of Edinburgh, 1705–1866, Edinburgh, 1867.

Lubbock, A.B., *The Opium Clippers*, Glasgow, 1933.

Lyon, D., *The Sailing Navy List: All the Ships of the Royal Navy Built, Purchased and Captured, 1688–1860*, London, 1993.

Morse, H.B., *Chronicles of the East India Company Trading to China, 1635–1834*, Oxford, 1926.

Mudd, D., *The Falmouth Packets*, Bodmin, 1978.

Napier, E.E., *Excursions in Southern Africa, Including a History of the Cape Colony*, London, 1849.

Nicholson, I.H., *Shipping Arrivals and Departures: Sydney 1826–40*, Canberra, 1984.

Nicholson, I.H., *Shipping Arrivals and Departures: Tasmania, 2, 1834-1842*, Canberra, 1985.

Nix, M., Portland: 'The Scotch Frigate'. Available at:
http://www.maritimescotland.org.uk/VESSELS/portland.htm, 2003.

Northcote Parkinson, C., *Trade in the Eastern Seas, 1793–1813*, London, 1966.

O'Byrne, W.R., *Naval Biographical Dictionary, Comprising the Life and Services of Every Living Officer in Her Majesty's Navy*, London, 1849.

O'Donnell, J., *1st King's Dragoon Guards, 1685–1912*, London, 1913.

Oxford English Dictionary, Oxford, 1989 (OED).

Parsons, R., *Ships of Australia and New Zealand before 1850*, Magill, 1983.

Paul, J. Balfour, *The Scots Peerage*, Edinburgh,1904–14.

Pendle, G., *A History of Latin America*, Harmondsworth, 1969.

Register of the Society of Writers to Her Majesty's Signet, Edinburgh, 1983.

Roff, W.J., 'Early Steamships in Eastern Waters', Gardiner, R., ed., *The Advent of Steam: The Merchant Steamship before 1900*, London, 1993.

Sexton, R.T., *Shipping Arrivals and Departures, South Australia, 1627–1850: a Guide for Genealogists and Maritime Historians* , Ridgehaven, South Australia, 1990.

Shaw, A.G.L., ed., *The Gipps–La Trobe Correspondence, 1839–1846*, Carlton, Victoria, 1989.

Smyth, W.H., *The Sailor's Word-book: an Alphabetical Digest of Nautical Terms*, London, 1867.

Spring, F.W.M., *The Bombay Artillery: List of Officers who have Served in the Regiment of Bombay Artillery*, London, 1902.

Steven, W., *History of the High School of Edinburgh*, Edinburgh, 1849.

Swinson, A., *A Register of the Regiments and Corps of the British Army*, London, 1972.

Syme, M.A., *Shipping Arrivals and Departures, Victorian Ports, 1798–1845*, Melbourne, 1984.

Syrett, D., and DiNardo, R.L., eds, *Commissioned Sea Officers of the Royal Navy, 1660–1815*, Aldershot, 1994.

Taylor, W.M. 'Account of the Ascent of Peter Botte Mountain (Mauritius) on 7th September 1832', *London Geographical Journal*, III.

The Clergy List for 1850, London, 1850.

The Cyclopedia of Tasmania (illustrated); An Historical and Commercial Review; Descriptive and Biographical, Facts, Figures, and Illustrations, Hobart, 1899?

Turner, J., ed., *The Dictionary of Art*, Basingstoke, 1996.

Turner, M., *Shipwrecks and Salvage in South Africa, 1505 to the Present*, Cape Town, 1988.

White, G.H., ed., *The Complete Peerage, or a History of the House of Lords and all its Members from the Earliest Times*, London, 1959.

Williamson, A.R., *Eastern Traders: Some Men and Ships of Jardine Matheson and Company and their Contemporaries in the East India Company's Maritime Service*, s.l., 1975.

INDEX

INDEX

VESSELS INDEX

The Victorian Naval Brigades

Lt. Commander A.L. Bleby, RN

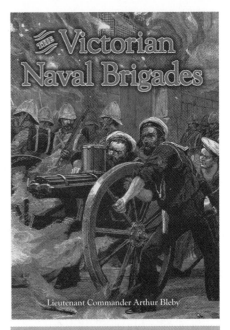

Lieutenant Commander Arthur Bleby

A record of the Naval Brigades' extraordinary exploits and achievements during eleven 'Wars of the Empire' in the 19th century

'This book is an important addition to British naval history ... definitely a standard work of importance on all the major Victorian Naval Brigade campaigns.'

— The Northern Mariner

'Commander Bleby has written a rattling good yarn of Victorian derring-do that will fascinate anyone who has Victorian naval ancestor.'

— Ancestors

ISBN 1-904445-25-X
240 x 170 mm • 192pp
illustrative maps and engravings
hardback • £20 + £2.50 p&p

There is a view that, in Victorian times, whilst the Army was engaged in a series of wars, the Navy enjoyed a peaceful existence – however, this was not the case. Complemented by authentic engravings, this book relates in fascinating detail the significant role that was played by the Naval Brigades in eleven 'Wars of the Empire' from the period 1854 to 1900. A naval brigade was a body of seamen of Royal Marines drawn from their ships and landed for active service under the orders of an army commander after a somewhat basic training.

The author relates how the crew of HMS Shannon, commanded by Captain William Peel, were involved in the Relief of Lucknow during the Indian Mutiny in 1857 whilst during 1867–68, the Naval Brigades under the command of Lieutenant General Sir Robert Napier played a crucial role in rescuing the British Consul who had been held in chains for three years within land-locked Abyssinia.

Contents: The Naval Brigade before Sevastopol, 1854–55; Naval Brigades in India, 1857 and '58; Naval Brigades of the Second Ashanti War, 1873–74; The Zulu War, 1878; The Naval Brigade in the First Boer War, 1880–81; The Naval Brigades in Egypt, 1882; The Naval Brigades in the Sudan, 1884–85; The Naval Brigades in the Second Boer War, 1899–1901; The Royal Naval Brigades in the Boxer Rebellion, 1900.

Whittles Publishing • Dunbeath Mains Cottages
Dunbeath • Caithness • Scotland •KW6 6EY • UK
Tel: +44(0)1593-731 333; Fax: +44(0)1593-731 400;
e-mail: info@whittlespublishing.com
www.whittlespublishing.com